A Tour in Baoding:
Introduction to Tourism of Baoding

游在古城

保定旅游业

（双语版）

主编　刘　宇　张建辉
编委　李　勤　管敬彬
郝凌霞　佘明君
郭咨丹　董　进

北京师范大学出版集团
BEIJING NORMAL UNIVERSITY PUBLISHING GROUP
北京师范大学出版社

图书在版编目(CIP)数据

游在古城:保定旅游业:双语版/ 刘宇,张建辉主编. —北京:北京师范大学出版社,2018.12（2019.12重印）
ISBN 978-7-303-24374-7

Ⅰ.①游… Ⅱ.①刘… ②张… Ⅲ.① 名胜古迹-介绍-保定-汉、英 Ⅳ.①K928.702.23

中国版本图书馆 CIP 数据核字(2018)第 282615 号

营销中心电话　010-58802755　58800035
北师大出版社职业教育分社网　http://zjfs.bnup.com.cn
电子信箱　zhijiao@bnupg.com

出版发行:北京师范大学出版社　www.bnupg.com
北京市西城区新街口外大街 12-3 号
邮政编码:100088
印　刷:北京虎彩文化传播有限公司
经　销:全国新华书店
开　本:787 mm×1092 mm　1/16
印　张:12.5
字　数:288 千字
版　次:2018 年 12 月第 1 版
印　次:2019 年 12 月第 2 次印刷
定　价:40.80 元

策划编辑:王云英　责任编辑:李云虎　朱冉冉
美术编辑:焦　丽　装帧设计:焦　丽
责任校对:韩兆涛　责任印制:陈　涛

前 言
Preface

保定是一座具有厚重历史底蕴的古城。这座中国历史文化名城，在数千年的文明进程中，见证了历史长河的沧桑巨变，也创造了数不尽的物华天宝。这些厚重文化与丰富资源，都为发展旅游业提供了天然势能。这座中国优秀旅游城市，在2.2万平方千米的地域内，形成和磨砺出形式多样、特色鲜明、品牌强大的保定旅游业。

本书以图文并茂的形式，对保定旅游产业概况及保定旅游资源做了一番细致全面的梳理。上篇详尽介绍了保定旅游业发展历程、发展现状、保定旅游市场及部分相关企业；下篇全面深入介绍保定人文与自然旅游资源。本书可供旅游业从业人员及游客查询资料，亦可以作为大专院校英语及旅游专业师生的学习参考资料。

本书在写作过程中，编者参阅了大量的保定旅游相关著作，并得到保定市旅游发展委员会的大力帮助和支持，在此表示衷心的感谢。

由于时间仓促，水平有限，书中难免有不当与疏漏之处，希望同行与读者批评指正。

Baoding is an ancient city with a long history. In the course of thousands of years of civilization, this famous historical and cultural city in China has witnessed tremendous changes in the long history and created countless treasures. The ancient culture and abundant resources provide natural potential for the development of tourism. This excellent tourist city in China, within 22000 square kilometers, has formed and sharpened Baoding tourism with various kinds, distinctive features and strong brand.

This book provides a respectable overview of the general situation of Baoding's tourism industry and tourism resources in the form of both pictures and texts. In the first chapter, the development history, current situation, tourism market and related enterprises are introduced in detail. The second chapter is a comprehensive introduction to Baoding's humanities and natural tourism resources. This book can be used as a reference for tourism practitioners and tourists, as well as for teachers and students majoring in English and tourism in colleges and universities.

In the process of writing this book, I have consulted a large number of Baoding tourism-related works, and received great help and support from Baoding Tourism Development Committee. I would like to express my heartfelt thanks.

There must inevitably be some omissions and deficiencies in this book, due to my limited time and my inadequate English proficiency, and therefore more comments and suggestions are sincerely welcome for future correction of this book.

目 录

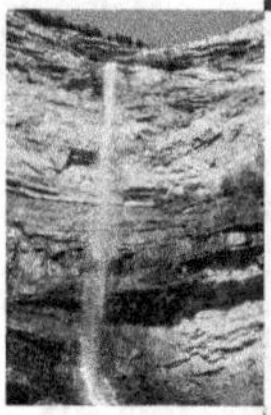

上篇　保定旅游产业概况

下篇　保定旅游资源简介

北岳庙

一、保定旅游业发展历程

保定地处京津石三角腹地，以“保卫大都，安定天下”而得名，现辖 25 个县（市、区），总面积 2.2 万平方千米，人口约 1200 万，是中国历史文化名城、中国优秀旅游城市。

5000 年前，轩辕黄帝在涞水釜山帝都的生活遗迹，印证了保定是华夏文明的肇始之地。保定是上古尧帝的故里，燕文化的发祥地。历史上燕国、中山国、后燕均在此建都。自汉建制，后唐立州，元设路，明易府，清设直隶总督署，中华人民共和国成立后两度为河北省省会。数千年的历史，孕育出汉昭烈帝刘备、宋太祖赵匡胤两朝开国皇帝，造就了古壮士荆轲、数学家祖冲之、戏剧家关汉卿、地理学家郦道元、杂剧家王实甫等名人志士。世界文化遗产清西陵、古北岳祭祀之地北岳庙、宋代五大名窑之首定窑遗址、一座衙署半部清史的直隶总督署、金缕玉衣的故乡满城汉墓、明长城紫荆关和倒马关、全国十大名园之一的古莲花池、有千雕艺术馆之称的王氏庄园等 69 处全国重点文物保护单位星罗棋布、凝古聚珍。

保定拥有 5A 级景区 3 处，4A 级景区 11 处，世界地质公园 2 处。百里峡艺术小镇、四季圣诞小镇、太行水镇、白石山温泉小镇、狼牙山花海小镇、世界门窗小镇、世界特产小镇、京南体育小镇、清河湾生态康养小镇、冀康现代休闲农庄、中华非遗小镇、休闲食品小镇、和道创意小镇、羊平雕刻小镇、秀兰文化小镇、龙泉关军事小镇、大汲店文创小镇等 21 家著名的旅游新业态小镇多彩多姿。

保定地理坐标介于东经 113°40′~116°20′，北纬 38°10′~40°00′之间。境内地势由西北向东南倾斜。地貌分山区和平原两大类，各占 1/2。境内群山西峙，沃野东坦。山区按高程及地貌划分为中山区、低山区及丘陵三类。西部为中山区，总面积 6790.5 平方千米，占全市总面积的 30.7%，海拔高程一般在 1000 米以上，最高峰为阜平县歪头山，海拔 2286 米。中山区东南部是低山区和丘陵区，呈条带形，总面积 4197.6 平方千米，占总面积的 18.98%，海拔高程除狼牙山为 1105 米外，一般在 500 至 1000 米之间，丘陵区海拔一般在 100 至 500 米之间。平原区系由大小不等的冲积扇构成，自北、西、南三个方向，向东部白洋淀倾斜，按其成因分山前洪积平原、冲积平原及洼淀区三部分。境内河流主要为海河流域大清河水系。永定河流经东北部边界。大清河主要分为南北2支，长10千米以上的山区河道有99条。南支主要有潴龙河、孟良河、孝义河、唐河、清水河、金线河、界河、府河、漕河、萍河、瀑河等汇入白洋淀。北支拒马河从铁锁崖分为南、北拒马河。境内有西大洋、王快、安格庄、龙门4大水库。

保定属南温带亚湿润气候区，春季干旱多风，夏季炎热多雨，秋季气候凉爽，冬季寒冷少雪，四季分明。年均气温差距较大，平原为12.7摄氏度，山区为7.4摄氏度。1月平均气温，平原为–5摄氏度，山区为–12摄氏度。7月平均气温，平原为27摄氏度，山区为22摄氏度（涞源）。极端最低气温为26.8摄氏度，最高气温43.3摄氏度（市区）。年日照2447~2871小时。无霜期165~210天。年均降雨量575.4毫米。年均径流量24.5亿立方米。

Being located in the area surrounded by Beijing, Tianjin, and Shijiazhuang, Baoding is named as "Protect the Capital, Pacify the World". It is a famous historical and cultural city and an excellent tourism city in China, which has 25 counties, with a total area of 22000 square kilometers and a population of about 12 million.

Baoding is the headstream of Chinese civilization, which could be confirmed from Emperor Huangdi's life remains in Fushan of Laishui County 5000 years ago. Baoding is the birthplace of ancient Emperor Yaodi and Yan culture, as well as the capital of Yan, Zhongshan and Later Yan. With the setting of the organizational system in the Han Dynasty, an ancient administrative division in the Tang and Yuan Dynasty, government office in the Ming and Qing Dynasty, Baoding acted as the capital city of Hebei Province twice after the founding of the People's Republic of China. It abounds in numerous celebrities over thousands of years of history, such as Emperor Liu Bei in the Han Dynasty, the first Emperor Zhao Kuangyin in the Song Dynasty, the ancient warrior Jing Ke, mathematician Zu Chongzhi, playwright Guan Hanqing, geographer Li Daoyuan, Wang Shifu, who was fond of a form of musical comedy in the Yuan Dynasty. There are 69 important monuments under the State Protection, such as the world cultural heritage of Western Tombs of the Qing Dynasty, sacrifice place of Beiyue Temple, a Song kiln ruins, the Viceroy Government Office of Zhili Province, the Tombs of the Han Dynasty, Zijing Pass and Daoma Pass, the Ancient Lotus Pond Garden and Manor of family Wang.

There are 3 5A-level scenic areas, 11 4A-level scenic areas, 2 world geological parks, and 21 characteristics towns, such as Baili Canyon Art Town, Four Seasons Christmas Town, Taihang Water Town, Baishi Mountain Hot Springs Health-care Town, Langya Mountain Flower-Sea Town, International Doors and Windows Town, International Specialty Town, Sports Town in the south of Beijing, Qinghe Bay Ecological Health-care Town, JiKang Modern Farming Leisure Town, Non-Material Culture Heritage Town, Leisure Food Town, Hedao Originality Town, Yangping Carving Town, Xiulan Culture Town, Longquan Pass Military Town, and Dajidian Creative Town.

The geographical coordinates of Baoding are between 113°40′~116°20′, 38°10′~40°00′ in the north latitude. The landforms are divided into two types: mountain and plain, each of which accounts for 1/2. With mountains in the west and plains in the east, the mountain area is divided into three types: medium-height area, low area and hilly area according to the elevation and geomorphology. The Western District is medium-height area, with a total area of 6790.5 square kilometers, accounting for 30.7% of the total area. The elevation is generally above 1000 meters. The highest peak is the Waitou Mountain in Fuping County, with an altitude of 2286 meters. The southeastern part of medium-height area is low mountain and hilly area, with a strip shape and a total area of 4197.6 square kilometers, accounting for 18.98% of the total area. The elevation is generally between 500 and 1000 meters except Langya mountain, and the altitude is generally between 100 and 500 meters in the hilly area. The plains are composed of alluvial fans of different sizes. They are tilted to the East Baiyangdian from three directions of north, west and south. According to their causes, they are divided into three parts: the piedmont plain, the alluvial plain and the depression area. The main rivers in Baoding are the Daqing River System in the Haihe River Basin. The Yongding River flows through the northeastern border. The Daqing River is mainly divided into 2 branches in the north and the south, and there are 99 mountain rivers over 10 kilometers long. The South Branch mainly includes Zhulong River, Xiaoyi River, Tang River, Meng Liang River, Qingshui River, Jin Xian River, Jie River, Fu River, Cao River, Ping River, Pu River, and they afflux into Baiyangdian. The North Branch of the Juma River is divided into the South and North Juma River from its cliff. There are four reservoirs named Xidayang, Wangkuai, Angezhuang and Longmen within the borders.

Baoding belongs to the warm temperate zone continental monsoon climate. It is often windy in spring, hot and rainy in summer, cool in autumn, cold and snowy in winter. It has in four distinct seasons. The annual average temperature gap is large. The plain is 12.7℃ and the mountain area is 7.4℃. The average temperature in January is -5℃ and the mountain area is -12℃. The average temperature in July was 27℃ in the plain and 22℃ in the mountain area (Laiyuan). The extreme minimum temperature is 26.8 ℃ ,and the highest temperature is 43.3 ℃(urban). The annual sunshine amount is 2447 to 2871 hours. Frost-free period is 165 to 210 days. The average annual rainfall is 575.4 millimeters. The average annual runoff is 2.45 billion cubic meters.

二、保定旅游业发展现状

保定作为首都南大门，是河北旅游先锋队，并且是首届河北省旅游产业发展大会的举办地。近年来，保定旅游业迎来持续快速发展的黄金期。2016 年，通过承办首届河北省旅游产业发展大会，保定成功打造了“京西百渡休闲度假区”，向世界呈现了保定最精彩的别样美。2016 年“十一”黄金周，“京西百渡休闲度假区”被国家旅游局评为全国“综合秩序最佳景区”“旅游服务最佳景区”。全市共接待游客 8000 万人次，旅游总收入 757.3 亿元，连续 5 年稳居全省第一。2017 年，首届保定市旅游产业发展大会在高碑店、定兴、白沟新城成功举办，以构建全域旅游大格局，建设“京畿文化名城”和“中国国际旅游目的地城市”。

保定旅游业迈入了转型升级、提质增效、加快发展的轨道。近年来，旅游总人数累计增长 135.45%，旅游总收入累计增长 323.46%，游客接待量和旅游总收入稳居全省第一梯队。

目前，全市已开放旅游景区(点)85 家，A 级景区 39 家(4A 级以上旅游景区 15 家)，星级饭店 51 家(四星级以上饭店 18 家)，旅行社 180 家(出境社 8 家)，拥有持证导游 4000 多名，特色旅游商品和纪念品 30 多个系列或品种，娱乐设施、大型购物场所和特色商业街等规模不断扩大，旅游配套产业形成规模化发展，旅游接待能力逐步提高。旅游业已经成为保定市国民经济的战略性支柱产业。

与此同时，保定积极响应全省 4A 级以上景区整改提升工作，全市 4A 级以上景区复核在全省名列第一，涌现出野三坡、白石山等一批全国知名的精品景区；高等级旅游景区创建工作持续推进，白石山、清西陵、满城汉墓、狼牙山、天生桥积极推动国家 5A 级旅游景区创建，白沟和道国际、徐水巨力刘伶醉成功创建为国家 4A 级旅游景区，涿州影视城、高碑店澳润顺达、易县易水湖、阜平云花溪谷等创建 4A 级景区工作基本就位。旅游业与其他产业融合不断加深，开发出文化游、乡村游、宗教游、商贸游、养生游、工业游等一系列特色旅游产品，汽车露营地等项目在部分县市陆续启动，《印象野三坡》等夜间演艺节目纷纷登台，新型旅游业态不断涌现。

结合农村面貌改造提升和美丽乡村建设，保定市旅游业也大力发展乡村旅游，初步形成了 8 大乡村旅游片区和 16 个省级乡村旅游示范村，博野被评为保定市第一个全国休闲农业和乡村旅游示范县。为深入推进旅游扶贫工作，阜平县成功创建国家旅游扶贫试验区，带动天生桥、城南庄等 6 个旅游小镇建设以及骆驼湾、顾家台等 40 余个乡村发展。在涞水、涞源、易县、曲阳等贫困县大力扶持种植、养殖、旅游商品和乡村星级酒店、农家乐等项目，仅野三坡景区就带动辐射周边 7 个乡镇、90 个村的乡村旅游迅猛发展，受益人口近 10 万人，旅游立县富民和旅游扶贫在山区县已形成共识。

保定市围绕“京畿胜境，醉美保定”旅游品牌形象，加强线上线下宣传推广。在中央电视台、高速公路、首都机场、京津社区、公交候车亭等平台投放广告，多次举办旅游精品线路推介会，多次到京、津、晋、内蒙古、辽、鲁、豫等地宣传促销，保定已设立营销中心 40 个，与 20 多个城市 260 多家旅行社订立了互送游客协议。保定还积极开展保定旅游产业博览会、保定旅游商品博览会、白洋淀新姿等一系列特色鲜明、影响力大的旅游活动，打造智慧营销平台，开通了“醉美保定”官方微信，并设立淘宝特色中国保定馆和京东中国特产保定馆，搭建了目前国内唯一的旅游商品、旅游购物信息资源一站式共享平台游购巴巴网。

保定市成立了旅游发展工作领导小组，对全市旅游业进行规范化管理，提升了旅游协会的服务和纽带职能，进一步加强了对星级饭店、乡村酒店和旅行社的管理和升级，加强了导游员队伍建设和培训，指导旅游重点县建立了旅游执法队伍，开通了“12301”旅游投诉咨询电话，建立了旅游法律咨询中心，旅游服务水平整体提升。坚持依法治旅，围绕“零负团费”“挂靠承包” “超范围经营”“强迫购物消费”等扰乱市场秩序的顽症，保定市开展了旅游景区整改提升、治理强迫消费、违反旅游合同擅自增加自费项目、旅游包车安全生产等专项检查，全市旅游市场秩序得到明显改善。

As the South Gate of the capital, the vanguard of Hebei tourism and the host of the first conference of Hebei Tourism Industrial Development, Baoding has entered in a golden period of sustained and rapid development in recent years. In 2016, by hosting the first conference of Hebei Tourism Industrial Development, it successfully built “Western Beijing Ferry and Resort”, presenting the most wonderful beauty of Baoding to the world. In 2016, during the Golden Week of National Day, “Western Beijing Ferry and Resort” was selected by the National Tourism Administration as “the Best Scenic Spot of Comprehensive Order” and “the Best Tourist Service Scenic Spot”. More than 80 million tourists visited Baoding, with a total income of 75.73 billion *yuan*, which is listed as Top One in the whole province for 5 years. In 2017, the first conference of Baoding Tourism Industrial Development was held successfully in Gaobeidian, Dingxing and Baigou, aiming at the construction of the pattern of region-based tourism and “Jingji Cultural City” and “China International Tourism Destination”.

Baoding’s tourism industry has moved forward into the track of transformation upgrading, quality and efficiency improving and development accelerating. In recent years, the total number of tourists has increased by 135.45%, and the total tourism income has increased by 323.46%. The number of tourists and the total tourism income ranked the first of the whole province.

At present, the city has opened 85 tourism scenic spots, 39 A-level scenic areas (15 scenic spots above 4A-level), 51 star-rated hotels (18 hotels above four-star), 180 travel agencies (8 outbound travel agencies), with more than 4000 tour guides, more than 30 series or varieties of tourism products and souvenirs. The scales of the entertainment facilities, large shopping malls and specialty commercial streets continuously expand. Tourism-related industries have formed large-scale development. The capacity of tourist reception is gradually increasing. Tourism industry has become a strategic pillar industry of national economy in Baoding.

At the same time, in response to the upgrading work of the 4A-level scenic spots in the whole province, the review of the city's scenic spots above 4A-level ranked the first in the province with the emergence of Yesanpo, Baishi Mountain and a number of national well-known scenic spots. The promotion of high-grade tourist attractions continues to carry forward. Baishi Mountain, Western Tombs of the Qing Dynasty, Mancheng Han Tombs, Langya Mountain and Tiansheng Bridge actively promote the creation of national 5A-level scenic spots. Baigou Hedao International, Liulingzui in Xushui Juli group successfully built national 4A-level scenic spots. Zhuozhou World Studios, Gaobeidian Aurun Shunda Window and Door Town, Yishui Lake in Yixian County, Fuping Yunhua Valley built 4A-level scenic spots in the basic work. The integration of tourism industry and other industries is deepening by developing cultural travel, rural travel, religious travel, business travel, health travel, industry travel and a series of tourism products. Car camping and other projects have been started in some counties. The night shows, such as *Impression of Yesanpo*, were performed on the stage. New types of tours are continuing to emerge.

With the transformation of rural areas and the construction of the beautiful countryside, Baoding tourism industry also vigorously develops rural tourism with the initial formation of the 8 rural tourism areas and 16 provincial rural tourism demonstration villages. Boye County was rated as the first national leisure agriculture and rural tourism demonstration county. To further promote poverty alleviation by tourism, Fuping County successfully created the National Tourism poverty alleviation pilot area, which has driven the construction of more than 6 tourist towns including Tiansheng Bridge and Chengnanzhuang Town, as well as the development of more than 40 villages including Camel Bay and Gujiatai. In Laishui, Laiyuan, Yixian, Quyang and other poor counties, the programs of planting, breeding, tourism commodities, rural hotels, farmhouses and other projects were supported vigorously. The development of rural tourism in 7 towns and 90 villages benefited a lot from the Yesanpo scenic spot, with a population of nearly 100 thousand people. There is a consensus on the mountainous county for the poverty alleviation of the county by tourism.

In order to create the tourism brand image of "Splendid Scenery, Charming Baoding", Baoding strengthened online and offline promotional campaigns. Through advertising on CCTV, expressway, Beijing Capital Airport, Beijing-Tianjin community, bus shelters and other platforms, and launching promotional campaigns of tourist routes, marketing many times in Beijing, Tianjin, Shanxi, Inner Mongolia, Shandong, Henan, Liaoning, and other places, Baoding has set up 40 marketing centers and has come into an agreement with more than 260 travel agencies in more than 20 cities. Meanwhile, Baoding actively carries out distinctive and influencial tourism activities, such as the Baoding Tourism Industry Exposition, Baoding Tourism Commodity Exposition and the Introduction of Baiyangdian. To build intelligence marketing platform, Baoding opened the official WeChat "Charming Baoding" and set up Taobao characteristic Baoding Pavilion of China, Jingdong Baoding Specialities hall, and Ugobaba Net, which is the only one-stop sharing platform of tourism commodities and tourist shopping information resources in China.

The establishment of the Baoding Tourism Development Leading Group aims at the standardized management of the city's tourism industry. The function of service and link of the tourism promotion association is promoted. The management and upgrading of the star hotels, rural hotels and travel agencies are further strengthened. The construction and training of the guide team are also strengthened. Baoding helped the tourism key counties establish tourism law enforcement team and set up the hotline "12301" for tourist complaints and consultation. Baoding also established tourism legal consultation center, so that the level of tourism services could be enhanced overall. Baoding upheld the rule of law on the tour. In order to solve the problems of "zero or negative membership fee" "affiliated contract" "out of scope business" "forced shopping" and other problems disrupted the market order, Baoding carried out tourism scenic rectification. Up till now, the city's tourism market order has been significantly improved.

三、保定旅游业特征分析

保定市位于河北省中部，冀中平原西部，地处北京、天津、石家庄三角腹地。市区南距省会石家庄125千米，北距首都北京140千米，东距天津145千米。素有首都南大门之称，北京护城河之誉。现辖25个县(市、区)，面积2.2万平方千米，人口约1200万。

(一) 战略地位突出

保定是京师门户，曾“北控三关，南达九省，雄冠中州”，是历史上燕国、中山国、后燕立都之地，清代八督之首，为冀北干城，都南屏翰。现为大北京经济圈中的两翼之一，北京主要卫星城。

(二) 人文历史灿烂

保定物华天宝，人杰地灵。古壮士荆轲、燕大夫郭隗、汉昭烈帝刘备、宋太祖赵匡胤、地理学家郦道元、数学家祖冲之、戏剧家关汉卿等名人志士辈出。保定教育渊源，人文灿烂，宋有州学，明有府学，清有莲池书院，北洋军阀冯国璋、清末状元刘春霖等一大批清代官员和教育家曾毕业于此。保定是留法勤工俭学运动发祥地，曾在此培养了蔡和森、赵世炎、周恩来、李维汉、李富春等一大批中国早期革命家。保定是将军的摇篮，保定军校曾培养出叶挺等1700多名将军。清末，保定被称为学生城。保定现有河北大学等11所高等院校。

(三) 文物古迹众多

保定是中国文物国保地级市第一大市，河北省第一文物大市。保定埋葬着清代4位皇帝的世界文化遗产——清西陵；有“一座总督衙署，半部清史写照”的全国保存最完好的清代衙署——直隶总督署；有出土金缕玉衣、长信宫灯的西汉靖王满城汉墓等69处国家级文物保护单位，109处省级文物保护单位，456处市(县)级文物保护单位，1600余处不可移动的文物点，有8万余件馆藏文物。

(四) 红色文化丰厚

保定是红色之城。保定人民有着光荣的革命斗争传统。毛泽东主席曾亲笔题词“抗日模范根据地”，也因此在中国现代文学史上诞生了以著名作家孙犁的“荷花淀”派为代表的保定作家群。《荷花淀》《红旗谱》《小兵张嘎》《敌后武工队》《青春之歌》《野火春风斗古城》《地道战》《狼牙山五壮士》《烈火金刚》《平原枪声》等著名电影、文学作品与保定享誉海内外，激励了一代又一代中国人。现保定有3处全国爱国主义教育基地，7处国家级红色经典景区。

（五）自然风光秀美

保定是兼有平原、湖泊、湿地、丘陵、山地、亚高山草甸的地区，有国家5A级景区3处、国家4A级景区13处、世界地质公园2处、国家重点风景名胜区1处、国家地质公园3处、国家森林公园5处。境内群山西峙，沃野东坦，植被繁茂，山明水秀，既有避暑的凉城，又有泛舟的湖泊。野三坡世外桃源，神奇俊美；白洋淀苇绿荷红，胜似江南；白石山、大茂山巍峨耸立，云蒸霞蔚；天桥瀑布、龙门天关飞流直下，气象万千；西胜沟峡谷龙潭，峰回路转；北岳庙历览千年，风采依然；万顷桃园"乱花渐欲迷人眼"，空中草原"浅草才能没马蹄"；紫荆关畿南第一天下险，古栈道地下长城世间奇！

（六）特殊旅游资源荟萃

保定是一个拥有43个民族的大家庭，形成了丰富多彩的民俗文化。保定现有5处国家非物质文化遗产，7处国家级工农业旅游示范点；有"千年药都誉天下，世界盛会喜迎宾"的安国药都；有"旅游名镇，购物天堂"的中国白沟；有全国四大名砚之一的易水古砚等特色区域经济。

（七）道路交通便捷

全国南北大动脉京广铁路，京珠高速和107国道纵贯市区，京原铁路、112国道横穿山区，保津高速连接京珠、津沪、津唐三大公路干线。境内50条公路纵横交错，形成以高速公路为"龙头"，以"五纵四横"为骨架，以县乡道路为依托的四通八达的公路网络。随着京津保城际高铁的开通，北京第二机场的建设及轻轨入保，保定构建了京津保一体化旅游大格局和"快旅慢游"的公共服务体系，为境外游客72小时落地免签奠定了基础。

（八）旅游接待水平北方领先

全市现有旅行社180家，星级酒店50家，其中五星级酒店4家，社会餐饮店数百家。保定还拥有河北省最大的旅游营销组织——保定金牌旅游线路联盟，为旅游行业提供培训服务和就业平台的金典导游服务公司，集旅游商品研发展示及线上线下销售于一体的河北直隶八珍旅游投资有限公司等。

Baoding is located in the center of Hebei Province and the west of Jizhong Plain. It lies in the interweaving area among Beijing, Tianjin and Shijiazhuang. Its downtown is 140 kilometers north to Beijing, 145 kilometers east to Tianjin and 125 kilometers south to Shijiazhuang. It is known as "the southern gate of Beijing" and "the moat of Beijing". It has 25 counties and districts, covers 22.1 thousand sq km, with a population of 11 million.

3.1 Great Strategic Position

Baoding is the entrance to Beijing. It connected the three passes in the north, 9 provinces in the south, and ranked the first in ancient China. In history, it had been chosen as the capital city by Yan state, Zhongshan State, and Late Yan state, and ranked the first among the eight great provinces in the Qing Dynasty. It is a major city in North China and is the southern entrance to Beijing as well. Now it is one of the two wings of Beijing economic circle, and a major satellite city of Beijing.

3.2 Brilliant Human History

Baoding is a fair place boasting of both outstanding people and historical sites. Since ancient times, a great number of famous people have emerged, such as the Hero Jingke, Yan minister Guohuai, Han Zhaolie Emperor Liubei, the first Emperor of the Song Dynasty — Zhao Kuangyin, geologist Li Daoyuan, Dramatist Guan Hanqing and so on. As for the education resources, the Lianchi Academy of the Qing Dynasty is the most famous one, from which many officers and educators in the Qing Period received their education, such as Feng Guozhang, a head of Beiyang military section, and Liu Chunlin, a number one scholar in the Qing period. It is also the base of "study-in-France" Movement, where a great number of early Chinese revolutionaries graduated, including Cai Hesen, Zhao Shiyan, Zhou Enlai, Li Weihan, Li Fuchun, etc.. Baoding Military School is the cradle of generals from which over 1700 generals graduated, such as Ye Ting. In late Qing period, Baoding was called as the Town of Students, and now there are still 11 higher education institutes including Hebei University.

3.3 Tremendous Cultural Relics and Historical Sites

Baoding boasts rich relic resources in Hebei. We take pride in our 69 national-level, 109 provincial-level, and 456 municipal/county-level protected sites and more than 1600 immobile historical sites. Among them, there are the Western Qing Tombs, where buried 4 emperors of the Qing Dynasty; the Provincial Governor's Office, the best preserved of its kind, as the saying goes, "one governor's office, half the Qing Dynasty's history"; the Tomb of the King Jing of Western Han, where the gold-and-jade garment and Changxin palace lantern were discovered. What's more, over 80000 pieces of relics kept in museums are all most precious and vivid records of the past.

3.4 Rich Red Historical Resources

Baoding is a city of red revolution. And Baoding people have a glorious tradition of revolutionary struggles. Chairman Mao praised it as "model anti-Japanese base". It had brought forth in modern Chinese literature history a group of Baoding writers, known as "the lotus-pond group", represented by the famous writer Sun Li. And Baoding also gets known along with some famous movies and novels, such as *The Lotus Pond*, *Song of the Red Flag*, *Little Soldier Zhang Ga*, *Story of the Armed Group*, *Song of The Youth*, *Wild Fires and Spring Winds*, *Tunnel Warfare*, *Five Heroes of Langya Mountain*, *Fires and*

Men, *Gun Fires In The Plain*, etc.. All these have encouraged Chinese people one generation after another. Now in Baoding, there are 3 national patriotism education bases, 7 national recommended tourists' destinations.

3.5 Beautiful Natural Sceneries

Baoding is an area full of plains, lakes, marshes, hills, mountains, and sub-highland grassland as well. It boasts 3 5A-level scenic spots, 13 4A-level scenic spots, 2 world geoparks, one national key scenery site, 3 national geological parks, 5 national forest parks. In the west there erects Taihang Mountain, while in the east, there lies vast plains. There are mountain areas and plains, forests, lakes, and cool cities as well, where people can enjoy the beautiful sceneries or spend hot summer days, or go boating. There are many scenic spots, for example, Yesanpo, Baiyangdian, Baishi Mountain, Damao Mountain, Tianqiao Waterfall, Xishenggou Valley, Beiyue Temple with a thousand years, peachland of a thousand *mu* (1 *mu* ≈ 666.67 m^2), grassland in the air, Zijing Pass, the Ancient Plank Road and the Great Wall underground.

3.6 Various Special Tourism Resources

Baoding is a big family of 43 nationalities, thus a marvelous folk culture has been cultivated. It boasts 5 national non-material cultural heritages, 5 national industrial and agricultural touring site models. What's more, it has become a great market of touring and shopping with characteristic economic areas. For instance, Anguo County, the town of Chinese herbs and medicines, is known for its long history of manufacturing Chinese traditional medicines. Baigou Town is known for traveling and shopping, and Yixian County is known for producing Yishui inkstone, one of the 4 great brands of its kind.

3.7 Fair Traffic Conditions

Beijing-Guangzhou Railway, the artery line linking the south and the north, Beijing-Zhujiang Expressway and national highway 107 run through its district. Beijing-Taiyuan Line and national highway 112 run through its mountain areas. Baoding-Tianjin Expressway connects together the three major expressways, namely, Beijing-Zhujiang Expressway, Beijing-Shanghai Expressway and Tainjin-Tangshan Expressway. With 50 highroads connecting one another within it, Baoding has completed a fair traffic network, in which expressways are the backbone, 9 highways are the framework, roads linking to counties and towns are the main body. With the opening of Beijing-Tianjin-Baoding intercity high-speed rail, the construction of Beijing second airport and the entry of light rail, the integrated tourism of Beijing-Tianjin-Baoding and the public service system of "fast travel and slow sightseeing" have been built, which laid the foundation for overseas tourists to sign for free 72 hours.

3.8 Leading Tourist Reception Level

There are 180 travel agencies in the city and 50 star rated hotels, of which 4 hotels are rated as five-star hotels and hundreds of social restaurants. There are also the largest tourism marketing organization Baoding Gold Tours Alliance, Golden Guide Service Company which provides training and employment service for the tourism industry, and Hebei Zhili Bazhen Tourism Investment Co., Ltd. which integrates tourism commodity development with online and offline sales.

四、保定旅游市场

（一）核心市场

核心市场是指河北省及京津地区。据统计，2015 年京津两市常住人口达 3717.45 万人，京津冀都市圈人口年增百万，私家车保有量超过 800 万辆，潜在出游力在全国排名分别为第 1 和第 7 位，随着京津冀协同发展的深入实施，保定将成为京津居民周末、小长假出游的主要目的地之一。同时，从近几年保定国内旅游前五大客源地来看，本省游客所占比例均在 50%左右，是保定最重要的客源市场。因此，京津冀地区是保定的核心市场。

（二）基本市场

基本市场是指山西、山东、河南、内蒙古、辽宁等周边省区。这些地区与保定空间距离远、时间距离近，高铁路网的建成大大缩短了到保定的时间，同时保定野三坡、白石山、白洋淀等景区在这些区域已形成较大的吸引力，因此将其定位为保定的基本客源市场。

（三）拓展市场

拓展市场是指长三角、珠三角及国内其他地区。该区域占据了全国多半客源。“十三五”时期，保定市在做强做大核心市场、稳步提升基本市场的基础上，要以交通变革为契机，加大对长三角、珠三角等远程市场的宣传促销与市场开发，不断扩大旅游市场半径。

（四）入境市场

近年来，保定市入境旅游客源虽有所增多，但所占比例仍然相对较少。为突破入境市场，如日韩市场、欧美市场，以及新加坡、马来西亚、泰国、印度尼西亚等东南亚市场，保定应加大宣传营销力度，积极争取过境免签、落地签、延长多次往返签证等市场便利性政策。保定还应借鉴珠三角地区 144 小时便利签证的政策经验，推动京津冀区域 144 小时落地免签政策的实施，外国旅游团进入本区旅游，不仅享受入境便利手续，可以在区域内互相流动，还可以从区域内不同城市、口岸出入境，提高入境市场竞争力。

4.1 The Core Market

It refers to Hebei, Beijing and Tianjin. According to statistics, in 2015, the resident population in Beijing and Tianjin reached 37174500. The population of Beijing-Tianjin-Hebei metropolitan region increased in millions annually. The present number of private cars is more than 8 million. And the potential travel capacity of the two cities ranked the first and the seventh respectively. With the further implementation of the coordinative development of Beijing-Tianjin-Hebei, Baoding will become one of the main destinations of weekend or holiday travel for Beijing and Tianjin residents. Meanwhile, from the analysis of the top five tourist generating regions, the proportion of tourists in Hebei Province accounts for around 50% , which is the most important source of tourists in Baoding. Therefore, the Beijing-Tianjin-Hebei region is the core market for Baoding.

4.2 The Basic Market

The regions like Shanxi, Shandong, Henan, Inner Mongolia, Liaoning and other surrounding provinces are far away from Baoding in space distance but short in time distance. The construction of high-speed railway network greatly shortens the time to Baoding. Meanwhile, such scenic spots as Yesanpo, Baishi Mountain and Baiyangdian Lake have exerted an intense attraction in these areas, so these areas are seen as the basic source market of Baoding city.

4.3 The Expanding Market

The regions of Yangtze River Delta and Pearl River Delta have contributed more than half of the country's visitors. During the "13th Five-Year Strategy" period, on the basis of the development of core market, as well as the steady enhancement of the basic market, the promotion and development of remote markets, such as the Yangtze River Delta and Pearl River Delta, should be highlighted based on the revolution of transportation, so as to expand the tourism market.

4.4 The Inbound Market

In recent years, the number of inbound tourists in Baoding has grown, but the proportion is still relatively small. In order to further promote the inbound market, such as markets of Japan and South Korea, European markets as well as Southeast Asia markets of Singapore, Malaysia, Thailand and Indonesia, we should launch more advertising and marketing campaigns, and actively implement such preferable visa policies concerning visa-free transit, visa on arrival and extended circulation visa. Learning from the 144-hour facilitation visa policy in Pearl River Delta region, Baoding should promote the implementation of the 144-hour landing visa-free policy in Beijing-Tianjin-Hebei region where foreigners could, if entering such regions, not only benefit from the convenience of entry procedures, but move about freely in different cities or ports in the region, thus improving its market competitiveness.

五、保定旅游企业

保定市现有旅行社181家，拥有强大的组团及地接能力，推出的系列精品旅游线路在京、津、冀、晋、内蒙古、辽等周边省份和高铁沿线有着非常高的知名度和数量巨大的游客群体。

（一）金牌旅游联盟

2014年，由保定市最具实力的七家旅行社注资组建河北金盟国际旅行社，以“6+1”联动形式发展，包括旅行社、酒店、餐厅、旅游商品、车队、导游及市县两级旅游局。金盟进入企业化运营发展，致力于规模化、网络化、品牌化发展。公司以“旅游兴市，地接为王”为宗旨，大力整合保定旅游资源，打造金盟旅游绿色通道。

（二）保定市中国旅行社有限公司

保定市中国旅行社有限公司是中国中旅集团成员之一，具备国际类旅行社资质。公司凝聚了高素质管理人员和专业团队，具有灵活的经营方式，丰富的组团接待经验及成熟的运作模式。公司实现电脑网络化办公，设有17个营业部，承办团体旅游、商务旅游、散客旅游、常规旅游以及各种体育交流、文化科技交流、自驾车、考察等特殊项目的旅游。

（三）中国国旅保定国际旅行社有限公司

中国国旅保定国际旅行社有限公司是中国国际旅行社总社唯一在保定直接投资控股经营的旅游企业，也是保定地区首家国家特许经营出境游旅行社。公司秉承了“中国国旅”的品牌理念和服务宗旨，与民航铁路交通、国内外相关旅行社、酒店、景区有着良好的合作关系，拥有一批文化素质高、业务能力强、服务周到的外联销售人员和翻译导游专业人员。先后获“国家级青年文明号”“河北省十佳诚信旅行社”等多项荣誉称号。

（四）保定正大国际旅行社

保定正大国际旅行社具有独立的出境资质，拥有一批勤奋敬业的员工和优秀导游员队伍，业务开展广泛，与国内多家兄弟社建立了良好的合作关系，旅游线路多，项目齐全。公司可根据不同层次客户的要求，任选标准、任选路线、灵活安排；经营范围包括入境旅游业务、国内旅游业务、出境旅游业务、会议服务、汽车租赁、代购火车票、代购机票、代购汽车票等业务。

（五）河北卓正国际旅行社有限公司

河北卓正国际旅行社有限公司是特许经营出境游资质的旅行社，与国家5A级景区白洋淀大观园、卓正国际酒店同属于河北卓正实业集团。公司设有“公民旅游中心”和“同业操作中心”两大板块。公民旅游中心下设组团部、商旅部、会奖部三大部门，主要从事国内及出境散客接待、商旅定制、单项服务、会议服务、奖励旅游、主题定制等多项业务；同业操作中心下设地接部、假日产品事业部、国内产品事业部、出境产品事业部四大部门，主要从事国内外来京津冀旅游团队的接待、周边汽车团队操作及同业销售、国内长线团队和出境团队的操作及销售等业务。

（六）保定市省青国际旅行社有限公司

保定市省青国际旅行社有限公司是经国家旅游局批准的具有特许中国公民出境资质的国际旅行社。公司下辖保定纵游旅游运输有限公司、保定市省青会议服务有限公司。2014 年底公司成立了保定市旅游咨询集散中心，是集旅游咨询、交通运输、门票预售、旅游宣传为一体的综合型旅游服务体。打造保定旅游航母，创建市场联合舰队，更好、更快捷、更高品质为广大游客服务是公司的最终目标。

（七）保定市神州国际旅行社

保定市神州国际旅行社具有独立的出境资质，被保定市旅游局评为首届旅游行业“十佳旅行社”称号。公司以“全心全意地照顾好身边的人”为企业文化，引进全国旅游连锁品牌“旅游百事通”，利用互联网平台和信息通信技术，把互联网和传统的旅行社门店结合起来，在新的领域创造出一种新的模式。

（八）涞水县野三坡隆兴旅行社有限公司

涞水县野三坡隆兴旅行社有限公司承接保定、野三坡、白洋淀、北京周边等地接业务，国内旅游、会议考察、预订酒店、代订火车票、代订飞机票、旅游包车及自驾游等业务，年接待人数近万人。公司宗旨是“信誉第一，宾客至上”。2013 年，公司被保定市旅游局评为“保定市十佳旅行社”。

（九）白洋淀水天旅行社有限公司

白洋淀水天旅行社有限公司位于安新县，成立于 2004 年，专业承接保定白洋淀、北京、天津等周边地接业务，以“宾客至上，诚信第一”的服务宗旨，赢得了游客和组团社的一致好评，实现了多年零投诉。在国家旅游局开展的“寻找最美导游”活动中，该社一名导游员曾获“河北省最美导游”的荣誉称号。

（十）白洋淀国际旅行社

白洋淀国际旅行社位于安新县，公司成立于 1989 年，因业绩突出曾获“全国巾帼文明岗称号”“河北省精神文明窗口单位”“保定市旅游行业先进单位”“保定市青年文明号”等荣誉称号。公司以“真诚服务每一天”为企业精神，坚持以“诚实服务，承诺是金”为服务宗旨，保持着从业 20 余年零投诉的纪录。

There are 181 travel agencies in Baoding with strong group and local reception capacity. The excellent tourist routes series have got a very high reputation and a large number of tourist groups in Beijing, Tianjin, Hebei, Shanxi, Inner Mongolia, Liaoning and other surrounding provinces alongside the high-speed rail lines.

5.1 Gold Medal Tourism Alliance

In 2014, Hebei Golden Alliance International Travel Agency was established with the investment of the most powerful seven travel agencies in Baoding. They developed in the form of "6+1" linkage, including travel agencies, hotels, restaurants, tourist commodities, convoys, tour guides, and municipal and county Tourist Bureaus. Golden Alliance International Travel Agency is dedicated to the development of enterprise operation, and is committed to the development of scale, network and brand. With the purpose of "tourism revitalizes the city, with emphasis of the local reception service", the company energetically integrates the tourism resources of Baoding and creates a green channel for the tourism of golden alliance.

5.2 Baoding China Travel Service Co., Ltd.

It is a member of Chinese travel group, and possesses the international travel agency qualification. The company consists of the high-quality management and professional team, which has the flexible way of management, the rich group reception experience and the mature operation mode. The company has computer network office, which is made up of 17 business departments, dealing with group tour, business tour, individual and regular tour, as well as various sports exchange, cultural and technological exchange, self-driving, and other special projects.

5.3 CITS (Chinese International Travel Service) Baoding International Travel Service Co., Ltd.

It is the sole tourism enterprise invested and owned by the Chinese International Travel Service head office. It is also the first national franchise outbound travel agency in Baoding. The company adhered to the "CITS" brand concept and service tenet, cooperating with the civil aviation and railway transportation, domestic and international travel agencies, hotels and scenic spots. It also has a group of high-qualified, professional and thoughtful sales personnel and tourism translators. It has been awarded a number of honorary titles such as "the National Youth Civilization" and "the Top Ten Faith Travel Agencies in Hebei Province".

5.4 Baoding Zhengda International Travel Agency

It has an independent exit qualification. It has a group of diligent and dedicated staffs and excellent tour guides. Its business has been extensively developed, and has established good relationship with many domestic businesses. With various tourist routes and complete programs, the company could select and arrange the standard or the route flexibly according to the requirements of different levels of customers. The business scope includes inbound tourism business, domestic tourism business, outbound tourism business, conference service, car rental, purchasing train ticket, air ticket, car ticket and so on.

5.5 Hebei Zhuozheng International Travel Service Co., Ltd.

It is an authorized travel agency for the outbound tours. It belongs to Hebei Zhuozheng Industrial Group along with a national 5A-level scenic spot, Baiyangdian Grand View Garden and Zhuozheng International Hotel. The company consists of two sections:" tourist center" and "business operation center". The Tourist Center is divided into three sections: group travel department, business travel department and award travel department. It is mainly engaged in a number of domestic and outbound tourist reception, business travel customization, individual services, conference services, incentive travel, theme customization, etc.; The Business Operation Center consists of four departments: local reception division, holiday products division, domestic products division and outbound products division, which is mainly engaged in the reception of domestic and foreign tourism teams, the operations and sales of surrounding cars teams, the operation and sales of domestic long-line trade teams and outbound teams.

5.6 Baoding Shengqing International Travel Agency Co., Ltd.

It is an international travel agency approved by the National Tourism Administration with the outbound qualification of chartered Chinese citizens. The company has the right to administer Baoding Zongyou Travel and Transportation Co., Ltd. and Baoding Shengqing Conference Service Co., Ltd. By the end of 2014, the company had established the Baoding Tourism Advisory Center, which is a comprehensive tourism service system consisting of tourism consultation, transportation, ticket pre-sale and tourism promotion. It is the ultimate goal of the company to build a Baoding tourist carrier and create a joint market so as to provide better, faster and qualified service for the tourists.

5.7 Baoding Shenzhou International Travel Agency

It has an independent outbound qualification. It was reputed as the first "Top Ten Travel Agencies" by the Baoding Tourism Bureau. "Serving the people around" is the corporate culture. Through the introduction of the national tourism brand "know-all tourism", by using the Internet platform and information and communication technology, it combines the Internet with traditional travel stores, so as to create a new pattern in new areas.

5.8 Yesanpo Longxing Travel Agency Limited Company in Laishui County

It undertakes the business around Baoding, Yesanpo, Baiyangdian, Beijing and other places. The business scope covers domestic tourism, conference inspection, hotel reservation, ticket booking, chartered car and self-driving business. The annual reception number is nearly ten thousand people. The principle of the company is "reputation first, guest first". In 2013, the company was named as "Top Ten Travel Agencies" by the Baoding Tourism Bureau.

5.9 Baiyangdian Shuitian Travel Agency Co., Ltd.

It is located in Anxin County and was founded in 2004, undertaking the business around Baoding, Baiyangdian, Beijing, Tianjin and other places. With the service tenet of "customer first, honesty first", the company has won the praise of tourists and travel agents for achieving zero complaints for years. In the activity of "searching for the most beautiful tour guide", the tour guide in the travel agency won the honorary title of "the most beautiful tour guide in Hebei Province".

5.10 Baiyangdian International Travel Agency

It is located in Anxin County, founded in 1989. It has won the honorary titles " National Heroine Civilized Post Title" "Hebei Province Spiritual Window Units" "Baoding Tourism Industry Advanced Unit" "Baoding Youth Civilization" due to its outstanding performance. The company takes the spirit of "sincere service provided every day" as the spirit of the enterprise, and insists on serving the purpose of "service honestly and keep commitments". It maintains a record of zero complaint for more than 20 years.

一、自然风景旅游资源

（一）野三坡

野三坡

野三坡位于涞水县城西北75千米处的太行山深处，总面积498.5平方千米，由百里峡峡谷风光游览区、拒马河避暑疗养娱乐区、佛洞塔奇泉怪洞游览区、龙门天关长城文物保护区、白草畔原始森林保护区及金华山寻奇狩猎游览区6个景区组成。景区内分布着上百个景点，是集山水泉洞、林木花草、鸟兽鱼虫、文物名胜于一体的综合性自然生态风景区。文物名胜无所不包，旅游资源独具风采，被誉为"京畿胜景"。

国家5A级景区百里峡，奇岩耸立，绝壁万仞；拒马河景区气候凉爽，环境清幽；龙门天关景区巍峨壮观，清流直泻。此外还有民族园、鱼谷洞、白草畔、金华山、三皇山等景区也会让人流连忘返。

野三坡地势由南向北逐渐增高，高度差异很大，又被称为盘坡，分为上中下三坡。上坡与下坡相差半月。三坡这个地名是由地形变化、气候不同而产生的。这里有嶂谷神奇的百里峡、森林繁茂的白草畔、风光旖旎的拒马河、神秘莫测的鱼谷洞、九瀑连环的上天沟。拒马河水川流不息，生态环境原始自然，历史文物稀有珍贵。这里浓缩了太行之深情、燕山之风采，再现了十多亿年来地质演化过程，传承着中华古老文明，融雄山碧水、春华秋叶、瀑布冰川、奇石异洞、长城古堡、摩崖石刻、名树古禅、高山草甸、空中花园以及《印象野三坡》大型舞蹈史话等自然与人文景观和旅游娱乐项目于一体。

野三坡是华北地质历史的缩影。它雄踞在紫荆关深大断裂带之上，多期强烈的构造运动和岩浆活动留下了一幅幅壮观雄伟的地壳演化的画卷。险峻、神奇、幽深的百里峡构造，气势磅礴的冲蚀嶂谷，巍然矗立的龙门天关花岗岩断裂构造，深邃莫测的鱼谷洞构造岩溶洞泉，是内容丰富、类型齐全、典型独特、珍稀无价的地质遗迹。

野三坡的地质遗迹典型、系统、完整，各类不整合面清晰，岩浆岩、沉积岩、变质岩三大岩类齐全，节理、断层、褶皱等构造遗址、山地夷平面、河流阶地、岩溶溶洞、古火山、古冰川等地貌遗迹丰富多彩。它是一部生动的地质教科书，是一座天然地质博物馆。它浓缩了华北 30 亿年来地质构造的演化史，是专家学者研究地球科学的最佳区域，是学生教学实习的理想基地，是科普教育的生动课堂。2004 年，它被批准为“国家地质公园”，2006 年，被评为“世界地质公园”。2014 年，入选“国家生态旅游示范区”，是河北省唯一入选景区。

野三坡风光

1. 百里峡

天下第一峡

百里峡被誉为“天下第一峡”，位于野三坡镇苟各庄村一带，总面积 110 平方千米，由三条峡谷组成。最外边一条被称作蝎子沟，全长 12.5 千米，因沟中遍生蝎子草而得名。中间的一条峡谷是海棠峪，因谷内遍布海棠花而得名。海棠峪是一条长 17.5 千米的洞壑，峡内翠壁耸立，直插云天，令人望而生畏。沿沟而上，有奇险的“老虎嘴”，是由一个巨大的弧形悬崖构成的圆洞，极像老虎张着的血盆大口；有狭窄的“一线天”，最窄处只有 0.83 米，悬崖峭壁，窄涧幽谷，天光一线，真有一种“双崖依天立，万仞从地劈”的意境；还有惟妙惟肖的“回首观音”、规模宏大的“上天桥”和“下天桥”等景观。

第三条峡谷被称作十悬峡，因沟内分布着数十处弧形悬崖而得名，长达 22.5 千米。进入峡谷，“抻牛湖”瀑布、灵芝山“水帘洞”、弧形悬崖形成的“不见天”、令人费解的“怪峰”、峭崖剔透的“雄狮出世”等景观映入眼帘。三条峡谷全长 52.5 千米，故此得名百里峡。峡谷幽深，日照时间短，所以在外面高达 40 摄氏度气温的情况下，峡谷内气温依旧是 20 摄氏度左右。另外，峡谷内负氧离子超过 20000 单位，氧气充沛，成为风光绮丽迷人的旅游养生佳地。由于景观奇特，这里成了央视以及许多古装剧的拍摄场地。比如，闻名中外的《三国演义》《水浒传》《西游记》等多部大型电视剧都曾在此拍摄。

2. 拒马河景区

拒马河畔为休闲避暑胜地。清澈的拒马河水唱着欢快的歌从万山丛中走来，水中一群石猴无忧无虑地嬉戏；一叶叶轻舟随风荡漾，小舟上一对对情侣放飞着绵绵情怀；岸边沙丘在阳光的照射下，发出迷人的光芒；《印象野三坡》中那思古颂今的悠扬歌声随风而至，让人如痴如醉；青山叠翠，尽享天然氧吧带来的酷爽；两岸花艳，让人尽饱眼福；仙人桥入目，引出万般遐思。

3. 鱼谷洞景区

鱼谷洞景区由古庙、奇泉、怪洞、古松组成。位于拒马河支流小西河流域，是游人猎奇览胜的佳境。鱼谷洞、鱼谷泉，自然天成，充满神奇。幽深莫测的鱼谷洞深约1800米，是出现在古生代石灰岩中的裂隙式溶洞。石灰岩成岩后，在1.4亿年间，地壳造山运动使厚大的石灰岩层中出现断裂和节理纹。水从裂缝中流动，将岩石中钙质溶解，形成长条状溶洞。由于裂缝常出现分叉状，故使溶洞出现洞连洞、洞生洞和洞中有洞的神奇迷宫状溶洞群。更有趣的是，由于部分水溶蚀了大量钙质，使其成为饱和钙溶液。这些水又纷纷将钙质沉淀或重结晶，生成多种钟乳石质的石笋、石柱、石龙、石帘、石瀑布等美景。

海棠女石像

同时这个溶洞中的泉水是一个间歇泉。受季节影响，每年到谷雨节气前后，泉洞中的泉水会不断外溢，并神奇地向外喷鱼，故称之鱼谷洞、鱼谷泉。其中的缘由也成为千古之谜。这甘洌清凉、长年涌流不息的泉水，因水中富含丰富有益于人体健康的多种矿物质微量元素，是难得的天然矿泉水。鱼谷洞中之鱼更是珍宝。因长期生活在含多种矿物质元素可供吸收利用的环境中，所以鱼的本身就富含钙质等多种矿物元素。因此该泉被列为世界“八大怪泉”之一，并被称为世界奇观。

4. 龙门天关景区

龙门天关景区由万仞绝壁、飞瀑流泉、摩崖石刻、古城堡、古长城、猿人谷等组成。龙门天关是历史上京都通往塞外的重要关隘，是历代兵家必争之地，明清两代均有重兵把守，因此留下了很多古迹。到这里游览观光，让人惊叹叫绝。

5. 白草畔景区

白草畔景区位于涞水县西北部东侧，与北京市为邻，海拔1893米。景区面积90平方千米，森林6600余公顷(1公顷=0.01平方千米)。它是河北省太行山唯一保留的以中生代火山岩为基础发育的火山岩石林与森林相匹配的生态系统。这里有华北地区特种动植物及暖温带垂直景观、北方最纯的天然山地泉溪、京西地区最佳的云雾、旭日观景台、风动石、冰川赏花、密林雪浪等多种奇观，具有观赏和科研价值。

该景区地质复杂，自然环境保存完好，山地气候独特。这里栖息生长着众多种类的野生动植物，是一个野生动植物的王国，有种子植物92科，713种，蕨类植物15科，65种。植物主要有油松、华北落叶松、白桦、榛树、侧柏、臭椿、香椿、黄栌、西伯利亚早熟禾、蒙古早熟禾、阿穆尔莎草、胡枝子、鸟巢兰、花楸、滨紫草、凤毛菊等。野生动物有700余种，其中脊椎动物184种。野生动物主要有野猪、袍子、青羊、狐狸、獾、松鼠、野兔、红隼、金雕、雉鸡、石鸡、褐马鸡、黑鹳、喜鹊等。

因海拔垂直变化大，这里形成了一年四季和上下不同的气候。山上垂直分布着4个植被类型，15个植物群系。山上清泉甘洌，花木繁茂，原始次生林分布山间，有太行山“绿色明珠”之美誉。紫丁香、野玫瑰、杜鹃花、照日白等各色山花漫山遍野。树木、花草随季节和山势的高低而变换色彩，使这里成为天然植物标本园。野生脊椎动物184种，其中鸟类125种，鱼类13种，两栖类2种，爬行类15种，哺乳类29种，其中被列为国家重点保护的野生动物有褐马鸡等15种。

白草畔景区分风动石、白草畔和石城岭三条旅游线路，主要景点28处，尤以石城岭日出、风动石和冰川赏花等景点引人入胜。石城岭为白草畔顶峰，是中国北方观日出、赏云海的胜地。天将破晓，登上峰顶，见那一望无际的云海和云霞中喷薄欲出的红日冉冉升起，壮观的场景使人赏心悦目。风动石是块直径10米、高4米的巨石，底部与崖面的两个接触点间是剔透的，两个支撑点的面积仅25厘米见方，偌大的巨石在两个支撑点上，历经千万年的地震、山崩、风暴等震动，依然固若磐石。称之为风动石，实际风吹它却不动，而是遇上风天林涛波动。由此攀上巨石，俯视林涛翻涌，感到足下巨石似乎在随风摇动。

冰川赏花奇观，是指五六月间已入初夏，在白草畔大山深处还能见到冰川。山谷一片银色，山脚没膝白雪，沟底丈深坚冰。而仰望两侧群山之腰，布满着粉红的杜鹃花，如冰川上的彩霞，似入仙境。该景区除自然景观外，人文景观亦较丰富，如老人官故居，把游人引入当年带有神秘色彩的民俗与社会制度。白草畔山下北边桥遗址出土的涞水智人化石，距今已有2.8万年的历史。

野三坡景区集名山、峰林、森林、湖泊、瀑布、云海景观、珍稀植物、野生动物、古人类遗址、避暑胜地等于一体，是旅游观光、休闲度假、探险与科研考察的好去处。这里民风古朴、山水独特、环境优雅。到过这里的客人都不会忘记那美丽的风景、周到的服务和热情的笑脸。

Yesanpo Scenic Spot lies in depths of Mt. Taihang, 75 kilometers northwest of Laishui County, covering a total area of 498.5 square kilometers. It consists of Baili Canyon Scenery Area, Juma River Summer Resort, Buddha Strange Caves and Springs

Area, Longmen Pass Great Wall Historic Reservation, Baicaopan Primeval Forest Reserve and Jinhua Mountain Hunting Area. There are hundreds of scenic spots in this area. It is a comprehensive natural ecological scenic spot, integrating mountains, rivers and springs, trees and flowers, birds and animals, fish and insects, cultural relics and places of interest. The tourism resources are unique and honored as "The Capital City and Her Environs Scenery".

Baili Canyon, national 5A-level scenery, features cloud-tapped grotesque peaks and cliffy precipice; the climate of Juma River is very cool and the environment is so quiet and serene; Longmen Pass is lofty and spectacular, with waters rushing down straightly. Besides, there are also Ethical Park, Fish Vale Cave, Baicaopan, Jinhua Mountain, Sanhuang Mountain and so on, all these scenic spots will catch people's attention thoroughly.

The terrain of Yesanpo ascends from the south to the north, and because of the difference of the altitude, it is named the spiral slope consisting of three parts vertically. The season change between the top and the bottom is about half a month. And Yesanpo is named with the change of the terrain and the climate. There exist the gorgeous Baili Canyon, the shady Baicaopan, the attractive Juma River, the mysterious Fish Vale Cave and the Shangtian Valley with nine continuous waterfalls. In this area, Mt. Taihang and Mt. Yanshan are popular for its constantly flowing Juma River, ecological and primitive environment, and precious relics, showing the process of geological evolution and the ancient Chinese civilization. With mountains, rivers, trees, flowers, waterfalls, stones, ancient castles, cliffs, meadows, and the splendid dancing—*Impression of Yesanpo*, Yesanpo Scenic Spot combines the natural landscapes with the cultural landscapes.

Yesanpo Scenic Spot is the epitome of the geological history in North China. It occupies the Zijing Pass where the great fault belt locates, and the magnificent crust-evolutionary drawings are created by the intense tectonic movement and magmatic activities. The construction of Baili Canyon is trenchant, amazing and quiescent. Besides, the corroded valley, the Longmen Pass made of straight but cracked granite and the deep Fish Vale Cave are the precious geological relics.

The relics in Yesanpo Scenic Spot are typical, systematical and complete. The surface of unconformity is clear, with magmatic limestone, sedimentary limestone and metamorphic limestone as its components. And the relics of joints, fissures and folds are abundant. The hilly planation surface, the river terrace, the magmatic caves, the ancient volcanoes and glaciers vary from one place to another. It is a vivid geological textbook and natural museum of geology. The evolution history of geological structure in North China for the past 3 billion years is concentrated, thus it is the best realm for experts to do research in geograph, the ideal base for graduates to do internship, and the vivid class for the science education. In 2004, it is authorized as "National Geological Park", and then it is recognized as the "Universal Geological Park" in 2006. In 2014, it is selected as the "National Ecotourism Demonstration Area", which is the only one included in Hebei Province.

1.1.1 Baili Canyon

It is renowned as the "First Canyon under Heaven", which locates in Gougezhuang Village, Yesanpo Town, covering an area of 110 square kilometers. and consisting of three canyons. The outmost one, Xiezi Ditch, is popular for the Girardinia cuspidata scattering all over, with the total length of 25 *li* (1*li*=0.5 km). The middle one is Haitang Ditch, which is famous for its permeating Chinese flowering crabapple. Haitang Ditch is a 35 *li* gully and the hills inside are covered with green plants soaring to the sky, which make people feel awesome about it. Going up along the ditch, one can see the amazing but dangerous "Tiger Mouth", which is a circular hole composed of arc precipice, looking like a tiger opening its dangerous and bloody mouth; then one can see the narrow "One-Line-Sky", with the narrowest pert of 0.83 meters. With the steep and cliffy precipice, the narrow gorge and the quiet valley, it forms the illusion of "With two precipices sitting in the sky, thousands of blades of mountains split the ground". Besides, the attractions, such as the flawless mimic "Turning Round Buddhism Goddess Guanyin" and the magnificent "Leading Bridge to Heaven" and "Leading Bridge to Earth" also located there.

The third canyon is called Shixuan Canyon, because there are ten arc-shaped precipices scattered inside, covering an area of 45 *li*. Entering the canyon, the waterfall "Chenniu Lake", "Shuilian Cave" in Lingzhi Mountain, the scenery of "Unseen Heaven" formed by the arc-shaped precipices, the "bizarre peak" and "the male lion" are all in sight. The total length of the three canyons is 105 *li*, thus gain it the name, Bali Canyon. Since the valleys are very deep, and the duration of sunshine is very short, when the temperature outside is about 40 ℃, the temperature inside is still about 20 ℃. In addition, the negative oxygen ion there is over 20000 units, making Baili Canyon the health-cultivation place of beautiful sceneries. It has also become the shooting place of CCTV (China Central Television) and lots of ancient plays. The TV plays known both at home and abroad are shot there, such as *Romance of the three Kingdoms*, *Heroes in Water Margin* and *Journey to the West*.

1.1.2 Juma River Scenic Spot

Juma River is the recreational summer resort, with a group of lifelike monkeys inside and many boats rippling at the mercy of the zephyr, and the couples on the boat singing love songs to each other, which make people intoxicated; the sand dunes under the inflection of the sun, beaming the wonderful light; also, the rising and falling melody in *Yesanpo Impression* is descended to the present, winning the heart of the listeners thoroughly; the verdant mountains covered with exuberant plants, bring the cool and fresh enjoyment; the flowers at the banks of the two sides, feasting the eyes totally; and the view of the Immortal Bridge, leading to ideas without limitation.

1.1.3 Fish Vale Cavity

It is composed of ancient temples, fanciful springs, bizarre caves and primitive pines. Being located at Xiaoxi River District, the branch of Juma River , Fish Vale Cavity is the wonderful place for tourists. The cave and fountain both are born by nature and full of amazement. Fish Vale Cavity is 1800 meters deep, which is discovered in the crusting karst cave in the Paleozoic limestone. Then during the period of 1.4 million years, the bigger and thicker limestone is turned into having crackles and veins under the effect of the crust movement. After that, the water snoozing from the crackles dissolves the calcium in the limestone, forming the bar-shaped karst caves. Due to the branches, the phenomenal maze of connected karst caves, continuously growing karst caves and karst caves inside another karst caves are formed. More interestingly, the calcium is turned into saturated calcium-contained water. Then the water put the calcium into sediments or crystalize it again, creating the comely scene of stalagmite, pillar, stone dragon, stone curtain and stone waterfall.

At the same time, the spring in the karst cave is intermittent. Under the influence of the season, the water in caves will snooze out. What makes it more astonishing is the spring of fish. Thus, it has the name of Fish Vale Cavity and Fish Vale Spring. The reason for this is a maze that cannot be explained. The sweet and fresh spring water is the uneasy-gained mineral water, because it is abundant in wholesome minerals and elements. The fish living in the water are more priceless, for the kind of fish is full of minerals due to the environment. All these give it the fame of one of the "Top Eight Bizarre Springs", and it is also regarded as the anecdote all over the world.

1.1.4 Longmen Pass Scenic

Longmen Pass Scenic consists of thousands of cliffy precipices, waterfalls and springs, inscriptions, ancient castles, ancient Great Wall, and Ape-man Valley. Longmen Pass is the paramount site to Beijing historically, thus it is the seizing place of two opposite parties and guarded by warriors in the Ming Dynasty and the Qing Dynasty. And a lot of relics are left there, making visitors cannot help complimenting.

1.1.5 Baicaopan Scenic

It sits on the eastern side of the northwestern part of Laishui County, bordering Beijing. The altitude of it is 1893, and the covering area is 90 square kilometers. with more than 6600 acres (1 acre=0.01 km^2) of forests. It is the only ecological system compatible with the stone forest based on the volcanic stone of the Mesozoic. There, one can see all kinds of amazing scenes, including the special animals and plants, the vertical scenery of warm temperate zone, the purest natural water, the best clouds of fog in Western Beijing, the platform for the viewing of rising sun, the wind-blowing stone, the icy flowers, the thick forests with snow, all of which are of high value of appreciation and scientific study.

The terrain in Longmen Pass is complex, with well-preserved natural environment. The mountain climate is unique, and a lot of wild plants and animals there make it the kingdom of wild lives. Among them, there are seed plants of 92 families and 713 kinds, and ferns of 15 families and 65 kinds. The plants there mainly consists of Chinese pines, larches in North China, white birches, filberts, platycladus orientals, ailanthus, cedrela sinensis, smoke tree, early-matured wood of Siberia, the early-matured corn of Mongolia, nutgrass flatsedge of Amur, lespedeza, orchidaceae, mountain ash, mertensia and saussurea. As for the wild animals there, more than 700 kinds are included, of which there are 184 kinds of spine animals, such as boar, roe deer, mountain goat, fox, badger, squirrel, hare, kestrel, golden eagle, chick, browned-eared pheasant, rock patridge, black badgers and magpie, etc..

With the great vertical change of the altitude there, the four seasons and different climates are all represented from the bottom to the top. There are four kinds of plants and fifteen series of plants growing vertically. The water is sweet and fresh, the flowers and plants are of intense scattering, winning it the name of "Verdant Bright Pearl". The wild plants are of pervasive state, like lilac, wild rose, azalea and the white-beaming flower of different kinds of color. The tree, wood, flower, and grass change their color according to the season and the height of the terrain, which makes it the garden of wild plant samples. Besides, there are 184 kinds of spine animals, among which there are 125 types of birds, 13 types of fish, 2 types of amphibian animals, 15 types of reptiles and 29 types of mammals. And 15 kinds of animals are listed as the national protective animal, like the brown-eared pheasant.

There are three routes to Baicaopan scenic, namely the wind-blowing stone, Baicaopan and the stone-wall ridge. There are 28 sites of landscapes, among which the most compeling sceneries consist of the rising sun in great stone wall, the wind-blowing stone and the icy flowers. The stone-wall ridge is the summit of Baicaopan, which is the best site to see the sun rise in North China and appreciate the sea of clouds. When the drawn comes, with unlimited sea of cloud and the rising sun deriving from the rosy clouds, one cannot help being occupied with pleasant emotions in front of such a scene. The wind-blowing stone is a piece of giant stone with the radius of ten meters. The height of it is four meters. The two interfaces of the bottom of it and the surface of precipice is crystal, and the acreage of two standing points is 0.25 square meters. Though the two points have been trembled by earthquake, landslide and storms, they still stand there without crashing. Therefore, it has the name wind-blowing stone. Actually, the stone never moves but the trees in the forest waves at the mercy of wind. If one climb onto the top of the stone from there, one would have the false sense that the gigantic stones under feet are wavering at the same time, with the ocean of trees in sight.

The unique glacier during the period of the early summer in the month of May and June can be seen at the bottom of the valley. The valley is sliver white and the ditch is full of sharp ice, but there is deep snow at the foot. Amazingly, pink azaleas permeate every ridge, like the rosy clouds in the immortal glacier. Except the natural landscape, the cultural landscape there is also of great amount. Take one as an example, the Dwelling of Old People, leading the tourists there to experience the mysterious customs and social rules. At the foot of Baicaopan, there is a Site of North Side Bridge, where the fossil remains of Laishui homo sapiens are unearthed, with a history of more than 28000 years.

Yesanpo Scenic Spot combines a lot of attractions together, including the famous mountains, peak forests, lakes, waterfalls, cloudy sceneries, treasurable plants, wild animals, site of ancient people and summer resorts. It is also a good place for sightseeing, recreational vocation, explosion and scientific study. The simple folk custom, the particular mountains and rivers, as well as the elegant ambience can all be experienced once for all. Visitors here would keep the attractive scenic landscapes, the considerate services and the warm smiling faces in mind.

（二）白石山

白石山位于涞源县城南15千米，雄踞八百里太行山北端，由大理岩构造峰林景区、十瀑峡花岗岩瀑布群景区、拒马源泉群景区等组成核心景区，总面积100余平方千米，是北京房山世界地质公园的一部分，国家5A级景区。白石山山体高大，最高峰海拔2096米，纵拔如屏，雄奇险幻，奇峰峭壁，登临其顶可以远眺狼牙山和五台山。白石山因其夏季平均气温21.7摄氏度，为北方避暑胜地。

白石山风貌

白石山景观多样，集峰林、怪石、绝壁、峡谷、瀑布、森林、云海、佛光、长城、庙观等景观于一体，地貌奇特，结构复杂，是中国古代“三十六洞天福地”之一。白石山最壮观的景致是大理岩峰林。大理岩峰林是中国峰林地貌的一种新的类型。17亿年前，白石山地区是海滨环境。到了1亿年前，经历了强烈的“燕山运动”，炽热的岩浆在白云岩盖层下剧烈运动，向上顶举，使白石山地区发生了两种变化：一是物理作用过程，简单地讲，就是岩浆巨大内应力将顶部的白云岩盖层顶起并顶裂、顶斜，之后由于重力崩塌和水流的搬运作用，形成了沟谷和山峰；二是化学作用过程，白云岩在高达上千摄氏度高温岩浆的烘烤下，发生了变质，转化成白云质大理岩，同时，在热液的作用下，花岗岩和白云岩的接触变质带生成了许多矿藏。

白石山奇峰林立，巨壑纵横。峰多、壁峭，形异、势险，堪称山岳景观中奇与险的代表。峰多：山脊山谷密集，山峰成丛成林。壁峭：直上直下，有棱有角，陡直壁立，如刀削斧劈。形异：山上的石头形体各异，如柱、如帆、如笋、如人、如兽。此处山石千奇百怪，或怪在其形，如坐佛石、象石、猪头石、人头石、蜗牛石、断剑石、将军石，妙趣横生；或怪在其质，如馒头石、千层石、龙壁石，不同石质，形态各异；或怪在其位，如悬石，好像悬挂在崖壁一小坎上半身在外。势险：山上巨石有的上大下小，有的欲倒而不倒，有的状如累卵，岌岌可危。

白石山由100多座高低错落、相对独立的山峰组成。峰林落差可达600米，谓之“雄”；峰林峥嵘，峭壁陡崖，谓之“险”；峰林如兽、如塔、如剑、如笋、如仙，鬼斧神工，谓之

“奇”；而夏秋时节，海拔1800米以上，常常云雾缥缈，若雨后初霁，波涌浪卷，缥缈难当，谓之“幻”。

白石山最高峰白石顶，每年夏季还常常会有神奇佛光出现。夏天白石山云雾缭绕的时节，摄身岩下云层中会幻化出七色光圈，中央虚明如镜，如彩绘佛像上的光环。观者背向阳光，有时会发现光环中出现自己的身影，举手投足，光环随人的移动而移动，而且每个人只能看见自己的光环，却看不到旁人的光环，这就是被人们向往亲见的佛光。

“白石晴云”为涞源古十二美景之首，意思是说，即使是晴天，白石山巅也会有层云盘绕。白石山云雾，首先是出现的机会多，夏季有三分之二的天气出现云雾，这一现象是白石山特殊的自然条件决定的，空气上升并有水汽不断补充是形成云雾的基本条件。白石山是山上之山，山体高大，比南麓群山高数百米，东南暖湿气流遇白石山爬升，含有大量水汽的气流，在爬升过程中气温降低，水汽凝结成雾。加之白石山林木茂盛，溪瀑繁多，空气湿度大，又有重峦叠嶂、深沟巨壑的阻拦与贮存，尤其是西面连绵陡峭的列屏峰与北部的主山脊将雾气严严实实地拦贮在峰林丛立的山坳里，又有暖湿气流不断从面向东南的喇叭口吹向山坳，空气湿度不断加大，从而形成了白石山的滚滚云雾。

“风云际会”是白石山的又一大奇观。白石山之景，晴不如雨，雨不如雾，雾不如云。云雾胜境总是出现在雨后初晴。在山谷中，在树林里，到处飘舞着的云雾自由自在、无所羁绊。当游客登上白石山的顶峰，无际无涯、缥缈浩瀚的云海就会显现在眼前。当山风骤起，衣袂飘动，游客就会有一种御风而行、飘然若仙的感觉。白石山的云雾胜境当属雨后初霁——沟谷之中的烟云缕缕，相继而行，袅袅上升，渐渐凝聚，成团成片，接着迅速弥漫，如万床棉絮，将谷壑填平。巨岩似浮岛，奇峰若仙山。

玻璃栈道

长城在白石山北侧逶迤盘旋，长约4000米。其大部分敌楼和墙体保存完好，是全国长城中保存比较完好的地段之一。

2014年9月中旬，白石山玻璃栈道对外开放。玻璃栈道全长95米，宽2米，是目前国内最长、最宽、海拔最高的悬空玻璃栈道。白石山玻璃栈道为混凝土框架结构，3.2厘米厚的双层夹胶玻璃与不锈钢龙骨架巧妙结合，每平方米承重达1000千克，为游客游览风光带来别样体验的同时并保障游客的安全。

Baishi Mountain is located 15 kilometers away from the south of Laiyuan County and occupies the north end of Taihang Mountains stretching 800 *li*. The core scenic area consists of Marble Mountain Peaks, Shipuxia Granite Waterfalls and the Springs to Juma River, covering a total area of 100 square kilometers. It is a part of Beijing Fangshan World Geopark and is a national 5A-level scenic spot. The Baishi Mountain is high and the altitude of the highest peak is 2096 meters. There are strange peaks and cliffs, with vertical peak like the screen, magnificent like the illusion. People can overlook Langya Mountain and Wutai Mountain after climbing to the top. Baishi Mountain is a summer resort in the north of China, as its average temperature ia about 21.7℃ in summer days.

Baishi Mountain has diversified landscape and integrates stone forest, bizarre rock, cliff, gorge, waterfall, forest, sea of cloud, Buddha's light, the Great Wall, temple and other landscape. With peculiar landform and complicated structure, it is one of the "36 cave paradises" in ancient China. The most splendid scenery of Baishi Mountain is marble stone forest. The marble stone forest is a new type landscape in China. 1.7 billion years ago, Baishi Mountain was in coastal environment. 100 million years ago, strong "Yanshan movement" occurred and fiery magma moved drastically under dolomite caprock and was raised upward to make Baishi Mountain subject to two changes. One is the physical process. Simply speaking, it is the huge internal stress of magma that raised the dolomite caprock upward and even create a big crack. Because of the collapse of gravity and the transport of water, the valleys and peaks were formed. The other is the chemical process. When baked under high temperature magma up to 1000 degrees Celsius, dolomite metamorphosed into dolomitic marble. At the same time, the contact and metamorphism of granite and dolomite generated a lot of mineral deposits under the action of hydrothermal solution.

Baishi Mountain has many magical mountains and staggered gullies. It is dense, steep, abnormal in shape and precipitous. It can be called representativeness of wonder and steepness in mountain landscape. This area has great concentrations of ridges and valleys, with peaks in clusters. Cliffs and precipices are as if they were cut by knife and axe, with clear corner angle. The stones of the mountain are various, like column, sail, bamboo shoot, man, beast. The stones have strange and witty forms in shape, like sitting Buddha stone, elephant stone, pig's head stone, man's head stone, snail stone, broken sword stone and the General stone. It is also strange in its quality, like steamed bun stone, thousand layer stone and dragon wall stone. With different quality of stones, the modality is various. It is strange in its place, like hanging stone, with the upper part hanging on the cliff ridge. Some giant stones almost collapsed and seemed extremely dangerous.

Baishi Mountain consists of more than 100 peaks of different height and they are relatively independent. The fall of stone forest can be up to 600 meters. It is magnificent with towering stone forest and steep cliffs and precipices. It is steep for the stone forest which is like beast, sword, bamboo shoot, immortal and extremely skillful. It is magical in summer and autumn. The altitude is over 1800 meters. Clouds and mists often encircle. If the sun shines again after rain, waves run high and it is dimly discernible. “Illusory Scene” can be reflected more.

In the highest peak of Baishi Mountain, Baishiding, magical Buddha's light often appears every summer. In the cloud-shrouded season, under the perturbed rock, seven-colored rings can be seen in the cloud layer, and the central area is as bright as mirror, which is like the halo above the colored drawings of the Buddha. If the viewers stand with the back to the sun, sometimes they can find their own figure in the halo, and the halo move along with the movement of people. People can only see their own halo, but can not see others'. This is Buddha's light people are yearning to see.

“Clouds in sunny day” is the oddest wonder among the Top Twelve Ancient Attractions in Laiyuan County. That is, even if it is a sunny day, Baishi Mountain is always shrouded with the cloud. In the first place, there are many opportunities for the emergence of cloud and mist in Baishi Mountain. Two thirds of the summer weather is cloudy. This phenomenon is determined by the special natural conditions of Baishi Mountain. The rising of the air and the continuous replenishment of water vapor are basic for the formation of cloud and mist. Baishi Mountain is tall and is about several hundred meters higher than mountains in the southern area. When the southeast warm air meets the mountain, it begins to climb with large amounts of water vapor. With the temperature decreasing in the process of climbing, water vapor condenses into mist. Together with countless trees, varieties of waterfalls, high humidity, the block and storage of precipitous mountains and deep giant ravines, the screen peak in the west and northern main ridge tightly stored the mist among the hills. And the warm moist air flow continuously blow from the southeast to the hole, with air humidity increasing, clouds and mist are formed in Baishi Mountain.

“Meeting of wind and clouds” is another wonder in Baishi Mountain. Mist scene always appears after raining. In valleys and woods, free and unrestrained clouds and mists wander everywhere, permeated with infinite leisureliness fluttering endlessly. When tourists climb to the top peak of Baishi Mountain, the boundless, misty and vast sea of clouds will appear in front of the eyes. When mountain breeze occurs abruptly and sleeves flutter, tourists may have a feeling of flying by virtue of wind and move with the calm serenity of a god. Mist scene of Baishi Mountain will occur after rain, cloud is generated in the gully in group and then rapidly diffuses as numerous cotton fiber to fill the gully. Enormous rock is like floating island and it is magical as spirit mountain.

The Great Wall winds its way in the north of Baishi Mountain with the length of about 4000 meters. Most watchtowers and walls are preserved well, being one of intact sections in the Great Wall nationwide.

In the midmonth of September, 2014, glass gallery road in Baishi Mountain was open to the public. It is 95 meters in overall length and 2 meters wide, being the longest, the widest and the highest suspended glass galley road in the country at present. Glass gallery road in Baishi Mountain is of concrete frame structure and 3.2 centimeters thick double-layer laminated glass is combined with stainless steel girder framework ingeniously. Each square meter can bear 1000 kilograms, It brings different experiences and ensure safety for tourists to tour scenery.

(三) 易水湖

易水湖位于易县县城西南30千米处，是20世纪50年代利用四周高耸的山势而修建的一座人工湖。水面面积27平方千米，最深处达48.5米。易水湖的水质为国家二级水质标准。湖的南侧与狼牙山相连，北侧是紫荆关，西侧是海拔高达1283米的五峰寨，东侧是九龙山。易水湖锁住易水河上游水流汇集成湖，水质清澈纯净，周围环境优美，景色宜人，因与漓江风光相媲美，被称为“北方小桂林”。

易水湖风光

老子峰是易水湖的精华。它山石林立，造型奇特。游客登临老子峰不仅可以体验大自然的鬼斧神工，更可体验中国易文化天人合一的境界。

组成老子峰的岩石，是距今10亿年前的中元古代时期在浅海、海湾、潮坪等海洋环境形成的。它是由各种燧石结核、燧石条带的白云质石灰岩以及纯灰岩、白云岩、绿色砂页岩等组成的沉积岩，称为“雾迷山组石灰岩”。这些岩石中含有藻类海洋植物形成的叠层石和原始的微古植物等化石。老子峰的地质遗迹保存了大量的地球演化、生物进化的信息，是一座天然的地质博物馆，是一本永存世间的“地学百科全书”。

湖的西北侧是五峰寨，那里经常有一条白色彩带似的迷雾从低处冉冉升起，将5个峰顶团团围住，久久不散，增添了神秘感。由五峰寨伸向湖边的五条支脉，如虎虎生威的5条巨龙，与易水湖大坝遥遥相对，把易水湖分割成块的中间半岛，是易水湖的心脏，也是易水湖秀丽景色的中心。半岛由大难坨、单寨、双寨、麒麟山等5个主要山峰组成，这5个山峰如同众星捧月，把最高峰威王山围在中间，像一朵盛开的莲花。在远离大坝的西部，由于山石长期受风雨侵蚀，山峰似斧劈刀削，又似精雕细刻，真可谓千姿百态，如在麒麟山巨壁峭岩上的几尊形似罗汉的石像，或盘膝，或默立，如静如动，形象逼真。另外三个峰尖，像三个巨人挨坐在那里，一个戴太子盔，一个戴扎巾盔，一个戴帅盔，就连穿着都是那样整齐。

易水湖是美丽的。她天生丽质，如出水芙蓉，但她更像一位藏在深闺人未识的大家闺秀。易水湖又是幸运的。她赶上了科学发展的新时代，有了出头露面、展示风采的好机会。易水湖所在的安格庄乡党委依托易水湖丰富的旅游资源，把旅游业作为本地的主导产业，积极优化环境，加大对易水湖的开发力度。目前，宽阔的龙安公路已经开通，各种车辆可以直接开到湖边，易水湖度假村、八里沟农家乐园、溪谷山庄、金坡餐饮一条街和附近的农家游已经具备了一定规模的接待能力。

Being located in the southwest of Yixian County, Yishui Lake is about 30 kilometers away from Yi County. It is a man-made lake built in the 1950s, making use of the surrounding mountains which are of high altitude. The lake totally covers the water surface of 27 square kilometers, with the deepest site of 48.5 meters. The south side of the lake is connected with Mt. Langya, the northern part to Zijingguan Pass, the west to Wufengzhai with an elevation of 1283 meters, and the east to Mt. Jiulong. The lake is formed through the collection of water coming from the upper river. With pure and clean water and splendid environment, it is termed as "little Guilin in the North China" since it rivals the Lijiang River in beauty.

The essential part of Yishui Lake is Laozi Peak, which is characterized with standing mountains and bizarre stones. Once tourists board the peak, the great workmanship of nature itself can be seen and the unification of heaven and man in Yi culture can be realized.

The rocks comprising the Laozi Peak is formed in the Mesoproterozoic Period 1 billion years ago. It is formed in the marine environment including shadow ocean, bay and tidal flat. And the sedimentary rocks there are composed of dolomitic limestone, pure limestone and sandy shales with the color of green, thus win it the fame of "Limestone of Wumishan Formation". Inside the rocks, the fossils like stromatolites and small primordial plants are formed by the sea plants belonging to algae. Now, Laozi Mountain is remarked as the everlasting "Textbook for Geographic Encyclopedia", because the vestige of the earth there reflects the process of biological evolution largely and it is also the natural museum of geology.

The Five-Peaks Stockade is located in the northwest part of Yishui Lake, with thick fog arising from the bottom, just like a white ribbon, which surrounds the five peaks for a long time and add mystery to them. The five branches stretching to the lake are like five Chinese dragons, facing to the dam of Yishui Lake. And the central island, separating the river, is the hub of the Yishui Lake. In terms of the island, it consists of five main mountains, including Danan Heap, Single-modle Stockade, Bimodal Stockade, Qilin Mountain and the highest one Weiwang Mountain in the center, forming the shape of blossoming water lily. In the western part far away from the dam, the glorious and varied peaks as if cut by the knives or axe, show their postures with the erosion of wind and rain. For instance, the Arhat-liked stone statues at the cliffy precipice, some cross-legged, while others silent-stood. The other three sharp peaks are like three persons sitting next to each other, with prince helmet, cloth helmet and general helmet on head. Whatever on their heads, they all wear neatly in terms of costumes.

Yishui Lake is born to be wonderful and charming, just like the water lily. To be more specific, it is better said to be an unknown fair maiden. Moreover, it is lucky enough because it caught the new era of scientific development, giving it the opportunity of showing its beauty and specialty. The Party Committee of Ange Village privileges tourism development as the major industry, making use of the resources and actively promoting the environment. At present, the Longan Road has been opened, so that all kinds of cars can be driven into the lakeside. The Vocational Village, the Baligou Farmhouse, the Xigu Mountain Villa, the Jinpo Catering Street, and the neighboring farmhouses all have the capability of accommodation.

(四) 狼牙山

狼牙山位于太行山东麓易县境内，因其奇峰林立、峥嵘险峻、风光绮丽，不仅有红色之城，更有绿色之韵。游客可尽享森林浴之妙：春天山花装扮，秋季红叶吐艳，半山腰有红玛瑙溶洞，景观神奇壮观。“狼山竞秀”为古易州十景之一。狼牙山现为国家4A级景区、国家级森林公园、国家级抗战遗址、河北省爱国主义教育基地、全国百家红色经典景区之一。

狼山竞秀

狼牙山是一座雄奇险峻、景色秀丽的名山，也称郎山。狼牙山由5坨、36峰组成，主峰莲花瓣海拔1105米，西北两面峭壁千仞，东、南两面略为低缓，登高远眺，可见千峰万岭如大海中的波涛，起伏跌宕。近望西侧，石林耸立，自然天成。大小莲花峰如出水芙蓉，傲然怒放，涧峡云雾缥缈，神奇莫测。狼牙山风光秀丽，漫山遍布苍松翠柏、飞溪流泉，拥有丰富的动植物资源。动物有黄羊、松鼠、锦鸡等。植物有松、柏、桦、枫等北方树种二三百种之多。狼牙山拥有丰富的林业资源，其森林覆盖率达80%，被称为天然氧吧。独特的地质环境、人文景观与自然景观交相辉映，使游客在接受爱国主义教育的同时，充分享受大自然的鬼斧神工和人文环境的熏陶。狼牙山是一处集教育、休闲、观光、娱乐于一体的旅游胜地。

1. 狼牙山五壮士纪念塔

狼牙山五壮士纪念塔是国务院批准的全国革命纪念建筑重点保护单位之一，位于狼牙山主峰棋盘坨。它由纪念塔、碑廊、凉亭、牌楼组成，建筑面积400平方米。碑廊有杨成武等12位领导人的题词。塔高21米，坐落于整座建筑物的中轴线，为中空正五棱柱体，上有琉璃瓦塔亭罩顶。塔内五级钢梯攀缘而上可直至塔顶小楼。站在小楼内极目远眺，可领略易县群山之壮观，观苍茫云海和日出。纪念塔是狼牙山第一胜景，有许多人在此举行革命纪念活动。

狼牙山五壮士

2. 五壮士陈列馆

该馆坐落在狼牙山山脚，馆内分为一、二两个展厅，陈列着当年中华儿女抗击日寇侵略的武器和根据地军民的生活用具以及革命先辈留下来的珍贵手迹和照片。人们在此缅怀英雄，强烈的爱国主义情绪油然而生，被激励着奋发图强。

3. 西天门

西天门是进入狼牙山的第一道关门，由此进入狼牙山奇险的境地。西天门旁的棒槌峰上立有一奇石，犹如一天将巍然屹立，顶盔掼甲，手执腰刀，长鬓挺直，威风凛凛。据说是天庭派来镇守此门的。在 1941 年的狼牙山战斗中，这里是第一次阻击战遗址，保存着较为完好的战壕遗址，向世人诉说着那段可歌可泣的历史。

4. 袖筒沟

袖筒沟是一狭长山谷，深长悠远，状如袖筒，似在洞中穿行。“阎王鼻”是一道窄窄的山梁，又叫“鲤鱼脊”。鱼头探向河谷，鱼尾搭在清水渠上，一条上山古栈道，挂在鲤鱼脊背上。石径宽不过盈尺，如绳飘忽，千回百折，若隐若现。小鬼脸沿石阶而上，一侧是巨大铁色石崖，如半壁山倾斜下来；一边深谷，崖下一条小径，人要紧靠崖壁行走，有时岩石会擦着耳朵蹭着脸，每迈一步都心惊胆战。

5. 棋盘坨

棋盘坨是狼牙山五指峰之一，坨顶地势平坦，多松柏树。棋盘坨共分三层，成梯状分布。最上层有块平坦光滑的青色巨石，上面清晰地刻有纵横十九条纹理，恰是一围棋棋盘。棋盘上有松柏遮日，中间一层也有一围棋棋盘，纹理稍浅，是假棋盘。旁有一千年古柏，树身分成 5 根，成 45 度角向四周伸展，丫丫杈杈，密密匝匝，冠盖如云，成巨伞状。最下层为一平地，松柏间浓荫处处。相传棋盘坨是王禅老祖和孙膑下棋练武之处。

总投资 1300 万元的狼牙山索道于 2004 年底建成，该索道从五壮士陈列馆后坡一直通往棋盘坨，全长 860 米，上下落差 300 多米，为箱式客运索道，乘索道可纵观狼牙山全貌。

狼牙山揽红色教育与绿色教育与一身，集爱国主义教育、山岳风光、溶洞、森林浴、三教文化五大优势于一体，独具特色，是教育、健身的最好游览地之一。

Being located at the eastern foot of Taihang Mountain in Yixian County, Mt. Langya is famous for its magnificent peaks, lofty steeps, beautiful scenery, revolutionary soul, and green rhyme. Tourists can enjoy flowers in spring, forest immersion in summer, and red leaves in autumn. The red agate cave, located half mountainside, presents a magnificent vista. The spectacular landscape, “The Langya Competition Show”, is one of the top ten famous scenic spots of ancient Yixian County. Now, Mt. Langya is categorized as a 4A-level tourist site, National Forest Park, Memorial Ruins for National Anti-Japanese War and the Base for Patriotic Education of Hebei Province, and one of the One Hundred Red Revolution Classic Attractions.

Mt. Langya is a famed mountain in terms of its magnificence, steepness and elegance, which wins it another name, Mt. Langshan. It consists of five ridges and thirty-six mountain peaks, the principal one of which is 1105 meters high. The cliffs are steep in the north and west, but low and flat in the south and east. Numerous peaks look like the fluctuating waves and tides in the sea. The stone forests in the west are created by nature with the Lotus Peak, resembling flowers in full bloom. The cloud and mist float in the valley making the atmosphere there more mysterious. Mt. Langya is covered with evergreen pines and springs and inhabited by a variety of animals and plants, such as mountain sheep, squirrels and golden pheasants are included, and more than two or three hundred kinds of plants such as pines, cypresses, birches and maples included. The Mountain possesses rich forest resource, which covers eighty percent of the whole area, thus it is called the Natural Oxygen Bar. Besides, the unique geographic environment, cultural and natural landscapes make visitors fully savor the nature and get educated with patriotic stories, and the influence of gorgeous workmanship of nature as well as the humanity of human society. Mt. Langya is a renowned tourist attraction for education, recreation, sightseeing and entertainment.

1.4.1 The Memorial Tower of Five Warriors on Mt. Langya

The Memorial Tower of Five Warriors is situated at the principal peak — Chessboard Heap, and it is granted as one of the important national revolution memorial sites under the State Protection. The tower consists of four parts, namely, the memorial tower, the tablet corridor, and the pavilion and memorial gate, occupying an area of 400 square meters. The inscriptions of twelve state leaders like Yang Chengwu and others are carved in the tablet corridor. And the tower is 21 meters high, located along the medial axis of the whole edifice. It adopts hollow structure and the shape of pentagonal prism with glazed tiles covering the top. Along the steel stairs of five floors, one can climb to the top of the tower, where the splendid view of the mountains, clouds and sunrise can be seen. Therefore, a lot of people chose it as the commemorative site for revolutionary activities as it is the top tourist attraction in Mt. Langya.

1.4.2 The Exhibition Hall for the Five Warriors

The Exhibition Hall for the Five Warriors lies at the foot of Mt. Langya and it is divided into two parts, displaying the weapons used for the fighting against the Japanese invaders by Chinese people, the utensils of soldiers and peasants, and the priceless manuscripts and photographs of precedents. When heroes are complimented here, the intense emotion of patriotism is motivated, compelling us to strive for the great prosperity of China.

1.4.3 The Western Heavenly Gate

The Western Heavenly Gate is the first pass to Mt. Langya. There is a strange stone on the Wooden Club Peak beside the Gate, looking like a person standing straight equipped with the helmet and armor. The spear as well makes him majestic-looking and commanding. It is said that he is sent there to defend the gate. During the war happened in Mt. Langya in 1947, the gate functioned as the blind for the first sniper shot and the trenches there are well preserved, reminding people of the inspiring and touching histories of warriors.

1.4.4 The Sleeve Valley

The Sleeve Valley is a long but narrow valley, making it looks like a sleeve. "Yama's Nose", also called "Carp's Spine", consists of a narrow ridge. With head probing into the valley and the end in the clean water channel, the archaic road just suspends in the spine of the fish. The radius of the stony road is no more than twenty centimeters wide, just like the wafting rope twisting thousands of times and looming there. Along the stony stairs, there is a giant rusty precipice like half of the mountain slanting to the valley; on the other side, there is a path along the deep valley. People have to walk closely to the cliff where sometimes people's face or ears may rub against the clamping rocks, which thrills the people who walk across there.

1.4.5 Chessboard Heap

Chessboard Heap is one of the Wuzhi Peaks, with flat terrain and numerous pines and cypresses on the summit. It is composed of three layers in the shape of ladder. At the uppermost layer, there is a piece of glazed giant stone with cut-crossing nineteen veins clearly inscribed. The "chessboard" is covered with pines and cypresses, which is the case with the middle layer. Beside it, there is an ancient tree of thousands of years, whose main body is divided into five branches extending to all directions with the angle of forty-five degree. The exuberant limps are as intense as clouds. At the bottom layer lies the flat ground. And the shades of pines and cypress covered almost everything. According to the legend, it is the place where Forefather Wang Chan and Sun Bin played chess and practiced martial art.

The cableway, with the total investment of 13 million *yuan*, was completed at the end of 2004. It starts from The Exhibition Hall for the Five Warriors to Chessboard Heap, stretching 860 meters and the depth between the top and the bottom is more than 300 meters approximately. The whole scene of Mt. Langya can be overviewed by the box-style cableway.

Mt. Langya is an ideal resort for patriotic and ecology education and mountainous sightseeing, with karst carves, forest exploration and Three Religions (Confucianism, Buddhism, Taoism) as its own advantage.

(五) 白洋淀

白洋淀地处京、津、石腹地，是华北最大的淡水湖泊，总面积达366平方千米。淀区被3700条沟壕、12万亩(1亩约为667平方米)芦苇、近10万亩荷花分割成大小不等、形状各异的143个淀泊，因白洋淀面积最大而命名，素有“华北明珠”之称和“华北之肾”之誉。白洋淀为国家5A级景区。景区凸显生态、历史、红色、民俗四大文化，有荷花大观园、白洋淀文化苑、怡欣园、鸳鸯岛、休闲岛、渔人乐园、元妃荷园、水上乐园、异国风情园、王家寨民俗村等景区。

白洋淀气候宜人，风景秀美，四季竞秀，水光天色，妙趣天成。春光降临，芦芽竞出，满淀碧翠；每至盛夏，“蒲绿荷红”“岸柳如烟”；时逢金秋，芦荡飞絮，稻谷飘香；隆冬时节，坚冰似玉、坦荡无垠。淀内沟壕纵横相连，芦荡、荷塘、渔村星罗棋布的地貌在全国独一无二。

白洋淀是鸟的王国，鱼的王国，多种水生植物的博物馆。淀内鱼、虾、蟹、贝、莲藕等水生动植物资源丰富，有着得天独厚的旅游资源。白洋淀是华北地区的“空调器”“晴雨表”，对于维护华北地区生态环境具有不可替代的作用。

荷花大观园

白洋淀文化底蕴深厚，历史悠久，民风独特，自古即为帝王巡幸之所，英雄辈出之地。康熙、乾隆多次到白洋淀游览，打水围，留下了许多脍炙人口的诗文和优美动听的历史故事，并修建了四处水上行宫。白洋淀是革命老区，具有光荣的革命传统。闻名中外的雁翎队谱写了一曲白洋淀人民抗日救国的英雄赞歌；著名作家孙犁先生的《白洋淀纪事》奠定了我国文坛“荷花淀”文学流派的基调;《小兵张嘎》《新儿女英雄传》等优秀文学作品成为我国现代文学发展史上一道绚丽的景观。白洋淀民俗文化淳朴，水乡渔民的生产生活具有浓郁独特的北国水乡特色。男捕鱼、女编织的渔民生活由来已久，捕鱼工具和方法名目众多，为全国之冠。苇箔、苇席产量一度占到全国的50%，并远销海外。造船业起于北宋，兴盛于清，誉满华北。白洋淀是艺术之乡，老调、昆曲等戏曲艺术种类繁多，民间花会活跃繁荣，苇编工艺独树一帜，放荷灯等民俗风情令人向往。

白洋淀是大清河水系重要的水利调节枢纽，上承九河，下注渤海，是海河流域重要的蓄滞洪区。它承接上游3.12万平方千米的洪沥水，承担着缓洪滞沥，保卫京津、华北油田、京九铁路等重要交通干线和周边地区人民生命财产安全的重任。

1. 白洋淀荷花大观园

白洋淀荷花大观园占地面积2000亩。这里建有六区、十二园、三十六景、七十二连桥，拥有666种中外名荷，各种水生植物366种，是目前我国种植荷花和水生植物面积最大、品种最多的巨型生态景区，被确定为“河北省名特优荷花繁育示范基地”“省级湿地自然保护区”“野生动植物繁育示范基地”。

白洋淀荷花大观园是集旅游观光、休闲度假、会议教学、拓展训练、水上运动于一体的综合性生态景点。

2. 白洋淀文化苑

白洋淀文化苑占地约2000亩。景点主题涵盖历史、传统、民俗、生态四种文化。有八处景观：康熙水围行宫、沛恩寺、钱屏、东堤烟柳、西淀风荷、水生植物园、嘎子村和雁翎队纪念馆。

白洋淀荷花

康熙水围行宫是按原来郭里口行宫而恢复的，分千岁殿和寝宫两院，供皇帝在水围之余处理政务和休息之用。沛恩寺分天王殿和大雄宝殿两处，寺内藏有康熙皇帝亲题石匾一额，甚为珍贵。钱屏是一种仿古游戏，类似“投壶”。东堤烟柳和西淀风荷为安新的八景之一，恢复再现了当年秀美之姿。1500米长的水上栈桥尤为壮观。水生植物园重点展示白洋淀“一花三宝”（荷花、芡实、皮条、菱角）。嘎子村以展示和体味白洋淀民俗为主题。雁翎队纪念馆再现雁翎神兵的风采，为爱国主义教育基地。

3. 白洋淀之窗

白洋淀之窗位于鸳鸯岛南侧，面积5000平方米，距离旅游码头10千米左右。里面以写实为手法，浓缩了白洋淀区域的古今文化、生态文化，以丰富的实物和珍贵的历史照片，详细地介绍了淀上神兵雁翎队的抗战史，淀区的自然资源和淳厚的白洋淀渔家的生活气息及浓浓的风土人情。内容布局为“六厅一园”，即导厅、人文历史厅、民俗厅、自然资源厅、英雄史诗厅、渔家民俗厅和水乡风情厅。

人文历史厅主要介绍了白洋淀几千年的发展历程，其中既有白洋淀的人文景点，又有美不胜收的自然景观。民俗厅以真实优美的彩照和实物，介绍了白洋淀多姿多彩的文化生活：华夏一绝的芦苇工艺、秀美的剪纸、具有传统水乡特色的花会、祈求吉祥的放荷灯活动等。

自然资源厅主要以白洋淀内的水禽、水生植物、鱼类来展示白洋淀“鱼米之乡”的丰富资源。英雄史诗厅以珍贵的历史照片，再现了雁翎队的烽火硝烟，展示了雁翎队员英勇杀敌的壮举。渔家民俗厅以各式各样的渔具、行动来反映白洋淀人对水的珍爱及热爱生活的真实写照。水乡风情园主要介绍了白洋淀别具特色的水乡风情。古老的大槐树、浓缩的渔家小院、儿童英雄张嘎子的家、雁翎队队部、戏台、古朴的小店铺和那典雅的枣花墙、石碾、石墨以及古老的鹰排船，定会让你感受到白洋淀浓浓的水乡特色。

Being located in the middle of Hebei Province, surrounded by Beijing, Tianjin and Shijiazhuang, covering the total area of 366 square kilometers with 3700 trenches, 120000 *mu*（1*mu* ≈ 667 m^2） reed, 100000 *mu* lotus, and 143 lakes, Baiyangdian Lake is the largest freshwater lake in north China, named by the largest lake of Baiyangdian. It is national 5A-level scenic spot. It is known as “the Pearl and the Kidney of North China”. The scenic highlights the culture of ecology, history, revolution and folk, consists of Grand Lotus Park, Baiyangdian Lake Culture Park, Yixin Park, Mandarin Ducks Island, Leisure Island, Fisherman’s Paradise, Yuan Imperial Concubine Lotus Park, Water Park, International Culture Park and Wang Folk Village.

The climate of Baiyangdian is pleasant, the scenery there is graceful and excellent with four seasons competing for the throne of beauty. And the color of the sky is reflected in the water, which is created by the amazing nature itself. When spring comes, bulrush germinates emulatively, and the whole lake is jade-green. In the midsummer, the leaf is green, while the lotus is red. Willows on the bank sway in the wind, just like smoke rolling up. In golden autumn, the flower of bulrush flutters and fragrance of paddy floats in the air. In cold winter, solid ice is like jade, boundless and even. In the lake, ditches are joined vertically and horizontally. The physiognomy of rippled reed, lotus pools and scattered fishing villages is unique in the whole country.

It is the kingdom of bird and fish and it is also the museum of a variety of aquatic plants. It is rich in aquatic animals and plants, such as fish, shrimp, crab, shell and lotus root. It also abounds in tourism resources. Baiyangdian is the “air conditioner” and “barometer” of Northern China, playing an irreplaceable role in maintaining the ecological environment.

Possessing of profound culture, long history and unique folk customs, Baiyangdian is the place for Emperor traveling and heroic deeds. Emperor Kangxi and Qianlong went there many times for sightseeing, leaving a lot of poems and historical stories praised universally. They also left four palaces above the water. Baiyangdian is the old revolutionary area, which is famous for its honorable glories and traditions. The Yan-Ling Group, known by domestic and foreign countries, composes a carol of the heros of Baiyangdian defeating the Japanese; the well-known author Sun Li wrote *The Matters of Baiyangdian*, which set the tone of the literature, Hehuadian; besides, the works *Little Solider Zhang Ga* and *New Biography of Heros and Heroines* become the magnificent and special scene. The folk culture there is simple and pure, and the production and living of the fisherman's lives feature with specialities of Northern China. The fishermen is in charge of fishing and their wives in charge of spinning, which has a long history until now. The tools and ways for catching fish are diverse and ranked the first in China. Also, the production of reed screen and reed mat was once counted fifty percent of total sales of the whole market in China and even sold overseas. Ship building derived from the Northern Song Dynasty and became prosperous in the Qing Dynasty with its reputation covering the whole area even in Northern China. It is also the town of art.There are many types of Chinese opera such as traditional opera and Kunqu Opera. The Folk-custom Festival is active and thriving. The craft for reeding pages "has a life of its own". The tradition of setting lotus lights on the river makes people yearn for it.

Baiyangdian is the most paramount water control junction of Daqing Water System, as its upstream is linked with nine rivers and pours into Bohai Sea. It is also the most important storage area of flood in Hai River Basin. It is linked with the flood of 31200 square kilometers. from the upstream. It also shoulders the responsibility of alleviation and drainage of the water, protecting Beijing and Tianjin, the oil field of Northern China, and the key trunk line of the Beijing-Kowloon Railway and insuring the safety of the people and properties in the surrounding area.

1.5.1 The Grand Lotus Park

The Grand Lotus Park covers 2000 *mu*, with 6 sections, 12 gardens, 36 scenes and 72 bridges built there. As for the species of lotus and other aquatic plants , it is ranked as number one in China in terms of the growing area and the variety, with 666 renowned kinds of lotus from both domestic and foreign countries and 366 types of aquatic plants. Thus, it is called the magnificent ecological scenery. All these account for its reputation as "Demonstration Base of the Reproduction of Outstanding and High-quality Lotus" "Provincial Wetland Reserve" and "Demonstration Base of of the Reproduction of Wild Animals and Plants".

The Grand Lotus Park is a comprehensive ecological scenic spot, functioning as a place for sightseeing, entertainment, conference and teaching, outdoor training, and water sports.

1.5.2 Baiyangdian Lake Culture Park

It occupies 2000 *mu*, with four themes contained, namely, histroy, tradition, custom and ecology. There are eight landscapes: Kangxi Shuiwei Palace, Peien Temple, Qian Ping, Willows in the Eastern Bank, Lotus in the Western Lake, Aquatic Plants Garden, Gazi Village and YanLing Group Memorial Hall.

Kangxi Shuiwei Palace is restored according to the primary Guolikou Palace, which is divided into the Hall of One Thousand Years and the King's Resting Place. They were used to deal with official affairs and rest by emperor. Peien Temple is composed of Hall of Heavenly Kings and The Main Hall of One Thousand Years, with treasurable tablet inscribed personally by Emperor Kangxi. Qianping imitates ancient games, which is similar to "throw arrows into the pot". Willows in the Eastern Bank and Lotus in the Western Lake are peculiar scenery among the "Eight View of Anxin", reviving the elegance and beauty in ancient times. The bridge above the lake, extending 1500 meters, is so magnificent to see. Aquatic Plants Garden mainly displays the "three treasures of lotus". Gazi Village majorly displays Baiyangdian folk customs. YanLing Group Memorial Hall reappears the perky demeanor of the soldiers of Yanling Group and become the base for patriotic education.

1.5.3 Window of Baiyangdian

It sits in the southern part of Mandarin Ducks Island, covering the land of 5000 square meters. And 10 kilometers away from the dock. The techniques used inside exbition is realistic, it condenses the ancient and modern culture as well as ecology. With abundant exhibits and precious pictures, the story of Yanling Group's valiant warriors, the natural resources, the fishermen's living conditions and customs of Baiyangdian are detailedly introduced. The configuration of Window of Baiyangdian is "one garden and six halls", which includes Introduction Hall, Culture and History Hall, Folklore Hall, Natural Resources Hall, Heroic Epic Hall, Fishermen's local Customs Hall and Water Township Hall.

The Culture and History Hall is the place for the introduction of the evolution of Baiyangdian during the past few years, highlighting both cultural and natural attractions. With real and splendid objects and color photographs, Folklore Hall demonstrates the colorful life of its culture, such as the amazing crafts for weaving reed, the comely paper cutting, the tradition-featured Flower Show, and the setting of lotus light. In terms of the six halls, Natural Resources Hall features with aquatic poultry, aquatic plants and fish to show that Baiyangdian is the land flowing with milk and honey. Heroic Epic Hall reappears the real scene of the war, showing the feats of the warriors of Yanling Group. Fishermen's local Customs Hall is characterized by different kinds of tools to reflect how beloved people feel about water and their life. Water Township Hall highlights the distinctive features of watery township. The tall pogoda trees, delicate fisherman's yard, the home of Zhang Gazi, the office of Yanling Group, the opera stage, the shop with primitive simplicity, and the exquisite wall of Zaohua, the grinding stone, and the primitive row boat, all of these will make you feel the features of the water township, Baiyangdian.

㈥ 天生桥

天生桥瀑布群位于太行山中段北麓阜平县境内，总面积50平方千米，植被覆盖率95%以上，集“中国北方最大瀑布群、中国最大片麻岩天生桥、罕见的原始次生林”于一体。天生桥瀑布群一沟九瀑，呈阶梯状相连，最大的瑶台银河飞瀑落差为112.5米，飞流直下，气势磅礴。

天生桥景区是一处以中山和亚高山地貌为特色的自然风景区，以山奇、水奇、桥奇、林奇、草奇、洞奇、冰奇而著称，是阜平优美自然风光的精髓和灵魂，被誉为“太行山深处的香格里拉”。境内峰峦叠嶂、苍山如海、溪瀑跌宕、植被茂密、奇险峻峭，是一个巨大的“天然氧吧”。

据专家考证，天生石桥已有28~29亿年了，一般发育于喀斯特地貌中，也有出现在硅铝层状地层之中，但在变质片麻岩中，这是我国首次发现的变质岩天生桥。它长27米，宽13米，高13米，与九大瀑布中最大的瑶台山银河飞瀑组成了一个天然的地质奇观。

瀑布

阜平地区在28亿年以前曾是一片海洋，后来经历了阜平运动(距今28亿年)、五台运动(距今25亿年)，地壳上升为陆地。距今18亿年以前又发生了吕梁运动，使得阜平地区与整个华北地区形成了统一的地台基底。阜平地区又经历了3亿年左右陆地剥蚀，距今15亿年左右，海水入侵。之后距今8亿年至5.5亿年，地壳又上升为陆地，距今4.4亿年的时候，阜平地区与整个华北地区一起上升为陆地。后来又受燕山运动和由于印度板块挤压产生的喜马拉雅运动的影响，形成了天生桥国家地质公园今日复杂的地形地貌景观。

阜平是我国太古界“阜平群”建立的经典、标准剖面所在地，在华北各地变质岩都以“阜平群”作为标准，进行对比和命名，阜平也是阜平运动的命名地，阜平还是出露为数不多的“陆核”之一，因此作为阜平人和到阜平旅游的朋友应感到无限骄傲和自豪。

景区内系温带大陆性半湿润季风气候，夏季温暖多雨，冬春干燥寒冷，植被垂直分布明显，从下至上分别为落叶阔叶林、针叶林和亚高山草甸，主要乔木有辽东栎、油松、落叶松、桦树、漆树、盐肤木、杨树、山榆等。灌木有蔷薇、玫瑰、平榛、大花溲疏、绣线菊、接骨木、暴马丁香等。其中国家二级保护植物有刺五加、核桃楸。还有许多变色植物，如青榨槭、黑荀子、元宝槭，花楸等，为秋季旅游增添靓丽与多姿。

来天生桥瀑布群旅游最关心的问题之一就是水源。该景区地表水丰富，各沟谷内都有溪瀑流宕，多水多瀑原因有三：一是变质岩透水性差，地表保水保土条件好；二是山区降水较多，随海拔升高降水量加大；三是植被茂密，含水量强。

天生桥风光

天生桥瀑布群，时宽时窄，曲折幽深。溪水时而轰鸣雄壮，激昂豪放；时而委婉轻柔，悦耳动听，充满无限生机和活力。溪流两侧的悬崖陡壁、奇峰怪石千姿百态，花草树木万紫千红，无论浓烈与恬淡，到处展现的是大自然的神奇与美丽。

天生桥瀑布群是中国北方最大的瀑布群，从上到下，高差从几十米到一百多米，分为九级，宛如九条巨龙从崖壁上飞流直下。其中落差最大的是瑶台山“银河飞瀑”，高达 112.5 米，如一幅白缎。微风乍起，它便散作无数条洁白的哈达。

天生桥国家地质公园博物馆内详细介绍了景区的地质发展情况并且陈列了许多非常有价值的岩石矿物标本。公园主峰百草坨海拔 2144.5 米，它和“手摸白云天，脚踏花草地”的玫瑰坨一脉相连，在阜平诸山中位居第三，号称“空中草园”，现有 6000 亩人工栽植的落叶松，有 70000 亩以白桦林为主的乔灌杂树共生的原始次生林，有大面积的亚高山草甸，还可以观看到晋冀两省层峦叠嶂的山貌。这就是鬼斧神工的天生桥国家地质公园。

Being located in Fuping County, the northern part of middle Mountain Taihang, covering the total area of 50 square kilometers with forest planting rate of more than 95%, the Tianshengqiao Waterfall is the largest one in North China, the largest natural gneiss bridge in China, and the unusual original secondary forest. There are nine waterfalls in one valley, terraced flying straight down, with the largest Yaotai Milky Way Waterfall falls to 112.5 meters.

The scenery of Tianshengqiao Scenic Spot features average-altitude mountains and relatively high mountains. The freakish mountains, the pure water, the unique bridge, the peculiar forest, the fanciful plants, the rummy caves and the picturesque ice there all make it known as "Shangri-La in Mountain Taihang". In a sense, it is the essence and soul of Fuping County. With numerous mountains, fluctuating streams and waterfalls, flourishing plants, it is a gigantic "Natural Oxygen Bar".

It is reported by experts that the natural stone bridge has been existed there for 2.8 to 2.9 billion years, which was usually bred from karst formations, with some derives from sialic crust. But it is the first discovery of natural arch made of metamorphic rocks in China. The fall of the highest Yaotai waterfall is 112.5 meters. The inartificial bridge is 27 meters long, 13 meters wide and 13 meters high, together with the highest Yaotai waterfall forming a natural marvelous spectator.

Fuping County used to be an ocean 2.8 billion years ago, it then experienced Fuping Movement (2.8 billion years ago) and Wutai Movement (2.5 billion years ago), so it became one part of earth. After that, about 1.8 billion years ago, the Lvliang Movement made it form a united base between Fuping area and the whole region of North China. About 1.5 billion years ago, the sea water invaded, and the press from both sides lasted for 300 million years. Then, the crust of this area was lifted as the terrain approximately 800 million years or 550 million years ago. About 440 million years ago, because of Yanshan Movement and Himalayas Mountains formed by the pressure of the Indian Plate, the complex topographic and geomorphic landscape of Tianshengqiao National Geopark was formed.

Fuping County is the site where the classic and standard section locates in Archaean group among the"Fuping Group", thus it is the norm of the metamorphic rocks of different places in North China. Fuping is the origin place of Fuping Movement. Now, Fuping is one of the few uncovered "continental crust", which makes the locals and the visitors feel proud indefinitely.

The climate in the scenic spot belongs to temperate continental semi-humid monsoon climate, warm and rainy in summer, cold and dry in winter. The vertical distribution of vegetation is obvious. From bottom to top are deciduous broad-leaved forest, coniferous forest and subalpine meadow. The spices of trees are mainly Liaodong oak, Chinese pines, larch pines, birches, lacquer trees, Chinese sumac trees, poplars and wild elms. And the bushes there consist of stinging plants, roses, hazels, big flower deutzia, spiraea, elderberries and syringe reticulates and the like. Besides, there are the national second-class protective plants, including Acanthopanax and juglans mandshurica. The color-changed plants, like Acer davidii franch, black xunzi, acer truncatum and mountain ash, add the beauty and variety to the autumn tourism.

The most worried problem of the tourists in Tianshengqiao Waterfall Group is the source water. The scenic spot is abundant in surface water, with creeks and rivers flowing in every valley. There are three reasons for the overflow of water and falls. Firstly, the permeable ability of metamorphic rocks is poor, thus the water and the soil could be kept on the surface. Secondly, the precipitation of mountain area is flourishing, with the elevation of altitude. Thirdly, the exuberant vegetation can retain a lot of water.

Tianshengqiao Waterfall Group characterizes with unpredictable and zigzag shape. As for the creeks, the sound of it is very loud. For a while, the sound becomes euphemistic and soft, filled with unlimited vitality and energy. The cliffs and steep mountains on both sides of the river are unique and fanciful, and the multi-colored plants with light and dark color all display the amazing power and beauty of nature itself.

Tianshengqiao Waterfall Group is the largest one in North China, for the drop varies from decades of meters to more than one hundred meters. It is divided into nine stages, looking like nine giant dragons diving into the valley from the cliff, among which the highest one, Yaotai Waterfall, is as high as 112.5 meters, just like the picture of white stain. When breeze comes, it is scattered as the pure and pristine hada (a piece of silk ribbon used as greeting gifts).

The museum introduces in detail the geological development of the scenic spot and displays a lot of valuable mineral rock specimens. The main peak, Baicao Heap, has an elevation of 2144.5 meters, which is linked to the Rose Heap. It is ranked as the third one among the mountains of Fuping County. Baicao Heap is known as the Garden in the Air. It has 6000 *mu* of planted larches, 70000 *mu* of original forest of bushes and trees which is represented by birches, and a large area of subalpine meadow. The mountain landscapes in Shanxi Province and Hebei Province are also in view. This is the extraordinary Tianshengqiao National Geo-park created by nature.

(七) 虎山

虎山风景区地处太行山东麓，曲阳县境内。它与古北岳恒山相邻，因其山顶一块被当地称为“义虎”的巨石而得名。景区面积30余平方千米。

虎山风貌

虎山山青水媚，花繁林茂，是一处自然山水风景区。景区地处大山深处，人迹罕至，保持了完好的原生态风貌。虎山的山体平缓、温柔、和谐、安宁，给人一种敦厚、庄重、质朴的美。这里山泉涌动、流水潺潺，游客能在行走中感受太行山的美丽，在悠然惬意中有一种禅意涌上心头。虎山景区是集山水观光、休闲度假、林果采摘、会议接待为一体的多功能风景区。

来虎山旅游，是华北黄金文化第一游。这里具有悠久的采金历史，采金遗址众多，文化内涵丰富，拥有深厚的黄金文化底蕴。据《曲阳县志》记载：“金，分布在县境西北之界三尖梁山麓，矿化带500米以上，厚1米左右，含金量5克/吨，元代曾有开采。”据当地传说，在唐宋时期，虎山就有采金活动。至今山中仍遗留着石屋遗迹、石碾、石磨等实物以及历代金矿遗址多处，有的矿洞长约千米。虎山采金一直延续到20世纪90年代中期，形成了高品质、独具特色的采金历史文化资源。当地人在山中采金时祭祀山神、财神等活动，给这里留下了极为深厚的宗教文化、民俗文化等诸多虎山特色文化。这些文化展示了虎山丰厚的人文资源，是虎山“黄金文化之旅”最重要、最独特的优势。

虎山

这里有最惊奇的长达千米的金矿洞，有最值得一看的“黄金文化展览馆”，介绍金矿的成因及开采，展出各种金矿石标本，告诉人们黄金是怎样炼成的，人类为什么崇拜黄金；同时，还有黄金与宗教、黄金与养生、黄金与货币等知识展板。黄金文化展览馆也称一号黄金馆，是华北首家实景场景式展示中心。在这里，游客还可以

淘金文化

参与淘金活动，将会体验到无穷的乐趣，获得意想不到的惊喜！

站在一号馆旁边的广场上，抬头就可以看到前面山上矗立着一尊被当地人称为“老虎石”的巨石。相传，古时候山下村中有兄弟二人，到太行山里挖金。回家时，弟弟欲独吞财宝，就将哥哥推到了崖下，正好落在山崖上的一个窄窄的高台上，惊动了旁边虎洞的老虎。这只老虎背上哥哥跃上山崖，并送他回家。老虎返回大山，走到这块巨石下面的时候，它累死了。哥哥为了纪念这只有着一颗仁义之心的老虎，就请人书写了一副对联：“见利忘义人不如兽，世间真情兽胜于人。”至今碑已无存，巨石还在，被称为“老虎石”。山下的小村庄因此也得名为虎山村。虎山还流传着许多与虎有关的故事，如虎护狐仙、虎化人、虎救刘秀当皇帝等。

Mt. Hushan is located at the eastern foot of Mt. Taihang, Quyang County. It is adjacent to Mt. Hengshan, the ancient Beiyue. The total area is more than 30 square kilometers.

Mt. Hushan is a natural scenic area with picturesque landscapes and luxuriant plants. The scenic spot is located in the deep mountain where few people tread, thus it maintains the intact ecological features. Mt. Hu shan is flat, gentle, harmonious and peaceful, giving the visitors an enchanted feeling. With surging springs and gurgling streams, visitors can feel the beauty of Mountain Taihang. Mt. Hushan is a multi-functional scenic spot, which integrates sightseeing, recreation, fruit picking and conference as a whole.

Mt. Hushan is distinguished by the gold culture in Northern China. It has a long history of gold mining, and there are a large number of gold mining sites with rich cultural connotation. According to the record of *Quyang County Annals*: the gold is distributed in the northwest county border, the foot of Sanjianliang, the mineral zone is 500 meters high, and 1 meter thick, the gold content of which is 5 grams in every ton, which used to be mined in the Yuan Dynasty. According to the local legends, in the Tang Dynasty and the Song Dynasty, there were gold mining activities in Mt. Hushan. Now there are still stone ruins, grinding stones and other sites preserved here, with the length of about one kilometer. The gold mining of Mt. Hushan had been extended to the middle of the 1990s, forming a high-quality and unique historical and cultural resource. The worship of the Gods of mountain and treasure endows a very deep religious and folk culture when gold-mining, showing the rich cultural resources of Mt. Hushan, thus form the most important and unique attractions of the gold cultural tour to Mt. Hushan.

Here is the most amazing gold mine hole lasting for miles, and the most worthwhile watching one is "Gold Culture Exhibition Hall", which introduces the cause of formation and the mining techniques, and exhibits a variety of gold ore samples telling people how to smelt gold and the reasons of the worship of gold. At the same time, there are exhibition panels concerning gold and religion, gold and health, gold and currency. The Gold Culture Exhibition Hall, also known as the No. 1 Gold Hall, is the first real scene displaying center in Northern China. Here, one can also participate in the gold rush activities to have endless fun and get unexpected surprise.

Standing on the square beside the first hall, one can see a statue known locally as the gigantic "Tiger Stone". In ancient times, at the foot of the mountain, it is said that there were two brothers in the village, and they went to dig gold in Mt. Taihang. On the way back home, the elder brother was pushed off the cliff because of the younger brother's greed of taking the whole treasure. Fortunately, the elder brother fell down on a narrow catwalk, alerting the tiger nearby. The tiger carried the elder brother and leaped to the cliff. Thus the elder brother was sent back by the tiger. When the tiger came back to the mountain, it was exhausted when arriving at the rock. In order to commemorate the benevolence of the tiger, the elder brother asked others to write a poetic couplet: "One who cares about money, but forgets about love is no better than a tiger. It is the tiger that cherishes true love." So far, the tablet no longer exists, but the gigantic stone, "Tiger Stone", is still there. At the foot of the mountain, a small village gained the name, "Mt. Hushan Village", in which many stories about tigers spread far and wide, such as *The Protection of Fox*, *Tiger-shaped Person*, *The Rescue of Emperor Liu Xiu*.

(八) 云花溪谷

云花溪谷风景区是一处因爱情而甜蜜，因浪漫而潇洒的景区。每逢春天来临的时候，野玫瑰花漫山遍野。山里、云里、小溪旁、幽谷里，无论你走到哪里，你所看到的到处都是玫瑰花和捧着玫瑰花的姑娘，所以就得了“云花溪谷”这样一个美丽的名字。

云花溪谷

云花溪谷景区位于阜平县下庄乡境内，距县城 50 千米，与佛教圣地五台山相距 30 千米，景区植被多为原始森林和次生林，各种动植物达 700 多种。坨顶千亩空中草甸，坦若平川，百花争艳，有“鸡鸣闻四县，花开两省香”的美誉。

景区面积 20 余平方千米，主要以花海、奇峰、飞瀑、森林而著称。云花溪谷自然资源极为丰富。景区重峦叠嶂，沟谷纵横，水碧山青，景色宜人。景区奇峰险峻，峭壁林立，怪石遍布。千米以上高峰有 90 余座，游龙山、罗汉山、笔架山、牛舌山形态各异，各具特色。主峰玫瑰坨海拔 2281 米，系河北五大高峰之一，有“太行第一坨”“燕赵第一峰”之称。登高望远是令人叹为观止的“一坨观八景”——金蛙昂首。黎明日出，游客可东眺王快、岗南水库，南俯五岳、天桂景区，西望五台五峰，北指百草坨。雨后初霁，天空湛蓝，山间云海浩渺，气象万千，座座山峰恰似大海中的小岛，极为壮观。山中怪石似柱似塔，如禽如兽。七级塔、神龟出海、石蛇千姿百态，形象逼真。尤其是坨顶最高处山岩令人叫绝，东看似一条黄鱼遥望雾海，西看似一金龟卧于山顶。

景区森林植被完好，降水充沛，加之相对落差大，山泉叮咚，水溪纵横，三步一瀑，五步一潭。树夹泉、冰泉等数十个清泉宛若串串明珠，晶莹剔透，清凉甘甜；银河瀑、马尾瀑、龙舌瀑等十几处瀑布飞珠溅玉，千姿百态；青石潭、三色潭、碧玉潭等十余处深潭，或方或圆，或深或浅，不拘一格，巧夺天工。

坨顶的空中花园堪称大自然的神奇杰作。十草九开花，千亩草甸宛若花的海洋，野玫瑰、金莲花、胭脂花、百合花、紫菊花、灯笼花……上百个品种，红、黄、白、紫、蓝各色一应俱全，此起彼伏，灿若云霞。传说花神私自到人间闲游，看到玫瑰坨风景如画，流连忘返，被巡视雷公查知，前来捉拿。花神惊慌逃跑时不小心倾斜了花篮，蓝中五彩缤纷的鲜花撒到坨顶上，自此坨顶百花盛开。花期长达半年，而以六七月份最佳。

景区原始森林、次生林、人工林密布，森林覆盖率高达 65%。物种丰富，共有植物 102 科 686 种，动物 100 多种，且呈现出华北地区罕见的植被垂直分布，从山顶的高山草甸渐为落叶松林带、桦木林带、针阔混交林带、落叶阔叶林带。尤其是上千亩成片的稀有树种——红桦，极为珍贵。这里古树众多，400 年以上树龄的古板栗树 100 多棵，近千年树龄的倒栽杨树上生树。

景区内山峰众多，海拔较高，森林茂密，气候凉爽宜人，盛夏如秋，夏季平均气温 18.9 摄氏度，属清凉极地。

云花溪谷景区位于阜平天生桥国家地质公园南侧，地处晋冀文化交汇地带，独有保存完好的农耕村落，村民日出而作日落而息，白发垂髫，怡然自得，宛如“世外桃源”。原始自然的淳朴民风是现代人静心养生、返璞归真的向往之地。优质的自然景观、原生态的人文环境、良好的区位交通造就了云花溪谷独特的开发优势。云花溪谷景区正在全力打造集旅游观光、旅游地产、生态农业、休闲度假、健康养生、文化旅游于一体的休闲度假胜地。

Yunhua Valley Scenic Spot is a sweet and stylish spot because of love and romance. When spring comes, the mountains and plains are full of wild roses. In the mountains, clouds, streams, and valleys, wherever you go, what come into view are roses and girls with roses in hands. So it has such a beautiful name, “Yunhua Valley”.

Yunhua Valley Scenic Spot is located in Xiazhuang Village, Fuping County, and 50 kilometers away from the county and 30 kilometers away from Mt. Wutai, the Buddhist shrine. As for the coverings, primitive and secondary forests are the main types, and there are more than 700 kinds of animals and plants. The top of the heap is covered with meadows, which is as flat as plain, and there are hundreds of flowers contending in beauty. Thus the heap has the fame “The fragrance of flowers permeated the air in two provinces”.

The scenic spot is 20 square kilometers, and these areas are mainly decorated with clouds of flowers, bizarre peaks, waterfalls, forests. Yunhua Valley is very rich in natural resources. The mountains and valleys there pile up, surrounded with blue rivers. And the steep mountains and cliffy precipice stand over there; craggy rocks also permeate all over. There are more than 90 mountains with the height of more than 1000 meters. Mt. Dragon, Mt. Luohan, Mt. Bijia and Mt. Niushe all have unique forms. The height of the Rose Peak is 2281 meters, one of the five highest peaks in Hebei Province. It is also called the “Top One Heap in Mt. Taihang”, and “Top One Peak in Yanzhao

Area". Golden frog looking in the sky is the magnificent scenery. At sunrise, one can overlook the Wangkuai and Gangnan Reservoir to the east, Wuyue Mountains and Tiangui scenic to the south, the five peaks of Mt.Wutai to the west, and Baicao Heap to the north. After the rain, the sky is blue, the clouds are splendid, majestic and grand, and the mountains are like islands in the sea with spectacular scenery. The rocks are of bizarre shapes. The seven-stage tower, sea turtles, stone snakes are in different poses and with different expressions. The top of the highest mountain is especially stunning. Seen from the east, it appears to be a yellow croaker overlooking the sea clouds, like a golden tortoise lying on the top of the mountain westwards.

The scenic forest plants are protected intact. The abundant precipitation, combined with relatively huge fall make the scenic spot full of springs and waterfalls. Dozens of pure springs are just like a string of pearls with crystal clear, cool and sweet. More than a dozen waterfalls, such as the Milky Waterfall, the Horse Tail-shaped Waterfall, and the Dragon Tongue-shaped Waterfall splash jade-like water beads in different poses and with different expressions. And more than a dozen ponds, such as the Green Stone Pond, the Three-color Pond, and the Green Jade Pond, are round or square, deep or shallow, the style and the workmanship of which excel that of nature.

"The garden in the air" is a wonderful masterpiece of nature. A variety of flowers are alternatively blossoming in due season, just like a sea of flowers. There are over one hundred kinds, such as wild rose, lotus, carmine, lily, violet chrysanthemum, and lantern-shaped flower, with the color of red, yellow, white, purple, and blue. And the colors of flowers make them as bright as the rosy clouds. The legend goes that the Flora wandered to the earth and met with the picturesque Rose Heap, and then she lingered there and forgot to return to the heaven. Thus she was arrested by the patrolling God of Thunder. The panic-stricken Flora escaped but accidentally tilted a basket of flowers, and the flowers scattered at the top of the mountain. Since then, the heap is bloomed with flowers. The flowering period is half a year, with the best time in June and July.

The primitive forest, secondary forest and artificial forest in the scenic spot are densely distributed, and the forest coverage rate is up to 65%. The plants and animals are also of great variety. There are 102 families, 686 species plants and more than 100 species of animals. The rare vertical distribution of plants in North China, from the top to the bottom, include of the alpine meadow, the birch forest belt, the coniferous broad-leaved mixed forest belt and the deciduous broad-leaved forest belt. There are acres of patches of rare species, red birch, which is very precious. The primitive trees of more than 400-year-old are more than 100.

There are many mountains in the scenic spot, with high altitude, dense forests, cool and pleasant climate, and the average temperature of 18.9℃, thus it is a cool place.

Yunhua Valley Scenic Spot is located on the southern side of Tianshengqiao National Geological Park in Fuping. It is also the cultural intersect of Shanxi Province and Hebei Province, with unique and well-preserved farming village in which people get up at sunrise and come back home at sunset. The old and the young are pleased with themselves. It is just likes the "Land of Idyllic Beauty ". The primitive natural simplicity of folk customs is what is wanted in modern society. Besides, the high-quality natural landscape, the primitive ecological environment and the location have given the scenic spot unique developmental advantages. Yunhua Valley Area Spot is now striving to create a multifunctional holiday resort, functioning as a place for sightseeing, real estate industry, eco-agriculture, leisure and holiday, health and salubrious travelling and cultural tourism.

(九) 大茂山

史籍明确记载，从传说中的舜开始，此后的周、秦、汉、隋、唐、元、明以来，“古北岳”都是指河北曲阳(现属唐县)的大茂山，也称神仙山。

大茂山

大茂山古称恒山，又名常山，其峰为神山尖，俗称奶奶顶。传说恒山有72座庙宇，由于战乱遭到破坏。现在山阳褶皱处，寺观遗迹随处可见。该山曾有数量众多的铜神像，其中一尊铜像的耳朵眼里能容4人打牌，遗憾的是铜像均被毁。

神仙山顶现有北岳庙、玉皇庙、三霄圣母庙、药王庙、眼光庙、关帝庙等寺庙。唐县和涞源县分别在大茂山东侧和北侧建有北岳行宫。阜平县祭北岳为农历二月初二至三月十五日，涞源县为三月十八日。神仙山为历代的战略要地。春秋战国时期，这里曾为燕、代、中山国和赵国的界山。五代时期的晋、汉、周及宋朝均以此山与契丹为界。中山、北齐及明代曾于此修筑长城。

神仙山海拔1898米，雄踞于保定阜平唐县涞源三县交界处。这里有众多野生植物，一年四季月月有花开，适宜游览、休闲、避暑和野生植物考察。神仙山不仅是这方人民心目中的北岳，而且更以其优美的自然景观和相应的服务设施吸引着众多的游客，朝山进香者络绎不绝。

更神奇的是神仙山的山顶是由流纹岩组成，是千里太行地区唯一的死火山。由于流纹岩坚硬，抗风化能力强，这里形成了风动石、两面观音等国家一级景点，而且形成了火山岩中著名的天眼石和镶嵌其中的黑白妖石，对称对等分布的奇异现象。经考证天眼石是火山喷发时从上地幔带到地表，压力减小，所含二氧化碳气体挥发所造成的空洞天眼。黑白妖石其实是火山岩喷发过程中产生2000摄氏度的高温，将地表灰色石灰岩烘烤成白色大理岩，黑色妖石是碳质泥岩。对称对等分布是距离火山口远近受风力的影响，自然分选的结果，十分神奇。

这里林涛云海，翠峰耸立，树密草丰，响泉飞瀑。有南方山林的秀姿，有北方草原的野趣，有黄山云海，有南岳云雾，是一个入伏不见暑的清凉世界。神仙山原始森林郁郁葱葱，遮天蔽日，脚下蜿蜒小路被横生的灌木挤得模糊不清。越往上爬，山势越险，山林越密，脚下云来如雾，林海生烟。20000多亩山林中，有油松、白桦、山榆、白杨、翠柏、山杏、核桃等多种林木。浓荫下，有人参、灵芝等中草药千余种，黄杨球、野山茶等千姿百态的野花点缀其间，狍子、黄羊、小山猫的身影忽隐忽现。

神仙山是唐河支流通天河的发源地。山内泉水汩汩，流水潺潺，高山瀑布飞流直下，雾气蒸腾，十分壮观。石人沟内的溪流清澈见底，成群结队的鱼儿往来嬉游，既可休憩观赏，又可持竿垂钓。"恒山积雪"为神仙山奇景之一。严冬时节，山峰多为积雪覆盖，至5月份才融化。春季游览，山顶白雪皑皑，山下流水淙淙，山间山花烂漫。此时的神仙山，既展示着严冬雪峰的晶莹与肃穆，又流淌着春天的柔情与温馨，置身其间，身感神受，是一种奇妙无比的享受。

神仙山于2005年12月被国家林业局批准设立国家级森林公园，总面积1353.33公顷。山高林密，动植物资源丰富。原始次生林郁郁葱葱，遮天蔽日，森林覆盖率达56.6%。山上长满了松、柏、杨、桦等树木，特别是那万亩翠绿的油松，挺拔刚健，生生不息，欣欣向荣。南山上有数百亩山桃。每当初春，那串串粉红色的花蕾在春风的抚摸下，由山下向山上逐层开放，花期持续20多天。从春到夏，漫山遍野的野花野草，万紫千红，竞相斗艳，宛如一片花海。飞禽走兽有野雉、山鹰、青羊、狍子、土豹、狼、狐狸、野鸡、小松鼠、红嘴鸟、鸦等野生动物，随处可见。它集太行山所有动植物资源于一体，呈现了生物的多样性，是生物链保护较好的一个生物王国。

神仙山山势高，雄浑伟奇，自然景观多，充满神秘感，是华北平原北部与太行山交接处和距保定120千米范围内最高的一座山。山上有奶奶庙，香火不断。横亘数百亩的开阔地叫作跑马梁，顾名思义，平坦开阔。据传，这里是杨六郎的练兵场。每到温热季节，这里绿草如茵，繁花似锦，徜徉其间，仿佛到了塞外草原。草地上搭建有五颜六色的帐篷。游客在这里野宿，清晨可以观日出。

神仙山有数不尽的自然景观，尤以石窟、溶洞为最甚。南端四面悬崖峭壁上有无数神秘的洞窟，仅有神话传说的就有金龙洞、黄龙洞、黑龙洞、无底洞、老君洞、白虎洞、野马洞等。金龙洞内常年流水不断，盛夏冰凉刺骨，洞深无底。最大的老君洞可容纳200多人。这些洞窟，在抗日战争时期曾做过兵工厂，住过八路军三个团，三个干休所。此外，小的道观遗址随处可见。万丈崖之上是数百亩的山顶大草原，相传是杨六郎驯马的地方。此外，神仙山的神秘还在于让人难识真面目。在不同的时间内，大山时隐时现，变幻莫测：日出日落时，随着温度变化，远看其貌，雾霭弥漫，紫气笼罩，放射着仙气灵光；阴天看其状，是一座黑黝黝的黛青色屏障，阴森恐怖；雨过天晴，空气清新，满山如洗，山顶被云雾包裹，与天相连，威严而神秘。

神仙山山清水秀，雄伟奇险，由20多座山峰组成。其主峰为太乙峰。那些奇峰异石和附会着美丽传说的石景，如石人沟、长寿石、老佛石堂、菩萨山、棒槌山等也都具有较高的观赏价值。

History clearly records that, from the beginning of the legend of Emperor Shun and later the Zhou Dynasty, the Qin Dynasty, the Han Dynasty, the Sui Dynasty, the Tang Dynasty, the Yuan Dynasty, and the Ming Dynasty, the "ancient Mt. Beiyue" refers to Mt. Damao, also known as Fairy mountain, which is located in Quyang County(now Tang County), Hebei Province.

Mt. Damao was called Mt. Hengshan in ancient times, which is also known as Mt. Changshan. The peak, which is the fairy mountain tip, is commonly called Grandma Top. It is said that there are 72 temples in Mt. Heng, which have been destroyed at wartime. Now in the south of the mountain, the temple ruins can be seen everywhere. The mountain once had a large number of bronze statues. The ear of one of the bronze statues can hold 4 people playing cards, but unfortunately they were all destroyed.

On the top of the Fairy Mountain exists Beiyue Temple, Jade Emperor Temple, Three Goddess Temple, Yaowang Temple, Yanguang Temple, Guan Yu Temple and other temples. Tang County and Laiyuan County respectively build Beiyue Palace at the eastern and northern foot of Damao Mountain. The sacrificial days in Fuping County are from the second day of the second month of the Chinese lunar calendar to March 15th, while in Laiyuan County, it's March 18th. The Fairy Mountain is the strategic place of former dynasties. In spring and autumn period, it was the boundary mountain area of the states of Yan, Dai, Zhongshan and Zhao. The Jin, Han, Zhou and Song dynasties also claimed the border by Fairy Mountain with Khitan. The state of Zhongshan, Northern Qi and the Ming Dynasty built the Great Wall there.

Fairy Mountain is located in the border of Fuping County, Tang County and Laiyuan County. It is 1898 meters high. There are many wild plants, and the flowers are blooming at all seasons. It is suitable for sightseeing, leisure, summer holidays and wild plant investigation. It is still the ancient Beiyue in the eyes of the local people and attracts thousands of tourists through the elegant landscapes and corresponding services and facilities, thus it had a constant stream of pilgrims.

What is more miraculous is that, the Hilltop of the Fairy Mountain is made up of rhyolite and it is the only dead volcano in the Taihang area. Because of the hard rhyolite and weathering-resistance capacity, it generates wind-flowed stone, two-side Guanyin (one of the Buddhas), and other first level scenic spots of the state. Besides, the eye stone and black-and-white demon stone embedded in the volcanic and the bizarre phenomenon of uniform distribution of symmetric sized stones become the eternal mystery. The research demonstrates that when the volcano erupts from the upper mantle to the surface, the pressure decreases and the eye stone are created with the volatilization of carbon dioxide. The black-and-white demon stone is actually processed through the volcanic eruption that produces a temperature of 2000 ℃, which bakes the gray limestone on the surface into white marbles, and the black stone belongs to carbonaceous muddy stone. The symmetric distribution is formed under the influence of the wind in terms of the distance from the volcano, and the result of natural separation is very magical.

The landscapes here, such as the sea of forests, green-covered peaks, dense trees and grasses, springs and waterfalls, combine the beauty of mountains and forests in the south and grasslands in the north, forming a cool and refreshing world. The Fairy Mountain primary forests grow in exuberance, getting no glimpse of the sky. At the foot of the mountain, a winding path is covered with shrubs and trees. The higher one goes, the steeper the mountains become, as well as the denser forests. Among more than 20000 *mu* of forests, there are pines, birches, elms, cypresses, poplars, apricots, walnuts and other kinds of trees. Under the shade, more than 1000 kinds of herbs like ginseng, ganoderma and other Chinese herbal medicines grow there. Also, the flowers, like the Boxwood ball, the wild camellia, permeate all area, and the deer, the gazelle, the small lynx appear now and then.

The Fairy Mountain is the birthplace of the tributary of Tanghe River — Tongtian River. The scene is quite spectacular with gurgling springs and plunging waterfalls. The water in the trench is so clear that one can see to the bottom where groups of fish swim here and there. It is the place both for recreation and fishing. "The snow in Heng Mountain" is one of the wonders of the Fairy Mountain. In winter, most of the peaks are covered with snow, which do not melt until May. In spring, the snow covers the mountain top, while the water gurgles at the foot. Meanwhile, the mountain flowers are in full bloom. At this time, the Fairy Mountain shows not only the crystal clearness and solemnity of the peaks, but also the tenderness and warmth of spring, which give this area an enchanted feeling.

The Fairy Mountain was approved by the State Forestry Bureau as the National Forest Park in December, 2005, with a total area of 1353.33 hectares. The resources of animals and plants are abundant. The primitive secondary forests are thriving with the forest coverage rate up to 56.6%. The mountains are covered with pines, cypresses, poplars and birch trees, especially the ten thousand *mu* of sturdy green trees, thriving to the sky and growing lively. There are hundreds of acres of mountain peach. When the early spring comes, strings of pink flower buds blossom from bottom to top of the mountain lasting more than 20 days. From spring to summer, the wild flowers cover all the mountains and plains, and the color is various, just like a sea of flowers. Birds and animals include wild pheasant, wild eagle, mountain goat, deer, leopard, wolf, fox, pheasants, squirrels, red-bill birds, crows and others, which can be seen everywhere. It integrates all kinds of animals and plants of Taihang Mountain, showing the biological diversity and making it a biological kingdom in terms of the protecting of biological chain.

The Fairy Mountain is full of mystery in terms of steep hillside and magnificent natural landscape. It is the highest mountain within the area of 120 kilometers from Baoding, sitting at the intersection of northern part of the North China Plain and Taihang Mountain. Granny Temple is located on the mountain, which is still used by the pilgrims. The open land of hundreds of acres is called the Horse-riding Ridge. Just as the name implies, this area is flat open. According to the legend, this is the training ground of Yang Liulang. When the weather is warm, this place is in full green grass and blooming flowers. When wandering about, one may feel like roaming the grassland beyond the Great Wall. There are colorful tents on the meadow, where one can also watch the sunrise in the morning.

There are countless natural landscapes in the Fairy Mountain, especially the grottoes and caverns. There are numerous mysterious caves on the four sides of the southern cliffs. Among them, Jinlong Cave, Huanglong Cave, Heilong Cave, bottomless Cave, Laojun Cave, Baihu cave and Yema Cave all have the fairy legends. In the bottomless Jinlong Cave, the flowing water is constant throughout the year, cold in summer. The biggest Laojun Cave can hold more than 20 people. These caves, in the period of Anti-Japanese War, were served as the arsenal for three regiments of the Eighth Route Army. It is also the place of retired elites. In addition, the remains of small Taoist temple can be seen everywhere. The prairie of hundreds of *mu* lies above the towering cliffs, which is said to be the place of horse training by Yang Liulang. Meanwhile, the mystery of the Fairy Mountain lies in the difficulty to see its true face. At different times, the mountain looms unpredictably. And at the time of sunrise and sunset, with the change of temperature, the mountain is misty seen afar; when it comes to cloudy days, its shape is just like a dark blue barrier, making terrible sense. After raining, with clean air, the top of the mountain is wrapped in mist and clouds, majestic and mysterious near the sky.

The picturesque and majestic Fairy Mountain is composed of more than 20 peaks.

Among the numerous peaks, Taiyi peak is the main peak. Those bizarre peaks and stones are attached to beautiful legends, such as stone people valley, longevity stone, Ancient Buddha stone, Buddha mountain, rod-shaped mountain, which all have higher value of appreciation.

二、人文景观旅游资源

（一）历史古迹之旅

1. 直隶总督署

直隶总督署位于保定市区，是我国一所保存完整的清代省级衙署。直隶总督署是清代直隶省最高行政长官直隶总督的办公处所。作为全省最高的封疆大吏，直隶总督具有“统治军民，统辖文武，考核官吏，修饬封疆”之责，管辖着直隶全省12个府、7个直隶州、3个直隶厅和127个州县。管辖范围要大于现在的河北省，包括河北，京、津两市以及山东、山西、河南、内蒙古、辽宁等的一部分。直隶总督设于清雍正二年（公元1724年），宣统三年（公元1911年）被裁撤，历经8帝187年的历史，共设有总督74人，99任次。直隶因地处天子脚下，有护卫京师之责。方观承、曾国藩、李鸿章等清代名臣都曾坐镇于此，这里发生过影响着清王朝政局的很多重大事件，可谓“一座总督衙署，半部清史写照”。

直隶总督署大门

直隶总督署修建于清雍正七年(公元1729年)，距今已有200多年的历史，虽然历经沧桑，但仍然保留着修建初期的建筑规模和建筑格局，保持着清代雍正、乾隆时期的建筑风格和建筑特色，是我国目前唯一保存完好的清代省级衙署，全国重点文物保护单位，国家4A级旅游景区。

总督署的前身可追溯至元代。元代时，这里是顺天路总管府所在地，明代相继做过保定府署和大宁都司署，清代曾做过大宁都司署和参将署，直到雍正七年（公元1729年)始成为直隶总督的办公处所。

直隶总督署规模宏大，南北长220米，东西宽130米，占地总面积30000余平方米。它严格按照清朝规制修建，坐北朝南，分为中、东、西三路，主体建筑大门、仪门、大堂、二堂、官邸、上房等院落全部集中在中轴线上，其他一些辅助建筑，如花厅、幕府院等则分列在东西两路。总督署均为布瓦顶、小式硬山建筑，是一座典型的北方衙署建筑群。

总督署的第一道门是大门，也就是俗话所说的衙门口儿。说到衙门口儿，很容易让人想起一句话：“衙门口儿朝南开，有理无钱莫进来。”实际上，中国古代建筑在方位和朝向上是非常讲究的，“衙门口儿向南开”取的是《易经》上所讲的“圣人南面而听天下，向明而治”的意思，不含任何贬义。要进大门，得先登上一米多高的台阶。大门是三开间的，明柱门板和门槛漆得乌黑铿亮。不光直隶总督署的大门是漆成黑色的，那些留存下来的衙门口，也都是黑漆漆的。黑色象征“清正廉明”，人们看到这黑色的大门，就像看到包公那张铁面无私的脸。

总督署的第二道大门称仪门，主要起到礼仪的作用，是主人迎送宾客的地方。官场上的迎来送往很有讲究。与总督官职相当，也就是平级的到署里来，要在仪门外下轿或下马，总督到仪门外迎接，宾主由仪门步入大堂。而品级低的官员来拜见总督的，在辕门外就要走出轿子或下马，低首敛眉小步而行，由两侧的便门进入，文官走东便门，武官走西便门，是不得由仪门而入的。平头百姓更是连进门的资格都没有。

过了仪门，进入的院落就是大堂院，大堂正中铺设甬道，在甬道左右两侧植有许多高大的古树，有侧柏、桧柏和国槐。它们栽种于明朝嘉靖年间，距今已有 480 多年的历史。这些古树不仅是历史的见证，还记载着许多有趣的故事和传说。总督署内有一奇特的景观，从每年的 11 月到第二年的 4 月，这些古树会被数百只猫头鹰所盘踞，给森严肃穆的古衙增加了一种神秘的色彩。传说保定曾经有过一次严重的鼠疫，身为总督的方观承心急如焚，一天夜里，他正在总督署内和师爷商量办法，忽然一只受伤的猫头鹰跌落在方观承的面前。他命人悉心照顾这只猫头鹰，还亲自给它换药。猫头鹰的伤治好后便飞走了。几天后的一个清晨，数十只猫头鹰飞到总督署院内，盘旋着落到了古树上。自此，这些猫头鹰昼伏夜出，很快消除了保定周围的鼠灾。

在古树的掩映下，甬道正中矗立着“公生明”牌坊，北面写有四句话：“尔俸尔禄，民膏民脂，下民易虐，上天难欺。”大体意思是：你的俸禄取自于民膏民脂，都是老百姓的血汗钱，为官办事要不徇私情、秉公执法。否则，即使老百姓好欺负，老天爷和皇帝也是不会饶恕你的。这座牌坊立在甬道之上，正对总督署大堂，对为官者起一定警诫作用，是一种官场箴规。据说这 16 个字是宋太宗钦定的，颁行天下的州县衙门，作为对官员的训诫，后来宋代书法家黄庭坚重新书写这 16 字箴言。这“戒石坊”，是州县衙门里必备之物。据说总督署里的“戒石坊”是后来建的。大概皇帝觉得那些封疆大吏觉

古柏群鹰

悟远比州县芝麻官要高，用不着这样的训诫了。

在牌坊的东西两侧有 18 间科房。东侧为吏、户、礼房，西侧为兵、刑、工房，是总督署对应朝中六部而设立的办公机构。它们分管官吏任免、土地户口、科举学校、军政、刑法和屯田水利。在甬道北侧矗立的是总督署内的权威性建筑——大堂，是总督举行重大政务活动和隆重庆典的地方。迎接圣旨、颁发奏折和每年秋审等重大活动都在这里举行。大堂处于整座建筑群落的中心，基地位于高 0.4 米、二踏步的月台上，门内的地坪又略高于堂外。大堂东西面阔五间，22 米，前有抱厦三间，立有四根平行的楹柱。楹柱上悬挂着的多幅匾额和楹联，分别是乾隆、光绪两位皇帝和慈禧太后赐给直隶总督方观承和李鸿章的匾额以及曾国藩题写的楹联。大堂现在的布置是照着李鸿章任直隶总督时复原的，因为直隶总督的职权到李鸿章时达到顶峰。

直隶总督署大堂

大堂正中悬挂着一方匾额，上面写的是“恪恭首牧”，这是大堂里最早的一方匾额，是雍正皇帝写给唐执玉的，夸他勤劳恭谨地治理着天下最要紧的地方。后来的历任总督也都把它高悬在大堂上。在匾额下有一扇屏风，上面绘着丹顶鹤和海潮。这是什么寓意呢？原来一品文官的官服上绣的图案是丹顶鹤，是一品文官的象征。“潮”者“朝”也，也就是入朝为官。大堂中间放着一张大大的公案，公案上摆放着官印，公案两边排列着兵器和仪仗。那些官职都一一写在职衔牌上，在这里摆放着。总督出巡的时候，把这些职衔牌打出来，加上那么多的仪仗，前前后后一大溜。总督的大堂可不像州县衙门大堂，公案也不放惊堂木、文房四宝和那些红绿头案签。

大堂之后即是二堂，二堂是总督日常办公和接见外地官员的地方，二堂的建筑布局为一明两暗，中间厅堂摆有三扇屏风，上面绘有麒麟图案。这又有什么寓意呢？原来在清朝一品武官的官服上绣有麒麟图案，与大堂的一品文官的丹顶鹤联系起来，说明总督是军、政、民全管的地方大员。同时，这里也是总督复审案卷的地方。总督为地方最高审级，不审理一般的民刑案件，只对流刑、死刑以上案件进行复审。直隶总督曾国藩在任期间，曾对直隶各类民刑案件的积案进行过突击审理。在他的努力下，只用了 7 个月的时间，全省共审结同治七年以前旧案 12074 起，新案 28121 起。可见曾国藩时期二堂的使用效率之高。

在二堂的东西两侧，各有一间暖阁，用来查找整理案卷和议事。二堂之后有一道内宅门，顾名思义，通过此门，便是总督署的内宅了。该门起到一种分割空间的作用，它把总督署中路建筑分为两部分，前朝后寝。平时有兵丁把守，署外人员无事不得入内。三堂正房五间，中间为穿堂间。是总督平时批阅来文及处理公务之所，室内有书桌、书架等办公用品。三堂西侧的房屋是总督的书房，是总督习经写字、著书立说的地方。总督多为正途入仕，是经过科举考试一步步走上仕途的。他们中的一些人在文学、书画等方面多有造诣。中路的最后一间院落是四堂，又称上房，是总督及其家眷生活居住的地方，十分幽雅静谧。

直隶总督署是清朝政治、经济、文化等制度的历史载体，是一部立体的教科书，有着丰富的历史内涵。

The Viceroy Government Office of Zhili Province is the resident office of the highest administrative official of Zhili Province in the Qing Dynasty. As the highest-ranked official of the province, this governor-general has the authority of overseeing military and civil affairs, rating administrative officials and military officers, as well as maintaining the border region. Zhili Province in the Qing Dynasty is composed of 12 urban prefectures, 7 independent sub-prefectures, 3 independent departments, and 127 counties, not only covering today's Hebei Province, Beijing and Tianjin but also part of Shandong, Shanxi, Henan, Inner Mongolia, and Liaoning provinces. The viceroy of Zhili was set up in the second year of Emperor Yongzheng's reign (1724 AD) of the Qing Dynasty, and ended in the third year of the reign of Emperor Xuantong (1911 AD). It witnesses 7 ruling emperors and lasts for 187 years. There are 74 viceroys in history of China and 99 tenures. Zhili Province is encompassing the imperial capital, playing an integral part in the defense of Beijing, thus many important ministers in the Qing Dynasty have ever assumed their office here, such as Fang Guancheng, Zeng Guofan, Li Hongzhang. Due to its indispensability and prevalence to the politics of the Qing Dynasty, the best summary of the Viceroy Government Office of Zhili Province is, "One Viceroy Government Office — half the history of the Qing Dynasty."

Construction of the Viceroy Government Office of Zhili Province begun during the 7th year of the reign of Emperor Yongzheng (1729 AD), and it has a history of over 200 years. Though it has experienced great vicissitudes in historical changes, it retains the architectural style and features as well as its original layout of the governmental offices during the reign of Emperor Yongzheng and Emperor Qianlong when it was initially built. It is the only well-preserved and complete provincial government offices of the Qing Dynasty in China. In 1988, it was listed as A Major Historical and Cultural Site Protected at the National Level, and then in 1999, it was granted a Base for Patriotic Education. In 2003, the corresponding tourism area is classified as a 4A-level scenic spot by the Chinese National Tourism Administration.

The predecessor of the Zhili Viceroy Government Office dates back to the Yuan Dynasty, when it was the resident office of the governor-general of Shuntian Capital Circuit. During the Ming Dynasty, it functioned as the office of the prefect of Baoding and subsequently the office of the Dusi (a provincial military leading organization) of Daning. Until the 7th year of the reign of Emperor Yongzheng (1729 AD), it was converted into the office of the viceroy of Zhili Province.

The Zhili Viceroy Government Office complex is grandeur and magnificent, about 130 meters wide from the east to the west and 220 meters deep from the south to the north. It covers around 30000 square meters. The present Zhili Viceroy Government Office is essentially in accordance with the specification of the typical governmental office of the Qing Dynasty. It is positioned south and faces north and divided into three pathways: the east, the middle and the west. Such main buildings as the Front Gate, the Etiquette Gate, the Main Court, the Second Court, and residence of the official and his families are all lined up on the axis. The attached buildings, such as the Hall of Flowers and the residence of the staff are located on both sides of the east and west pathways. It has a hipped-gable roof covered with tiles. It is a building complex of architectural characteristics of the governmental office in the north of China.

The main entrance to the Zhili Viceroy Government Office is the Front Gate, which is also widely known as "ya men kou" in colloquial Chinese. When people hear this, it is naturally associated with the old saying, "Yamen gates may always open to the south, but not to the poor." In fact, there are well-established laws for the location and orientation of the governmental buildings in ancient China. The statement of "Court gates open to the south", derives from those words of Classic of Changes "The emperor sits on the north with his face to the south while giving audience to affairs of the country, and he administrates his states with his face towards the bright sun", initially carrying no negative connotations of an arrogant and corruptive bureaucracy. One has to climb steps which are over 1 meter high to reach the Front Gate. The gate is three purlins in width, and its columns, planks and threshold are painted brightly black. In ancient China, almost all the gates to the government offices are painted black, since black symbolizing honesty and uprightness of the government officials.

After entering the gate, to the north side, there is the Etiquette Gate, symbolizing following etiquette. It is the place where the host greets and sees off the guests. In ancient Chinese officialdom, the governmental officials clung to certain established rites when welcoming and parting with guests. When the military officers and administrative officials of a rank comparable to that of a Viceroy come to the office, they have to get off the sedan chair or dismount the horse outside of the Etiquette Gate, and the Viceroy comes out to greet them, then the guests and the host enter the Court through the Etiquette Gate together. When the lower-ranked officials came to pay visits to the Viceroy, they, who are not qualified to go through the Etiquette Gate, ought to get off the sedan chair or dismount the horse outside of the Front Gate, then walk forward humbly on small steps to enter the sides doors, administrative officials through the east door while the military officers through the west door. Nevertheless, the civilians are even allowed to enter any door.

Passing through the Etiquette Gate, one reaches the main courtyard, with a paved passage running through in the middle. There are many tall old trees planted on both sides of the passage, including arborvitaes, Chinese junipers and Sophora japonicas. They were planted during the reign of Emperor Jiajing in the Ming Dynasty, with a history of over 480 years. These trees not only witness the changes in history but also tell of many interesting stories and legends. There is a unique wonder in the Main Court courtyard. During the period from November to April in the following year, hundreds of owls perch in these old trees, adding a forbidding, solemn and respectful ambience to the Viceroy Government Office of Zhili Province. It's said that Baoding once had a severe plague of rats. Fang Guancheng, the incumbent Viceroy of Zhili Province at that time, was distraught. At one night, when Viceroy Fang Guancheng was consulting his brain man for solutions, suddenly a wounded owl fell in front of Fang Guancheng. He ordered people to take good care of this owl, and gave it a medical dressing change in person. The owl flew away after it was cured. One morning after a few days, dozens of owls flew to the Viceroy Government Office and perched these old trees. Since then, these owls were out in the night, quickly eliminating the rat plague in Baoding.

Amidst these old trees, the "Gongshengming" Stone Archway stands in the middle of the central passage. On the north side of it is carved 16 Chinese characters in calligraphy. The main meaning of it is that "As an official, your salary comes from the lavish taxes on the grassroots. Therefore, he is expected to decide cases in justice and perceive everything in fair. Otherwise, even though it were easy to abuse the people, it is difficult to cheat justice endowed by the Emperor and Heaven." The reason why the archway is erected here and faces the Main Court is that it functions as a motto of the officialdom to warn officials from corruption and dereliction of duty. According to the accounts, these words were enacted by the Emperor Taizong of the Northern Song Dynasty as a warning for officials and then issued for the enforcement by all governments of the prefecture as well as lower levels. Later, these 16 characters were rewritten by the famous calligrapher Huang Tingjian. The Warning Stone Archway becomes an integral part of the governments of the prefecture as well as lower levels.

On the east and west sides of the "Gongshengming" Stone Archway, there are 18 department houses. The east side is the offices for the civil officials of Personnel, Revenue and Rites; while the west side is the Department of Defense, Department of Justice and Penalty, Department of Public Works. These administrative offices in the Viceroy government are established in correspondence to the six ministries of the central government, and respectively take in charge of appointing, rating and demoting of officials, gathering census and land data, managing imperial examinations and schooling, handling military affairs, supervising judicial and penal processes as well as maintaining farmlands and water conservancy. On the north side of the central passage is the main building of the government office — the Main Court. The Main Court is the venue to handle important political affairs and hold great celebrations. For example, such activities as receiving imperial decrees and annual Autumn Trial and Execution are held here in the Main Court. Situated on the center of the building complex, the Main Court has a base which is located on a 40cm-high, two-stepped platform. Its inside ground floor is a little higher than outside. The main court is 22 meters in width, and 5 rooms wide from east to west. A porch with three bays is in its front side. There are 4 paralleled frontal columns, on which hang many plaques and couplets. Those plaques were awarded by Emperor Qianlong, Emperor Guangxu and Empress Dowager Cixi to Fang Guancheng and Li Hongzhang, who served as the Viceroy of Zhili Province, and the couplets were inscribed by the Viceroy of Zhili Province, Zeng Guofan. The present layout of the Main Court was remodeled from that when Li Hongzhang assumed his office in Zhili Province, since during his tenure as the Viceroy, the influence and authority of the Viceroy of Zhili reached the peak.

In the middle of court hangs a plaque, on which are written four Chinese characters "ke gong shou mu", meaning loyalty to duty, respectfulness and submission. The characters were inscribed by Emperor Yongzheng for Tang Zhiyu, the Viceroy of Zhili Province, to praise his diligence and prudence in his governing the most importance province of the whole country. Subsequently, all Viceroys, successor to Tang, hung this plaque in place. Below the plaque stands a folding screen, in middle of which are painted a red-crowned crane and sea tide. Why do these images mean? Originally, the images of the red-crowned crane and sea tide are embroidered on the official robe of the first rank official of the imperial court of the dynasty. Only the first rank officials are eligible to share this kind of painting, thus making these images the symbol of status. In Chinese, the pronunciation of "tide" resembles that of "imperial court", symbolizing an official in the imperial court of the dynasty. In the middle of the Main Court lies a big legal case table, on which is placed the government seal. On both sides of the table, there are ranges of weapons, ritual implements and title plates. On each plate is written one official title. When the Viceroy is conducting tours of inspection, all title plates, along with those ritual implements, are held to form a magnificent lineup. Unlike the canton and county governmental courts, there are no such tools as the official gavel, Four Treasures of the Study, green and red broad prods for deciding civil and criminal cases in the court of the Viceroy.

Going through the Main Court, one enters the Second Court, the place where the Viceroy meets officials from the outside districts and handles daily official business. The Second Court has one opening hall and two recesses. In the middle of the hall stand a three-leaf folding screen, painted with the image of the kylin. In the Qing Dynasty, only the first rank military officers are eligible to embroider the image of Kylin on their official robe. Coupled with the re-crowned crane imagery associated with the first rank officials, it indicates that the Viceroy is the most important and powerful post to oversee both the military and civil affairs. In addition, the Second Court is also the place where the Viceroy re-examines cases. The Viceroy Government is the supreme regional court, which does not decide ordinary civil and criminal cases, but only re-examines those cases that involve exile penalty or death penalty. During the tenure of Zeng Guofan as the Viceroy of Zhili, he ever concentratedly tried various long-pending cases in a short time limit. Via his efforts, the Zhili Government concluded 12074 unfinished old cases which had firstly filed in the 7th year of Emperor Tongzhi's reign or earlier, and 28121 new cases, suggesting the high frequency of use of this Second Court.

On the east and west side of the Second Court, each has a cabinet, which is reserved for the staff to look for and manage legal documents as well as discussing official business. Through the Second Court, one reaches the door to the inner chamber. The name tells that going through this door, one would come into the inner mansion of the Viceroy and his families. The door serves as the dividing line of the central buildings of the Viceroy Government Office of Zhili Province, the forepart being the office while the rear part the residence. Normally, the door is guarded by soldiers and those who are not the government staff are not allowed to go into the third court unless on business. Entering this door, one arrives at the Third Court, which has five rooms, with a lobby in the middle. The third court is the place where the Viceroy writes instructions on the incoming files and deals with official business. There are office furniture in these rooms, such as desks and bookshelves. The west-side room functions as the study, the place where the viceroy practices calligraphy, ruminates on classics as well as conduct academic and literal research. Normally, viceroys achieve the office mainly through the success in the imperial examination, so most of them have a profound knowledge in literature, calligraphy and painting. The courtyard in the rear part of the axis is the Fourth Court, which is also known as the main house. It is the residence of the Viceroy and his families, extraordinarily tranquil and reclusive.

With profound historical implications, the Viceroy Government Office of Zhili Province is a mirror to the history of the Qing Dynasty on its institution, politics and culture, thus making it a vivid and three-dimensional historical textbook.

2. 古莲花池

古莲花池是我国北方著名的古典园林之一，地处保定市区中心，始建于元太祖二十一年（公元1227年），原名雪香园，距今已有近800年的历史。它的创建人是元代汝南王张柔元帅。金末元初，为张柔的副帅千户侯乔维忠的园地。明代，它为官府所用，是达官贵人饮宴聚会的乐园。由于湖中荷花历年不衰，故明代以后称“古莲花池”。

清代，这里曾作为乾隆、嘉庆、光绪三朝的行宫和慈禧的行宫御苑。清雍正十一年(公元1733年)，直隶总督李卫在此修建了闻名遐迩的莲池书院。乾隆十一年（公元1746年），工匠建造了巧夺天工的十二景，被誉为“城市蓬莱”。以后，古莲花池虽几经修复，但已无法恢复盛世时的情景。古莲花池现占地面积69.7亩。1956年，古莲花池被公布为河北省重点文物保护单位；2001年，被公布为全国重点文物保护单位；1988年，被收录在《全国十大名园》丛书。

古莲花池

古莲花池这座古园林，充分体现了我国南北园林艺术的风格与精华，其秀美和造园艺术更为园林界和文物界的专家所赞赏。在全国十大名园中，它融园林、书院、行宫三位于一体，展示历史文化的变革与沧桑。莲池书院造就了许多有志之士，更为莲池这座古园林展示了丰富的历史文化内涵，在我国教育史上曾占有非常重要的地位，清末保定因此为学生城。

游客步入古色古香、端庄厚朴的莲池大门时，首先映入眼帘的是一座坐南面北的古典门楼，门楼歇山翘角，三门三楹，朱漆彩绘，中门高悬民国初年大总统徐世昌亲书的“古莲花池”大字横匾，门前一对石狮雄踞左右，十分威武壮观。

进入莲池大门，看到的是乾隆时期修建的莲池十二景的第一景“春午坡”遗存，此景以太湖石精做而成。步过牌楼，方可领略荷塘情趣，体味那“接天莲叶无穷碧，映日荷花别样红”的古诗意境。1908年，卢靖任直隶提学使时，重新把莲池建成治学之所，成立直隶最早的图书馆并对外开放。馆南相连的是端庄秀丽的“水东楼”，楼上豁敞的阳台可凭栏俯瞰园中佳景，其西与“君子长生馆”隔岸相望。楼下东南角有著名的唐代碑刻及王阳明诗碑和西夏文经幢，它们均有很高的学术研究价值。

从水东楼向南，有两塘相通的弧形渠道，环抱一座奇石林立的假山，山体有体态空灵

园内风光

的四角小亭，往下可眺望莲叶参差、碧波荡漾的北塘，故曰“观澜亭”。其间以具有典型元代风格，园中最古老的元代桥相连。走过元代桥是“寒绿轩”，轩前修竹成林，是原莲池书院师生谈宴之处。沿台阶西行下山可见“不如亭”，是莲池书院谈宴之所，一些落榜书生，看到亭南农夫在园中耕耘获果，思量读书屡试不第，老死科场贻误终身的可悲境遇，感叹仕途艰难，还不如回家种田，遂有人提笔改为“不如亭”。从这里回转再过元代桥便是“藻泳楼”，1919 年，五四运动时期，直隶保定各校的志士仁人在这里成立了联合会，莲池成为河北中部爱国人士宣传科学与民主，唤起民众思想觉悟的活动中心。

下一个就是十二景之一的“宛虹亭”。它巧妙地将北塘分割成东大西小两塘，登亭环顾，景色尽收眼底。古莲池的园中园，名“昆阆”，又叫西小院取义于传说中神仙的居所——昆仑山阆苑，为小型庭院，南面是客厅，东、西、北三面为庑廊。张裕钊宫岛大八师生纪念碑即在北廊正中。宫岛大八是日本留学生，因慕院长张裕钊之名，于清光绪十三年（1887 年）来莲池书院就读，回国后广泛传播张派的书法艺术。1986 年，由日本善邻书院出资，保定市文物管理处主持，建成此碑。碑名由日本东京教育大学前教授上条信山书丹，碑额“谊深学海”由北京师范大学教授启功题写；背面“张裕钊宫岛大八师生记”由启功撰文，上条信山书丹。

从西小院往北走就能看到一座小巧玲珑的建筑——“小方壶”。“小方壶”匾额为清代书法家梁同书所书，因匾额“壶”字写得太草，游客到此多念为“台”。因这一带清静幽雅，宛如仙境，故以神话中的东海仙山“方壶”命名。当年，反映抗日战争和解放战争的小说就是在这里编纂而成的，这里也曾是河北作家群的办公地点。小方壶的北面是“君子长生馆”，面阔五间，抱厦三间，歇山顶，四周明朗宽畅，彩绘雕梁十分华丽。从这里可以看到“水中亭”的亭顶，十分像翻转的莲花叶上托着一个大仙桃。

古莲花池不仅景物秀美，而且因其人文内涵丰富而著名。受古代“钟灵毓秀”思想的影响，人们认为书院必须有一个良好的学习环境，因此，莲池书院建立在“古莲花池”这人杰地灵的风水宝地。同时进一步修缮完善园林的风景，使学堂和校舍与园林风光融为一体。乾隆十一年(公元 1746 年)，古莲花池被辟为行宫。乾隆、嘉庆、光绪三朝帝后均曾来此巡幸，仅乾隆皇帝就曾六次来莲池行宫游赏，三次亲临莲池书院视察学生的课业，大力褒奖莲池书院的成效。毛泽东主席在 1952 年来到莲池视察，就曾提出，莲池有名是因为有莲池书院。

说起莲池书院的创建，不得不提起直隶总督李卫。雍正十一年（1733 年），李卫响应朝廷命令建立官办书院，经过精心选址，决定把书院建在古莲花池。从碑记来看，实际上在莲池北部划出两块地，东边建宾馆，西部是书院。同时在莲池东南角建亭台楼宇，房屋40多间。建筑形式丰富多样，既可供莲池学员切磋学问，也可以留宿往来于保定的客人。书院建设工程进展很快，仅三月即落成。书院的建设费用除动用公费外，李卫还捐出了自己的养廉银。书院建成后，马上招聘教师，招收学生。为了使书院得到永续的发展，李卫延请名师主持教务，以保证教学质量；用千金购买良田，出租后用地租来解决办学经费。

直隶图书馆

莲池书院的高起点奠定了其雄厚的基础。直隶作为“畿辅首善之地”，在李卫之后的历任直隶总督对莲池书院都倍加重视，不仅在办学经费方面给予支持，还经常巡视书院，考量学员们的功课。乾隆十年（1745年），莲池被建为行宫，莲池书院又得到皇帝的关注。书院与行宫一墙之隔，学子们的读书声自然能传到来此巡幸的皇帝耳朵里。乾隆皇帝曾六次亲临莲池书院，考查学员的课业，这是其他书院所不能比的。乾隆写诗勉励书院师生：“处为传道器，出做济世匠。”——称赞直隶重视文化的风气，就像春午坡上盛开的鲜花一样生机勃勃。

莲池书院的办学很有特色。书院面积不大，实行开门办学，每年招生时没有任何地域的限制，被录取的学生无论是住宿还是走读，待遇都没有区别；每次考试时，还允许不在书院的各地读书人参加，成绩优异者照样给予奖金，并与书院的学生相同，这就使莲池书院声名远播，成为远近读书人向往的地方。

如今在莲池北岸，回廊复道的北部，有一栋彩绘如新的建筑，房檐下的匾额上书写着“万卷楼”三字，为当年方观承所书。该建筑建造于元代初年，里面收藏从南方各地搜罗来的图书档案。到了清代，虽然万卷楼原始的藏书可能已散失不存，可是文脉并没有中断。书院建成后，雍正皇帝亲赐了书院一些图书，万卷楼成了书院的图书馆。据记载，万卷楼的图书在清朝三聚三散，购书最多的一次是李鸿章任直隶总督时，他拨银1500两，买书33710卷，大大丰富了万卷楼的藏书。可惜的是，这些图书大部分于1900年被英、法、德、意联军烧毁，剩余的部分一直流传至今，保存在保定市图书馆。

莲池书院的知名不仅是因为有名师执教，更因为书院培养了众多出类拔萃的人才。例如，末科状元刘春霖，后升为直隶省教育厅厅长。光绪十年（1884年），日本汉学家冈千仞游历中国。因为他久慕张裕钊院长的文名和莲池书院的教学成果，特地到莲池书院进行学术交流。光绪十三年（1887年），莲池书院招收外国留学生，开风气之先，对传统书院开放办学起到推动作用。在张裕钊主持莲池书院期间，中国的旧教育已在一片改良声中开始从传统到近代的转型。在这种形势下，吴汝纶接掌莲池书院，开设东、西文学堂，聘请英国人和日本人教授英语和日语，从教学方法、教学内容和教学形式上都不同以往。

到清末，由于教学制度改革，光绪二十九年（1903 年），莲池书院部分改建为直隶省第一模范小学。第二年，莲池书院改为校士馆，是书院的尾声。

Being located in the downtown area of Baoding, the Ancient Lotus Pond Garden is one of the most famous classical gardens in the north of China. This garden, with a history of about 800 years, originally named Snow Fragrance Garden, was first built in the 21st year of the reign of the first emperor of the Yuan Dynasty (1227 AD) by Marshal Zhang Rou who was the king of Runan Kingdom. During the period of the last years of the Jin Dynasty and the early years of the Yuan Dynasty, the garden belonged to Qiao Weizhong, who was the deputy marshal to Zhang Rou and given a fief of a thousand households. In the Ming Dynasty followed, it was expropriated by the government and converted into a garden exclusively for the feasting and meeting of aristocrats and senior officials. For the reason that the centerpiece of the garden is a pond plated with lily pads and blooms for centuries, this garden has been known as "Ancient Lotus Pond" since the Ming Dynasty.

In the Qing Dynasty, the Ancient Lotus Pond Garden used to serve as the temporary imperial palace for the Emperor Qianlong, Emperor Jiaqing, Emperor Guangxu as well as Empress Dowager Cixi. In the 11th year of Emperor Yongzheng's reign (1733 AD), Li Wei, the Viceroy of Zhili, built the reputable Lotus Pond Academy. In the 11th year of Emperor Qianlong's reign (1746 AD), the exquisitely-designed Twelve Views were constructed, and thus making the garden bear the honored title "Fabled Abode of Immortals in the Downtown Area". Since then, despite several rounds of renovation, the garden can never be restored to its initial brilliance. Currently, this garden covers an area of 69.7 *mu*. In 1956, the Ancient Lotus Pond Garden was listed as a Major Historical and Cultural Site Protected at the Provincial Level, then in 2001, as a Major Historical and Cultural Site Protected at the National Level. In 1988, it was included in the book *Top Ten Famous Gardens in China*.

The Ancient Lotus Pond Garden fully displays the cream and the incorporated style of both the north and the south of China, and its beauty and high-profile gardening arts are highly valued by experts in garden and cultural relics. Among all the ten top gardens in China, the Ancient Lotus Pond Garden features its multifunction as the garden, academy and temporary imperial palace, demonstrating the change and vicissitudes of history and society. The Lotus Pond Academy cultivates many people with lofty ideals, thus adding rich cultural and historical implication to this garden. And it has an important place in Chinese educational history. Baoding was known as "The City of Promising Students" in the late years of the Qing Dynasty.

Entering the quaint and elegant gate to the Ancient Lotus Pond Garden, one first meets the classical gate tower, which faces the north. It is of a saddle roof construction with up-turned eaves. It has three gates and three vermilion pillars decorated with lacquer paintings. A plaque is hung above the central gate. On the plaque were written four Chinese characters, meaning "The Ancient Lotus Pond", which was written by Xu Shichang, the fourth president of the Republic of China. A pair of majestic stone lions stands in front of the central gate, with the male lion on the right and the female one on the left.

Entering the gate, one can see the remains of "Slope of Spring Afternoon", one of the Twelve Views established during the reign of Emperor Qianlong of the Qing Dynasty. It is a rock formation of stones from Taihu Lake. Going through the archway, the visitors can appreciate the ambience of the lotus pond as well as the feelings expressed in the ancient verse "To the horizon, emerald lotus leaves seem to extend infinitely; in the sunshine, blossoming lotus flowers go bright scarlet distinctively". In 1908, Lu Jing, the director of Education Board of Zhili Province, converted the garden to a place of learning and built the first library in Zhili Province and subsequently opened to the public. On the south side of the library is an elegant and graceful building called "East-flowing Stream Pavilion". Its terrace on the second storey is spacious. Leaning against the balustrades, one can overlook the view of the garden. There is another pavilion, called "Virtuous Gentleman's Longevity Pavilion", to the west of the library on the opposite bank of the pond. On the southeast corner of the East-flowing Stream Pavilion stand famous stone tablets of the Tang Dynasty and poems written by scholar Wang Yangming, as well as the Tangut dharani pillars, all of which are of remarkable academic worth.

Further to the south from the East-flowing Stream Pavilion, there is a rockery made of exquisite and rare stones, which is enclosed by arch channels connecting two ponds. A terrace with four wings opening to all sides sits atop the rock formation. Standing on this terrace and looking down, one can have a panoramic view of tiers of lotus leaves and the north pond with ripples. Thus, based on this inspiration, this terrace is named "Pavilion of Viewing the Surging Waves". The two ponds, the north one and the one in the south, are connected by an old bridge built in the Yuan Dynasty and with noticeable architectural features of that time. Crossing the bridge, one reaches the "Cold Emerald Veranda", in front of which grow bamboo groves. Going down the stone steps westward, the visitor arrive at the Pavilion of Lesser Likelihood of Success. Originally, it is a place where students of Lotus Pond Academy held feast and did academic discussion. It is not uncommon that some candidates who failed the imperial examination lamented their sufferings and misery they met in order to rise to the imperial office. By contrast, when viewing farmers in the south of this pavilion got their harvests by their toil, someone realized that it is of lesser likelihood to succeed in life by taking imperial exams than by farming, so he named this place "Pavilion of Lesser Likelihood of Success". Turning back and crossing the bridge of the Yuan Dynasty again, one gets the Pavilion of Drifting Water Bloom. In 1919, during the May Fourth Movement, intellectuals with lofty ideals from schools of Baoding set up an association here in this building, thus making the Ancient Lotus Pond Garden the center in the central part of Hebei Province to promote science and democracy as well as enlighten the people.

The next attraction is the Rainbow-like Pavilion, one of the Twelve Views which subtly divides the north pond into two parts, the east is big while the west is small. Looking around in the pavilion, one can have a panoramic view of the garden. There is an inner garden which is called "Palace of Kun", also known as the West Small Courtyard. It takes its name from the legendary, Palace of Heaven in the Kunlun Mountain, the dwelling place of various gods and goddesses. It is a miniature courtyard, in the south sits a guest hall with a portico on the east, west and north side. A monument of Zhang Yuzhao and his student Miyashima Oya is mounted in the center of the north portico. Miyashima Oya is an overseas student from Japan, who travelled to China to study in the Lotus Pond Academy for admiring the president of Zhang Yuzhao in the 13th year of the reign of Emperor Guangxu (1887 AD). On his return to Japan, Miyashima Oya began to disseminate the calligraphic art of Zhang Yuzhao in Japan. In 1986, funded by Japanese Calligraphy Academy of Shanlin, Office for Cultural Relics of Baoding took in charge of the construction of this memorial. The name of the stone tablet is written by Kamijou Shinzan, a former professor of Tokyo Education University in Japan, and the four Chinese calligraphic characters on the head of this monument, meaning "Enduring Friendship and Oceanic Knowledge" are written by Qi Gong, a prominent professor of Beijing Normal University. The inscription on the back, "A Memorial to the Friendship of Zhang Yuzhao and His Student Miyashima Oya", is composed by Qi Gong, and written by the famous Japanese calligrapher Kamijou Shinzan.

Going northward from the West Small Courtyard, one can see a small but exquisite building , on which hangs a plaque with "Miniature Immortal Island of Fanghu" by prominent calligrapher Liang Tongshu of the Qing Dynasty. As the Chinese character "hu" is so cursive that many visitors misrecognize it as "tai", meaning terrace. Due to its tranquility in this region, like a fairyland, it takes its name after Fanghu, the dwelling place of immortals in the East Sea. Once, it was also the office of groups of writers of Hebei Province, and those novels which reflect the anti-Japanese War and the Wars of Liberation are composed here. On the north side of the Miniature Immortal Island of Fanghu is the Virtuous Gentleman's Longevity Pavilion, which is five rooms wide and has three bays. It is open to four sides with hipped gable roofline, making it spacious and bright. Meanwhile, it is decorated with lacquers and wooden carving beams. Standing inside the pavilion, one can capture the view of the roof of another pavilion, "Pavilion Drifting on Water", which resembles a big peach set on upturned lotus leaves.

Besides its superb scenery, the Ancient Lotus Pond Garden is famous for its rich cultural connotation. Influenced by the philosophy of "The region well-endowed with fine spirits of nature is conducive to breeding talents" in ancient times, Chinese believe that schools ought to be built in an appropriate natural environment, thus the Lotus Pond Academy was set up in the Ancient Lotus Pond Garden which is a propitious geomantic treasure land. Along with the construction of the academy, the garden is also renovated in order to keep the teaching buildings in harmony with the ambience of this garden. In the 11th year of the reign of Emperor Qianlong (1746 AD), the Ancient Lotus Pond Garden was used as the temporary imperial palace for the emperor. Emperor Qianlong, Emperor Jiaqing, Emperor Guangxu and their empresses all had lived in this garden for a short time. Emperor Qianlong had been here for six times. Meanwhile, the emperor in person ever supervised the study of students of Lotus Pond Academy for three times, and announced considerable acclaims to the achievement of the school. When Chairman Mao Zedong came to visit the Ancient Lotus Pond Garden in 1952, he proposed that the reputation of the Ancient Lotus Pond Garden derives from the academy which is located inside.

Concerning the establishment of the Lotus Pond Academy, Li Wei, the Viceroy of Zhili Province, can never fail to be mentioned. In the 11th year of Emperor Yongzheng's reign (1733 AD), Li Wei decided to build an academy operated by the government in accordance with the order of the emperor. After elaborately choosing, he decided to choose the Ancient Lotus Pond Garden. According to the inscriptions of the stele, two lots in the north part of the garden were set apart to build a guesthouse in the east and an academy in the west. In the meantime, in the southeastern corner of the garden, pavilions were built, containing more than 40 rooms. There buildings vary in architectural style, functioning as the place both for holding academic seminars and accommodating guests. The construction of the academy progressed rapidly and was completed in only three months. In addition to the funds from the government, Li Wei, the Viceroy of Zhili Province, donated a proportion of his own salary to finance the construction. On the completion of the academy, teachers and students were recruited without any delay. In order to achieve the sustainable development of the academy, Li Wei hired famous teachers to preside over the academy to ensure the quality of teaching; meanwhile, he bought hectares of fertile farmland with large sums of money and then rented it to finance the operation of the academy.

Based on the good starting point, Lotus Pond Academy has a solid foundation. Referred to as the "the most important place in proximity to Beijing", Baoding is attached great importance by governors of Zhili Province and his successors. They not only allocated great amounts of funds for the operation of the academy, but also inspected it now and then to supervise the study of its students. When the Ancient Lotus Pond Garden was converted into the temporary imperial palace for the emperor in the 11th year of the reign of Emperor Qianlong (1746 AD), the Lotus Pond Academy captured the attention of the emperor. The academy and the palace are separated by a wall, and understandably, the students' reading could meet the Emperor's ears. Emperor Qianlong had been ever here in person to supervise the study of students of Lotus Pond Academy for three times, which was not rivaled by its counterparts. Reputedly, Emperor Qianlong wrote poems to encourage the faculty and students of the academy: "Be a great teacher in the mundane life, while be a prominent minister in the imperial court." Besides, the emperor spoke highly of the practice of Zhili Province to give priority to education , thus making the literal ambience here vibrant and luxuriant like those blooming flowers on the Slope of Spring Afternoon.

The operating of Lotus Pond Academy was of unique characteristics. Small as it was, its recruitment was open to whole China, irrespective of the region where applicants come from. Once admitted, the students, living on campus or out of campus, could enjoy grants and offers equally. Furthermore, all the intellectuals, whether studying in this academy or not, were allowed to take exams held here, and those outsiders who performed well in the exam could be granted scholarships equivalent to that received by the academy students. This made the Lotus Pond Academy widely known, and became a place that most scholars yearned for.

Now, on the north bank of the pond, a building decorated with colorful paintings which are as good as new stands in the north of the circular corridor. A horizontal plaque is hung below the eaves, which is inscribed with "Hall of Scripts and Books" by Fang Guancheng. This building was built in the early years of the Yuan Dynasty, with a huge collection of archives and literature all over China. When the Qing Dynasty ruled China, though many of the original collections were lost, the literal heritage was carried forward. After the completion of the construction of the Lotus Pond Academy, Emperor Yongzheng bestowed some books and thus converted it to the library of the academy. According to the records, the collections of the Hall of Scripts and Books have gone through loss and recollection for three times in the Qing Dynasty. The largest addition to the collection was carried out by Li Hongzhang, the Viceroy of Zhili Province. He allocated 1500 taels of silver to buy 33710 books to add to the collection of the building. Regrettably, most of the books were burned in 1900 by the allied forces of Britain, France, Germany and Italy, and the remnant books are preserved now in the municipal library of Baoding.

The Lotus Pond Academy is well-known not only because of the teachers, but also those outstanding talents cultivated by it. For example, Liu Chunlin, the last primus scholar in the Chinese imperial examination in Chinese history, graduated from the Lotus Pond Academy, and later became the director of the Education Board of Zhili Province. In the tenth year of the reign of Emperor Guangxu (1884 AD), Oka Senjin, who is a famous Japanese expert in Chinese, traveled to China. Due to his admiration for the achievement of the Lotus Pond Academy and its principal Zhang Yuzhao, he specially went to the Lotus Pond Academy for academic communication. Two years later, the Lotus Pond Academy began to recruit overseas students for the first time in the history of China, prompting other Chinese schools' openness internationally. When Zhang Yuzhao presided over the academy, China's outdated education system has begun to transform from the conventional to the modern style to meet the demand of reformation. Against this background, Wu Rulun, the successor to Zhang Yuzhao, commenced to reform the academy from its teaching method and content. He set up departments of Chinese literature and Western cultures, and employed British and Japanese to teach foreign languages.

At the end of the Qing Dynasty, due to the reform of teaching system, in the 29th year of the reign of Emperor Guangxu (1903 AD), part of the Lotus Pond Academy was converted into First Model Primary School of Zhili Province. In the following year, it was changed into the Hall of Alumni, indicating the closing down of the academy.

3. 大慈阁

保定是一座古老的历史文化名城，文化底蕴十分深厚，在风景名胜方面有“上谷八景”之说，大慈阁即位居八景之首，称“市阁凌霄”。

大慈阁位于古城保定老城区中心地带，在北大街与东大街交汇处，在地势上是古城区的制高点。大慈阁作为保定市古建筑的代表，本身具有非常丰富的文化内涵，它的雄伟、高大为文人墨客所吟诵，甚至这里的一砖一瓦都有动人的故事。因此，人们常说：“不到大慈阁，等于未曾到保定。”

大慈阁

元太祖八年(公元 1213 年)，蒙古军攻陷保定，大肆烧杀抢掠，屠城三日，将整个保定城夷为平地。大慈阁就是元代蔡国公张柔于南宋宝庆三年（公元 1227 年）至绍定五年（公元 1232 年），在蒙古军屠城十五年之后的废墟上建起来的，原名叫大悲阁，距今已有近 800 年的历史。现在的大慈阁是清代乾隆年间被焚后经多次重修的建筑。2006 年 5 月 25 日，大慈阁被国务院批准列入第六批全国重点文物保护单位名单。大慈阁自古为佛教活动场所，现为保定市佛教协会所在地。

大慈阁是一组雄伟壮观的古建筑群体，坐北朝南。大慈阁重檐三层，歇山布瓦顶，面阔五间，进深三间。过去登上三层阁楼，可以鸟瞰保定全市景致。大慈阁占地 1600 平方米，建筑面积 600 平方米，现存主要建筑有山门、天王殿、钟楼、鼓楼、大慈阁和关帝庙。

大慈阁石像

大慈阁前面的钟楼、鼓楼和天王殿是清顺治年间维修大慈阁时增加的建筑，最前面的三个山称作山门。一般在寺院中称中间略大一些的门叫“空门”，左边是“无作门”，右边为“无相门”，这是 1983 年维修大慈阁时依照北京法源寺山门造型建造而成。

这座单檐歇山顶建筑就是原来的山门，因门中有天王殿，故又称殿门。门楣上有“真觉禅寺”四字，这是大慈阁的别称。史料显示，在道光二十六年（公元 1846 年）重修大慈阁，碑记上首次出现这个名字。

天王殿也叫弥勒殿，中间原有面南弥勒佛像一尊，背后是一尊韦驮塑像，左右分立四大天王塑像。解放后，所有塑像都被毁，只留空屋三间。

钟楼和鼓楼均为二层结构，高为 10.9 米，顶为十字脊，小巧玲珑，显得古朴典雅。楼内的钟和鼓在解放后均遗失，目前正筹划复原。

天井共有石碑四通。东西两侧是深色的石碑，字迹比较清楚，容易辨认；其他两座石碑现今字迹已模糊不清，难以辨认，但都有拓片保存。

沿台阶而上，游客会看到一座石砌，其高为 4.6 米，共有 22 级台阶。据保定老一辈人说，过去在维修台阶时，有人曾见到台阶后面有一碹门，据此推理，可能基座内有一地宫，到底有没有地宫，地宫内又有什么，现在还是一个谜，这又给大慈阁增添了神秘的色彩。基座石条颜色深浅不一，上半截略深一些，这是乾隆年间大慈阁因雷击被毁重修的明显痕迹。

鼓楼

大慈阁通高古人称高达九丈九，现在实际测得为 25 米，重檐三层，歇山式布瓦顶，底层面阔五间，进深三间，前后均施六抹格扇门，周围是玉石栏板望柱。大殿内观音菩萨木雕像高度为 5.5 米，原佛像在“文化大革命”中被毁。佛像身上共有 42 只手臂，分别执有各种法器，据说每只手有 25 种功能，每只手心都有一只眼睛，所以佛像又叫千手千眼观音。佛像神态安然，慈眉善目，好像正在劝告人们弃恶扬善，脱离苦海。在它的东西两侧墙壁，绘有十八罗汉画像及经变的故事，因年久及人为破坏，壁画下部已残破模糊，但上部仍色彩鲜艳，清晰可辨，这是大慈阁内遗存的艺术珍品。

在大殿的第二层回廊向四周眺望，游客就可以体会到“市阁凌霄”的意境。历史上大慈阁周围曾是古城闹市区，车马行人川流不息，商贩云集，熙熙攘攘，非常热闹。但是若在大慈阁居高临下俯视，只见人头攒动，车水马龙，却听不到半点喧嚣之声，大有横空出世、凌霄仙境之感。二楼殿内有一尊佛像——佛祖释迦牟尼，重达 300 千克，高为 1.6 米，金光闪闪，给人以佛光普照之感。

在钟楼二楼，大慈阁和关帝庙的屋脊和檐角上有造型逼真的人兽雕刻，屋脊两端各有一龙形雕兽，身上插一把剑，这在古代建筑中是常见的，这是传说中“龙生九子”中的一位龙子。关于这一龙子的一种说法是，由于这一龙子能喷浪成雨，故将它装饰在屋顶的正脊两端，取喷水镇火之意；这座关帝庙与大慈阁本不是同一建筑群体，据说关帝庙有镇邪作用，所以在保定旧城区，曾经有许多关帝庙，目前仅剩这座面朝北大街，也就是

天王殿

北城门的关帝庙。殿内有泥塑关公坐像，两旁侍立的是其义子关平、爱将周仓。整个殿内气氛一派威武，令人肃然起敬。

近年来在大慈阁周围进行了大规模的旧城改造，建成了集休闲、旅游、观光、购物为一体的大慈阁广场和步行商业区，吸引了大批中外游客。

As a city with a long history and an ancient civilization, Baoding enjoys a profound cultural background. As for the places of interest, Baoding boasts "Eight Views of Shanggu", among which the Temple of Mercy, known as the "Zenith of the City", is rated the top.

The Temple of Mercy is located in the central downtown of Baoding, on the intersection of the North Avenue and the East Avenue. It is naturally of high elevation in the urban area. As the masterpiece of ancient architecture in Baoding, it is rich in cultural implications and magnificence, thus making it constantly the preferred subject in the works of men of letters in China's history. It is not exaggerated to say that each part of this place bears its own story. Therefore, it is often said that he who has not visited Temple of Mercy can never claim that he has ever been to Baoding.

In the eighth year of the reign of Emperor Taizu of the Yuan Dynasty (1213 AD), the army of Mongolia conquered Baoding, and the soldiers looted this city wantonly and massacred for three consecutive days, leaving it in ruins. The Temple of Mercy was thus built upon the ruins by Zhangrou, the Caiguogong (defender duke) of the Yuan Dynasty, during the period of 1227 AD and 1232 AD, and it was initially named Temple of Grief , with a long history of more than 800 years. The current Temple of Mercy is actually the fruit of several renovations after burning down in the reign of Emperor Qianlong of the Qing Dynasty. On May 25,2006, the Temple of Mercy was placed on the list of "The Major Historical and Cultural Sites Protected at the State Level" at the sixth-round assessment. Since its founding, this temple has been the place of Buddhist activities and now is the seat of the Buddhist Association of Baoding.

The Temple of Mercy is a complex of magnificent ancient buildings, facing south. It is of triple-eave saddle roof construction covered with tiles and 5 rooms wide and 3 rooms deep. Once standing on the third storey, one could have a bird's-eye view of the whole city. The Temple of Mercy covers an area of 1600 square meters with a floor space of 600 square meters. The main extant buildings are the Mount Gate (the main entrance), the Hall of Heavenly Kings, the Bell Tower, the Drum Tower, the Pavilion of Mercy and the Temple of Guanyu.

The Hall of Heavenly Kings, the Bell Tower and the Drum Tower, which lie in front of the Pavilion of Mercy, were added to the Temple in the reign of Emperor Shunzhi of the Qing Dynasty when the temple was renovated. The main entrance to the temple is also known as the Mount Gates. Generally, gates of a Buddhist temple are usually built in a row with a bigger one in the middle and a smaller one on each side of the three gates, the bigger one is called "Kongmen" (emptiness freedom), the left gate is "Wuzuomen" (non-desire freedom) and the right gate is "Wuxiangmen" (non-aspects freedom). And it was built in 1983, modeling the Mount Gate of Fayuan Temple in Beijing.

This single-eave building with gables and a hip roof is the original main entrance to the temple. It is also referred to as Hall Gateway since it houses the Hall of Heavenly Kings. The plaque of the lintel is inscribed with "Zhen Jue Buddhist Temple", which is another name of Temple of Mercy. According to relevant historical data, this name first appeared in the 26th year of the reign of Emperor Daoguang in the Qing Dynasty on the inscription of the stele pillar, which was built in honor of the rebuilding of the temple.

The Hall of Heavenly Kings is also called the Palace of Maitreya. It originally housed a statue of the Maitreya (known in China as the laughing Buddha) facing south, with his back to a statue of Skanda (a high ranking heavenly general and defender of Buddhist law). The statue of the Maitreya is flanked on the left and right sides by statues of four heavenly kings, each representing one fourth of the universe. After 1949, all the statues in the temple were ruined, only three vacant rooms are extant.

Both the Drum tower and the Bell Tower are double-storey, with 10.9 meters in height. They have the cross-ridge roof, whose design is simple and exquisite, quaint and elegant. The drum and bell that used to be installed inside were lost after 1949, and now the authorities concerned are scheduled to restore them.

There are four stone tablets in the courtyard. The inscriptions on the tablet of the east and west side is easy to identify because of the deep color of the stone material, while the characters on the other two are hard to recognize but the rubbings are now well-preserved.

Escalating along the steps, visitors will see a stone platform, with a height of 4.6 meters and 22 stone steps. Some local people of the older generation recollect that an arched brick door was found behind those steps when the steps were restored, thereupon, some assumed that there probably exists an underground palace beneath the platform. It is still uncertain whether the underground palace exists or if it does, what is placed inside. This unsolved mystery only adds appeal to the Temple of Mercy. The stone slabs in the base are of various shades of color, a little deeper in the upper part, which clearly indicates the sign of its restoration during the ruling of Emperor Qianlong of the Qing Dynasty after the temple was struck by the lightning.

The Pavilion of Mercy was once alleged to be 9.9 zhang high (1 *zhang* ≈ 3.33 meters), but it is actually 25 meters high according to precise measurement. It is of triple-eave, saddle roof construction, and covered with tiles. The first storey is 5 rooms wide and 3 rooms deep, each of which is installed with screen doors with the hollow design of hexagon. The first storey of the pavilion is enclosed by baluster column made of jade stone. The 5.5-meter high wooden statue of Avalokitesvara is placed inside the hall, though the original statue was destroyed in the "Cultural Revolution". The statue has 42 arms, each holding varied Buddhist ritual percussion instruments. It is said that each hand has 25 kinds of supernatural power. There is an eye in each palm. 25 times 40 make 1000, so the Buddha is named "The 1000-handed and 1000-eyed Bodhisattva". The look of the statue is composed and benignant, seeming as if he is teaching people to desert evils and promote virtues and to readily answer the cries and pleas of all sentient beings and to liberate them from their own karmic woes. On the east and west walls are painted frescoes, depicting 18 arhats and stories deriving from Buddhists in scripture. Undermined by years of neglect and destroyed intentionally, the lower part of the murals has been broken and blurred, but its upper part remains brightly clear and recognizable. These precious frescoes are the only art treasure that is still extant in the Pavilion of Mercy.

Standing in the circular balcony of the second storey of the pavilion and looking around, visitors can have true understanding of the mood of reaching up to heaven. Once in history, around the Temple of Mercy was the downtown area, where the streets were crowded with traders and pedlars. From up here on the second storey of the pavilion, one could watch the heavy traffic and streaming people, but without the disturbance of any cacophony, which making one feel in the celestial palace exclusively belonging to immortals. In the hall of this storey sits a statue of Sakymuni. It is 1.6 meters high and weighs 300 kilograms. The statue is gold-plated, symbolizing the mood of Buddha's brilliance illuminating all as sunshine.

The ridges and the tips of eaves of the second storey of the Bell tower, the Pavilion of Mercy and the Temple of Guanyu are decorated with lifelike carvings of figures and animals. Both ends of the ridge are adorned with a dragon-shaped carved animal with a sword penetrating its body, which is common in Chinese ancient buildings. This animal was one of the son in the legendary of "Nine Sons of the Dragon". It is always carved here because it can spurt water so as to quench the fire that is undisputedly a catastrophe for any building. The Temple of Guanyu was, in fact, independent of the compound of The Temple of Mercy. Since Chinese believe that the Temple of Guanyu can exorcize evil spirits, many Temples of Guanyu were ever constructed in the ancient city proper. At present, only this Temple of Guanyu has survived, adjacent to the North City Gate and facing the north main avenue. In the Temple of Guanyu stands a sitting clay statue of Guanyu, with Guanping, his adopted son and Zhoucang, his general, standing in attendance at two sides of the statue. The hall is stately and solemn, arousing visitors' awe and respect naturally.

Recently, the massive-scale urban renewal has been implemented surrounding the Temple of Mercy, and a commercial square and a pedestrian business street have been constructed surrounding the Temple of Mercy to provide service of leisure, tourism and shopping, attracting a host of domestic and foreign visitors.

4. 陆军军官学校遗址

保定陆军军官学校是中国近代军事教育史上第一所规模较大、设施完整、学制正规、门类齐全的军事学府。它开创了近代中国军事科学教育的先河。一大批毕业生成为风云人物，在中华民族的生死存亡时刻，为捍卫国家和民族做出了巨大贡献。在抗日战争中，保定军校的学生陆续走上抗日战争的正面战场，从主要指挥官到团长、营长，从统帅部到各战区、集团军，占 80%之多，参与指挥了正面战场几乎所有的重大战役，为国捐躯者不计其数。

军校纪念馆

鸦片战争以后，清政府屡遭帝国主义列强入侵，不平等丧权辱国条约相继签订。残酷的现实，迫使清政府革新军制，编练新军，并在保定开办新式军事学堂，培训新军军事人才。自 1902 年至 1911 年，清政府在保定先后开办了学堂 14 所，学员共有 3000 余人，使保定成为全国最大的陆军训练基地。北洋政府成立后，于 1912 年在保定原有的基础上创办了陆军军官学校，至 1923 年 8 月共创办 9 期，培养了各类军事人才 6500 余人，其中成为国共两党高级将领的即达千余人，所以保定有“将军摇篮”之美誉。

光绪二十七年（公元 1901 年）11 月，袁世凯接任直隶总督兼北洋大臣后，在保定设立“北洋军政司”，以保定为基地，开始编练北洋常备军，并以新军为骨干，编成拥有七万多名士兵的北洋陆军六镇。在编练过程中，需要大批各级军官，所以袁世凯决定开办军事学堂以求解决所需人才。自光绪二十八年(公元 1902 年）至宣统三年(公元 1911 年)，袁世凯在保定共开办近代军事学堂 14 所。

现存保定军校旧址已被列入全国重点文物保护单位、河北省爱国主义教育基地。曾在中国现代史上产生过重要影响的保定军校旧址，目前已被整修一新，建成了军校广场和保定军校纪念馆，是国家 2A 级景区。

保定军校原占地 3000 余亩。1948 年 7 月，军校校舍被当时的国民党驻军拆毁修筑工事。保定解放后，军校旧址成为河北省农场，后改为保定畜牧场。1993 年 7 月，军校旧址成为河北省文物保护单位。1995 年，保定市政府在军校旧址上建起了保定军校纪念馆第一期工程。后来，保定市政府又投资修建了军校广场，扩建了军校纪念馆，修复了军校检阅台。新扩建的保定军校纪念馆总投资 200 多万元，占地 12 亩，包括军校大门、东西耳房、东西配房、东西厢房、尚武堂(校长室)及部分校舍，主要建筑均仿照原军校式样，为青砖灰瓦，小式硬山。军校检阅台也进行了修复，基本恢复原来的历史风貌。

清末建校所占的地方，本是被八国联军侵占保定时焚毁的一处关帝庙旧址及周围庙产。据史料记载，当初的校区分为校本部、分校、大小操场和靶场等。校本部居中，墙外有护河环绕，北面是生活区，南面是军校的中枢和教学区，又各分为东、中、西院落，各房舍间有走廊相连，形成分布严整的格局。现在的军校纪念馆大门，据说是仿照了当初可与总督署相比的军校大门建造的。用作展厅的“尚武堂”正门两侧的楹联参照了当年张之洞所做的楹联。

对于名著史册的保定军校，历来记述的文字很多，查阅起来也并不难。它虽然不像黄埔军校那样保留了一些旧迹，但却是黄埔军校的前辈。包括校长在内的黄埔军校的教学和管理力量，基本上都是出身于保定军官学校。保定军校的学生骨干，后来大多成为“黄埔系”的将领，这些将领也大多成为抗日战争时期正面战场上的指挥官。

Baoding Military Academy is the first large-scale military institution in the history of modern military education in China, with complete facilities, formal schooling and comprehensive military subjects. It set a precedent of military science education in modern China. A large number of its cadets played prominent roles in the political and military history of China, and made tremendous contributions to safeguard the country and its people when the nation met the crisis of life and death. During the Anti-Japanese War, the cadets from Baoding Military Academy successively entered the battles, and played a key role in the battlefield. The cadets from the chief commander to the commander of regiments and battalions, working both in the commander's headquarters and the group armies, accounted for as much as 80% of the military officers in total. They participated in and commanded almost all major battles in the frontal battlefield and countless graduates nobly sacrificed their lives.

After the Opium War, the Qing Dynasty was repeatedly invaded by the imperialist powers from the West, and the unequal humiliating treaties were signed successively. The harsh reality forced the Qing government to innovate the military system, to train the new army, and to set up a new-type military academy in Baoding, training military personnel for the army. From 1902 to 1911, 14 military schools were set up successively in Baoding, with over 3000 cadets, thus making Baoding the nation's largest army training base. After the establishment of Beiyang government, Baoding Military Academy was set up in 1912 based on the original military school. The Baoding Military

Academy closed in August, 1923, and until then it had trained more than 6500 military personnel of various kinds, among whom over 1000 became senior generals of the Kuomintang(KMT) and the Communist Party of China(CCP), so Baoding is reputedly called "The Cradle of Generals".

In November of the 27th year of the reign of Emperor Guangxu of the Qing Dynasty (1901 AD), Yuan Shikai was appointed the Viceroy of Zhili Province and the Minister of Beiyang. And then he set up Beiyang Military and Administrative Office in Baoding. Taking Baoding as the headquarter, Yuan Shikai began to form and train the standing army of Beiyang Government. Based on the New Army predominantly, the standing army was shaped, with 70 thousand soldiers and six full divisions. In order to meet the demand of military talents, Yuan decided to open military schools. From the 28th year of the reign of Emperor Guangxu of the Qing Dynasty (1901 AD) to the third year of the reign of Emperor Xuantong (1911 AD), he set up 14 modern military schools of different levels.

The extant Baoding Military Academy has been included in the list of A Major Historical and Cultural Site Protected at the National Level, and listed as Provincial Patriotic Education Base in Hebei Province. The former site of Baoding Military Academy, which has exerted prominent influence on modern Chinese history, has been renovated, and a Baoding Military Academy Plaza and Baoding Military Academy Memorial Hall have been built, ranking 2A-level national scenic spot.

The original Baoding Military Academy covers an area of over 3000 *mu* (about 2 million square meters). In July, 1948, some teaching buildings of the academy were demolished to build defense works by the KMT. After the liberation of Baoding, the site of the military academy became a farm in Hebei Province and later became Baoding Livestock Ranch. In July, 1993, it was listed as the major historical and cultural site protected by Hebei Province. In 1995, the first phase of the construction of Baoding Military Academy Memorial was completed on the site of the Baoding Military Academy. Later, Baoding government invested in the construction of the Military Academy Plaza, the extension of the Military Academy Memorial, and restoration of the reviewing stand of the academy. The newly expanded Baoding Military Academy Memorial Hall costs more than 2 million *yuan* and covers an area of 12 *mu*, consisting of the main gate, east and west penthouses, east and west side-houses, east and west wing-rooms, Shang Wu Hall (principal's room) and some school buildings. The newly buidling is a replica of the original counterparts, with blue bricks and grey titles and the roof of the hard summit of hill. The reviewing stand was also renovated, taking on what it looked like originally.

The place where the school was built in the late Qing Dynasty was originally the site of a Temple of Guanyu and the surrounding temple buildings that were destroyed by the invading Eight-Power Allied Forces when they took over Baoding. According to the historical records, the original campus is divided into several parts, including school headquarters, branch campus, sized playgrounds, shooting ranges and so on. The main campus lies in the central part, surrounded by a river outside the wall. To the north is the living area. To the south is the military academy's center and teaching area, each of which is divided into 3 courtyards, which are east, middle and west. All houses were connected by in-between corridors, thus forming a well-distributed pattern. The gate of the current military academy is said to have been modeled after the gate of the former military school, which was originally comparable to the Viceroy Government Office of Zhili Province. The couplets on both sides of the main entrance of the Shang Wu Hall, which is used as the exhibition hall, are composed with reference to the famous couplets made by Zhang Zhidong at that time.

Baoding Military Academy enjoys a niche in history, and one needn't take much effort to refer to the pertinent profuse accounts. It is not well preserved as the Whampoa Military Academy, but it is the predecessor of the Whampoa Military Academy. A majority of the teaching and management personnel of Whampoa Military Academy, even its principle included, graduated from Baoding Military Academy. The elites of the cadets of Baoding Military Academy basically become generals later in the Whampoa clique, most of these generals also became commanders of the frontal battlefield during the Anti-Japanese War.

5. 清西陵

易县城西 15 千米永宁山下的丘陵地带，有一处世界文化遗产——清西陵。它是中国最后一个封建王朝——清朝的陵墓建筑群之一。清西陵有 80 个陵墓，安葬了 4 位清朝皇帝：雍正、嘉庆、道光、光绪。

庄严肃穆的清西陵

清入关前，努尔哈赤、皇太极以及清朝皇帝宗室远祖，分别埋葬在“清初三陵”。清朝入关以后的 10 位皇帝，除末代皇帝溥仪没有设陵外，其他 9 位皇帝都分别在河北遵化市和易县修建规模宏大的陵园。由于两个陵园各距北京市区东、西 100 余千米，故称“清东陵”和“清西陵”。清西陵是 4A 级旅游景区，全国重点文物保护单位。2000 年 11 月，清西陵与明朝皇帝陵墓以及清初三陵、清东陵一起，列为世界文化遗产。

西陵周边近 100 千米，外围原有红、青、白三层界桩，每层之间相距 5 千米，界桩 10 千米为官山(系指西陵界外的皇家园林)，不许老百姓涉足。清政府为了加强陵区的管理，设立了一套机构，历代皇帝均任命泰宁镇总兵兼西陵大总管大臣统管西陵，并派辅国公、镇国公两个王公作为皇室的代表，设置东府、西府，专门守陵。

清西陵陵区周界约 100 千米。陵区保护范围 8300 公顷，重点保护面积 1842 公顷，陵区范围 800 平方千米。在清代三处陵园中，占地面积最大。清西陵自然风光秀美，北依层峦叠嶂的永宁山，南傍蜿蜒东流的易水河，绿草萋萋，松柏参天，与古桥、古牌坊、碑楼、朝房、隆恩殿、明楼、宝顶等古建筑融为一体，构成了一幅庄严神圣、静谧肃穆的皇陵园林景象。

三孔石桥

清西陵自雍正八年（1730 年）始建泰陵，至 1915 年光绪的崇陵建成，历经 185 年，共建有 4 座皇帝陵，分别是泰陵、昌陵、慕陵、崇陵；3 座皇后陵：泰东陵、昌西陵、慕东陵；3 座妃陵：泰妃陵、昌妃陵、崇妃陵；4 座王爷、公主、阿哥园寝等 14 座陵墓。另有行宫永福寺两处附属建筑及衙署营房遗址。这里埋葬着雍正、嘉庆、道光、光绪4位皇帝，9位皇后，57位嫔妃，2位王爷，2位公主，6位阿哥等共计80人。

隆恩殿

西陵建筑面积为50000多平方米，陵区内矗立着1259间宫殿和单体建筑，122座石建筑，构成了一个规模宏大、富丽堂皇的建筑群。其建筑形式和规制明显体现着封建社会的典章制度。4座帝陵、3座后陵均用黄色琉璃瓦盖顶；嫔妃陵、王爷陵为绿色琉璃瓦，公主陵、阿哥陵为灰布瓦盖顶。这些古建筑被15000株苍松翠柏环抱。永宁山屏立于陵寝之后，易水河流淌在大红门之前，使规模宏大的清西陵更显乾坤聚秀。这些古树减少了外界风沙的侵袭，以及热气、寒流的影响，为西陵营造了一个特别的小气候，使陵寝处于一个独立完整的自然环境之中，使这里的建筑，尤其是石雕建筑得以很好地保存。

关于清朝入关在建有清东陵的情况下，为什么还要建清西陵？清朝入关后，顺治、康熙两代皇帝的陵墓都建在了遵化市的清东陵，他们的后妃也都葬在清东陵，开创了“子随父葬，祖辈衍继”的埋葬制度。雍正皇帝登基后，根据风水大师的建议，在清东陵外另选陵址，首辟西陵，从而打破了传统。清朝皇帝在选定万年吉地的时候，十分注重“山脉水法”和“形势理气”，他们把具备了这些自然条件的地域称为“乾坤聚秀之区，阴阳交汇之所”。为了把这些天造地设的风水宝地建设得更完美，他们在营建规模宏伟的皇家陵寝时，要在陵区大面积栽植常青树，弥补青山绿水不能替代的庄严、肃穆气氛。清西陵自清朝入关后的第三代皇帝雍正建泰陵开始，到民国四年光绪皇帝的崇陵完工，历时185余年，共栽植松柏等常青树20余万株。这些树木增添了陵寝气氛，美化了西陵环境，同时也寓意了封建帝王渴望江山万代的心愿。时过境迁，清王朝已经成为历史，但保留下来的15000余株古松与清西陵一起成为珍贵的文化遗产。

清西陵4座帝陵及附属陵寝的建筑，无论在规模和形制上都反映了清王朝由盛至衰的演变过程。泰陵、昌陵完整宏伟的陵寝规模，反映了清王朝鼎盛时期的辉煌，慕陵建筑的裁剪，崇陵陵寝规模的减小，真实记录了清王朝从强盛走向衰亡，由封建走向半封建、半殖民地的历史轨迹。葬在清西陵崇陵及妃园寝的光绪皇帝和珍妃的命运，更记录了慈禧太后独霸朝廷、丧权辱国的屈辱历史。末代皇帝的陵寝工程由于清王朝被推翻而终止，更是中国两千多年封建历史结束的实物例证。就保存状况而言，清西陵是中国陵寝建筑群中保存最完整的陵寝之一。

Being located at the foot of Mt. Yongning 15 kilometers to the west of Yixian County, Western Tombs of the Qing Dynasty is a large-scale imperial mausoleum and architectural complex. It is buried 4 emperors of the Qing Dynasty, including Emperors Yongzheng, Jiaqing, Daoguang, and Guangxu.

Before the Manchurian came to Central China, the first and second emperors of the Qing Dynasty were respectively buried in the Three Mausoleums of the early Qing Dynasty. After that time, except the last Emperor Puyi, nine of the ten emperors constructed their large-scale cemeteries in Zunhua City and Yixian County of Hebei Province. Since the two cemeteries are more than 100 kilometers away from the east and west of the downtown of Beijing, so they are called Eastern and Western Tombs of the Qing Dynasty. Western Tombs of the Qing Dynasty is a 4A-level national scenic spot and National Culture Relic Protection Units. It was listed as the World Culture Heritage altogether with the Ming Tombs, Three Mausoleums of the early Qing Dynasty and Eastern Tombs of the Qing Dynasty in November, 2000.

Nearly 100 kilometers around Western Tombs of the Qing Dynasty, there were originally three layers of boundary posts with the colors of red, cyan and white, each of which is 5 kilometers apart. Mt. Guan is 10 kilometers away from the boundary post which is a royal garden outside Xiling and the civilians are not allowed to set foot in. In order to reinforce the management of the cemetery, a set of institutions were built in the Qing Dynasty. Generations of emperors nominated garrison commander of Taining town and chief minister of Xiling to administer Xiling. Furthermore, the positions of Fuguogong and Zhenguogong which represent the power of royal palace and the Government Offices of Dongfu and Xifu were set up to guard the mausoleum specially.

The perimeter of Western Tombs of the Qing Dynasty is 100 kilometers. The protected area of Western Tombs of the Qing Dynasty is 8300 hectares, in which 1842 hectares are specially protected. Western Tombs of the Qing Dynasty occupies the largest area among the three cemeteries of the Qing Dynasty. The natural scenery, such as green grass and ancient trees, of Western Tombs of the Qing Dynasty is beautiful, towering Yongning Mountain in the north, south to the Yi River. The ancient constructions, such as the ancient bridges and memorial archways, waiting rooms for officials, Longen Palace, Ming Tower, and Baoding, constitute a solemn and quiet scene of imperial mausoleums.

Tailing Tomb was first built from the eighth year of the reign of Emperor Yongzheng (1730 AD), and Chongling Tomb of Emperor Guangxu was completed in 1915AD. The construction of Western Tombs of the Qing Dynasty was lasted for 185 years. There were already 14 mausoleums, namely four mausoleums of emperors, including Tailing Tomb, Changling Tomb, Muling Tomb and Chongling Tomb; three mausoleums of empresses, including Taidongling Tomb, Changxiling Tomb and Mudongling Tomb; three mausoleums of concubines, including Taifeiling Tomb, Changfeiling Tomb, and Chongfeiling Tomb; as well as four tombs for prince and princess. There are also two auxiliary constructions, Xing Gong(a temporary imperial palace) and Yongfu Temple, as well as a site of government office in feudal China. A total of 80 people were buried in Western Tombs of the Qing Dynasty.

Covering an area of 50000 square meters, there are 1259 palaces and single buildings, 122 stone constructions standing in the burial area, which constitute a large-scale, magnificent architectural complex. The architectural form and regulation embody the system of the feudal society visibly. The tombs of the four emperors and three empresses are covered with yellow glazed tiles while the tombs of concubines and royal highness are decorated with green glazed tiles, with grey tiles for princes and princesses. These ancient architectures are surrounded by 15000 green pines and verdant cypresses. Mt. Yongning is standing behind the mausoleum while the Yishui River is flowing in front of the Large Red Door; these surroundings make the large-scale tombs more magnificent. These ancient pine trees provide a special climate for this area through reducing the attack from the outside sandstorm and the influences of the hot-gas and cold current, which leads to independent and complete natural environment and well-preserved architecture.

Since Eastern Tombs of the Qing Dynasty had already been built, why bother to construct Western Tombs of the Qing Dynasty? After the Manchurian came to Central China, the tombs of Emperor Shunzhi and Kangxi were constructed in Eastern Tombs of the Qing Dynasty in Zunhua City, Hebei Province. Their concubines were also buried there, so the burial system of "The following of one's father's burial site" was set. After Emperor Yongzheng ascended the throne, he selected the other burial site outside Eastern Tombs of the Qing Dynasty according to the suggestion of the geomantic masters, which broke the tradition. Emperors of the Qing Dynasty laid emphasis on "the site of the mountain and river" and "the invisible power" when selecting their mausoleums. The suitable region was called "The geomantic and treasured site which is more favorable and blessed for the emperors". In order to perfect these geomantic and treasured sites, they planted extensive pine trees in the mausoleum while constructing the magnificent mausoleums to create the aura of solemnity. From the construction of the tomb of Tailing by the third generation of Emperor Yongzheng to the completion of the tomb of Chongling of Emperor Guangxu in the fourth year of the Republic of China, it lasted more than 185 years and over 200000 evergreen trees were planted, such as pine and cypress, have covered every corner of the mausoleum region, which added solemnity to the mausoleum and beautified the environment of Western Tombs of the Qing Dynasty. At the same time, these evergreen trees also implied the aspiration of emperors yearning for everlasting generations. As time went by, the rule of the Qing Dynasty had been the past; however, the preserved 15000 ancient pine trees and Western Tombs of the Qing Dynasty had become the valuable cultural heritage for the later generations.

The affiliated constructions of the four tombs of emperors all reflect the evolutionary process from prosperity to decline of the Qing Dynasty whether in scale or shape. The complete and majestic scale of Tailing Tomb and Changling Tomb reflect the glory in the prosperous period of the Qing Dynasty; the reduction of the Muling Tomb and Chongling Tomb record the trace of history of the Qing Dynasty from prosperity to decline, from feudalism to semi-feudalism and semi-colonialism veritably. The destiny of Emperor Guangxu and his concubine buried in Chongling Tomb and Concubine mausoleums recorded the humiliating history of Empress Dowager Cixi who dominated the court and forfeited its sovereignty. The mausoleum project of the last emperor was terminated due to the decline of the Qing Dynasty. It is also the physical evidence of the end of the feudal history of China for more than 2000 years. In terms of the conserved condition, Western Tombs of the Qing Dynasty as a whole is one of the most intact architectural complex in China.

(1) 泰陵

泰陵是清朝入关后第三代皇帝雍正的陵墓，也是清西陵中建筑最早、规模最大、体系最完整的一座帝陵。

泰陵从雍正八年（公元 1730 年）开始营建，历经八年，于 1737 年竣工，命名为泰山陵，简称泰陵。成本材料费白银 240 多万两，用工 233.6 万人次。鉴于雍正皇帝对中国历史做出的贡献，所以他的陵寝用泰字命名 。

泰陵

泰陵是一处清朝盛世遗存下来的古建群体，从它的选址、规划布局都反映出当时国家的强盛以及政局的稳定。在建筑用料、工程技术、传统工艺等方面亦非常考究。

泰陵陵址名曰太平峪，地处永宁山主峰下。根据“陵制与山水相称”，即“天人合一”的宇宙观，清代建筑学家与风水学家把形态端庄的元宝山作为泰陵的朝山，永宁山作为泰陵的靠山。泰陵不仅讲究规划布局，而且建筑布局也非常考究，完全依照帝王生前所居宫廷布局，按礼制的需要而规划。以中轴线贯穿南北，主体建筑设在中轴线上，一律坐北朝南，地宫坐落在中轴线的北端，其余建筑沿中轴线排列开。这些建筑都以准确的尺度，灵活巧妙的手法进行配置和空间组合，使陵寝的纪念性、礼制性主体有条不紊地展开并不断深化。

泰陵是雍正的陵墓，埋葬着雍正及他的皇后孝敬宪、皇贵妃敦肃。其建筑序列从南向北，于 2.5 千米长的神路上以居中或对称的形式依次修建了五孔石桥、石牌坊、石獬豸、大红门、更衣殿、平桥、圣德神功碑楼、华表、望柱、七孔石桥、石像生、龙凤门、三孔桥、神道碑亭、神厨库、朝房、班房、隆恩门、焚帛炉、配殿、隆恩殿、三座门、二柱门、石五供、方城、明楼、宝顶等建筑。

石五供

明楼属于纪念性的建筑物，高高耸立在方城之上，使人置身于仰崇桥山的氛围之中。它朱红色的墙体、金黄色的瓦顶与湛蓝的天空构成一幅绚丽的画卷。

当游客踏上南门外远眺时，心中涌现一种无比自豪的感觉。正前方 2.5 千米之外的东西华盖山、九龙九凤山形成的自然门户，郁郁葱葱的古松树弥漫于 15 千米内外。座座殿宇、桥梁、门房、树木、山川疏密相间，错落有致。这种巨大的皇陵在中国的建筑史上留下了辉煌的一页，是中华民族的骄傲。英国著名科学家李约瑟说："皇陵在中国建筑制式上是一重大成就，它整个图案的内容也许就是整个建筑部分与风景艺术相结合的最伟大的例子。"

Tailing Tomb was built for the third generation of Emperor Yongzheng. It is the earliest, the biggest, and the most systematical tomb among the Western Tombs of the Qing Dynasty.

Tailing Tomb was built from the eighth year of the reign of Emperor Yongzheng (1730 AD), and was completed in 1737 AD. It was named Taishanling, with the abbreviated form of Tailing. It cost more than 2.4 million taels of silver and 2336000 workers. Taking account of the contributions Emperor Yongzheng have made to Chinese history, the tomb is named Tai.

Tailing Tomb is an ancient building complex in the Qing Dynasty. The site and the layout could reflect the prosperity and stability of the whole nation. Also, the building material, engineering technology and traditional arts all deserve studying.

The site of Tailing Tomb is called Taiping Valley, which is at the foot of the main peak of Mt. Yongning. According to the world outlook of "the match of the tombs and natural landscapes", that is, "the unity of heaven and earth", the architects and geomantic scientist regard Mt. Yuanbao as a place to make sacrifice and Mt. Yongning as the backing mountain of Tailing Tomb. The layout of the building is very elegant, fully in accordance with the palace before the emperor's death. The central axis of the tomb runs through the south and north with the main building facing to the south. The underground palace is in the northern end of the axis, with others spreading along the axis. With the exquisite combination of the buildings, the memorial and social theme is deepened.

Tailing Tomb is made up of a group of tombs of Emperor Yongzheng and his wives, such as Xiao Jingxian and Dun Su. Along the 2.5 kilometers long sacred way symmetrically built many buildings, including the Five-hole Stone Bridge, the Stone Paifang (Chinese architectural arch or gateway), the Stone Xiezhi (a mythical animal), the Red Gate, the Dressing Hall, the Flat Bridge, Beilou (the Memorial building), the Ornamental Column, the Baluster Column, the Seven-hole Stone Bridge, the stone animals, the Dragon and Phoenix Gate, the Three-hole Stone Bridge, the Stele Pavilion, the Sacred Kitchen, the Pilgrimage Room, the Jails, the Longen Gate, the Burning Furnace, the side halls, the Longen Hall, the Three-bottom Gate, the Two-column Gate, Shiwugong (five stone vessels filled with offerings), Fangcheng(mahjong layout), Minglou, and Baoding (the dome).

Minglou belongs to the memorial building type, sitting straightly on the square castle, making one intoxicated by the atmosphere. It draws a colorful picture by combining the scarlet walls, golden yellow tiles and pure blue sky as a whole.

Stepping onto the south gate of Minglou, unprecedented feeling is activated simultaneously. 2.5 kilometers right in front of Tailing Tomb lie in the east and west Mt. Huagai and Mt. Jiulongjiufeng. With pervasive old pines spreading 30 miles, the palaces, bridges, gates houses, trees and mountains are well-placed. The mausoleum is a big success in architectural history of China. It deserves the pride and compliments in the history of China. Take the quotation of Joseph, a famous British scientist, as instance, "The achievement of the imperial mausoleums is of great importance in the history of Chinese architectural model, the content of which is the perfect unification of the building pattern and the arts of landscapes.

(2) 昌陵

昌陵位于泰陵西 0.5 千米处，是清朝入关后第五代皇帝——嘉庆的陵墓，内葬嘉庆皇帝及其皇后孝淑睿，该陵与泰陵平行走向。

在清西陵的 4 座帝陵中，昌陵是唯一一座能与泰陵相媲美的陵墓，其建筑规模之宏伟、环境风貌之聚秀、文化内涵之丰富，均堪称清陵中的上乘之作，凝聚着古代劳动人民的心血和智慧，是嘉庆王朝政治、经济、文化发展水平及宫廷生活的真实缩影。

昌陵自 1796 年开始修建到 1803 年竣工，历时 8 年，使用白银 200 多万两，用工 204.4 万人次。它是东、西陵中较有特色的一座，是研究清代陵寝制度不可多得的实物见证。在清代所有陵寝中，昌陵是唯一一处由太上皇选定的陵址。

石像生

从泰陵大红门内三孔平桥以北、圣德神功碑亭以南，有神道向西、然后北折，即为昌陵圣德神功碑亭。从南到北依次为：五孔桥、石望柱、石像生、龙凤门、三路三孔桥、神道碑亭、隆恩门、东西班房、东西朝房、神厨库、井亭。隆恩门内两侧为燎炉、东西配殿。隆恩门后面是三座琉璃花门，二柱门位于琉璃花门内并与之咫尺相对，还有石五供、方城、明楼、宝城、宝顶。

昌陵的建筑规模虽小于泰陵，但昌陵的许多单体建筑，如圣德神功碑亭、隆恩殿、隆恩门、明楼、东西配殿在高度面积上又比泰陵有所增益，使昌陵更显宏伟壮丽，比泰陵并不逊色几分。

另外，昌陵隆恩殿明柱包金饰云龙，金碧辉煌。殿内的地板是由 1168 块 62 厘米见方的紫花石铺墁的，这在清代 9 座帝王陵墓中独树一帜。紫花石(又叫豆瓣石、花斑石)，黄色底面，以示高贵，紫色花纹，更显华美，使昌陵隆恩殿又平添几分富丽多彩的气氛。

昌陵隆恩殿的东暖阁佛楼分上下两层，它的金漆木雕花纹图案细腻玲珑，堪称佳品；昌陵地面上的建筑不仅令人叫绝，而且清宫档案记载的昌陵地宫亦是一座佛雕艺术的宝库，据现存的“雷氏图纸”中考证，昌陵地宫结构比泰陵还要宏大，雕刻十分精美，为“四门九券”且有佛像经文雕刻，与现已开放的清东陵境内乾隆的裕陵地宫规模装饰相近。同样昌陵的地宫也具有诱人的魅力，券顶外的宝顶封土内也有石雕，其结构造型与陵寝宫殿的瓦脊、勾滴等相同，先按地面建筑的要求营造好地宫，然后再覆土掩埋，形成清代皇帝陵寝地宫结构中独具特色的风格。

Changling Tomb is located at the place 0.5 kilometers away from the Tailing Tomb, which is the tomb of the fifth Emperor Jiaqing since the Manchurian came to Central China. It was buried the Emperor Jiaqing and his wife, Xiao Shurui, paralleling with Tailing Tomb.

Among the four tombs of Western Tombs of the Qing Dynasty, Changling Tomb is the only one that can rate with Tailing Tomb. It is the masterpiece in terms of the area of construction, the surrounding environment, and the cultural connotation, which condenses the painstaking work and wisdom of ancient laborers. It is also the miniature of the level of political, economic, cultural development of Jiaqing Dynasty and the real life of the imperial palace.

Since the construction of Changling Tomb from 1796 to the completion year of 1803, more than 2 million taels of silver and 2.044 million workers were used. Changling Tomb is relatively characteristic and rare. It is the material witness for researching on the mausoleum system in the Qing Dynasty and the only one tomb chosen by the overlord.

To the north part of Sankong Flat Bridge inside the Red Gate of Tailing Tomb, there is a divine path wandering to the west, then to the north, that is where the Divine and Moral Pavilion stands. From the south to the north, there are the Five-hole Bridge, the stone pillar, the stone statues, the Dragon and Phoenix Gate, the Three-hole Bridge, the Immortal Path, the Longen gate, the jails in the west and east, the reception rooms for officials, the kitchen and the pavilion. On both sides of the Longen Gate, there are stoves and affiliated palaces in the west and east. Behind the Longen Gate, there are three doors made of glass with Erzhu Gate in the opposite direction within one foot. Besides, there are Shiwugong (used for making sacrifice), Fangcheng, Ming building, Baocheng and Baoding.

Although the size of Tailing Tomb outnumbers that of Changling Tomb, there are exceptions, the Divine and Moral Pavilion, the Longen palace, the Longen gate, Ming building, and affiliated palaces in the west and east, all add glory to Changling Tomb.

In addition, the pillars in Longen Palace are inscribed with glorious clouds and dragons. The floor in the palace is decorated with sixty-two squared purple pieces of stones with the total number of 1168, which is unique among the nine tombs of emperors. The purple stone is called bean-shaped stone or color-spotted stone. The bottom of it is yellow, demonstrating the dignity and elegance. And the purple veins on the stones add beauty to the palace, which make the atmosphere charming and colorful.

The Buddha building in the east pavilion in the Longen Palace is divided into two floors, with the pattern of gold lacquer woodcarvings, delicate and exquisite. The buildings on the Changling Tomb are amazing. The underground palace recorded in the Qing Dynasty collection is also the treasure of the arts of Buddha sculptures. According to the extant "Lei Family Blueprint", the underground structure of Changling Tomb is larger than that of Tailing Tomb, and the woodcarvings there are delicate. It consists of four doors and nine halls with Buddha sculptures inscribed on them. This decoration is similar to the opening-up Yuling underground palace. Similarly, the underground palace in Changling Tomb is also inviting, with woodcarvings in the Baoding outside the hall. And the tile ridges and rain drainage ditches are identical with that of the palace on the ground. Changling Tomb is first built according to the standard of the buildings on the ground, and is buried thereafter, forming the characteristic style of Imperial Palace of the Qing Dynasty.

(3) 慕陵

慕陵是清朝入关后第六代皇帝——道光的陵墓。

慕陵位于西陵陵区最西端的龙泉峪，兴建于道光十二年至十六年间，由宠极一时的大臣穆彰阿主持建造，使用白银250万两左右，总用工87.6万人次。慕陵在选址时吸取清东陵宝华峪陵寝渗水的教训，选择了高平之地龙泉峪，鉴于地势的限制，道光对慕陵的建筑规制进行了大胆的改革和创新，建筑规模显著缩小，仅有建筑27座，占地45.6亩，同时对主体建筑结构进行了改革。地宫由四道石门改为两道，地宫内增设龙须沟；隆恩殿由重檐改为单檐，殿外不设石栏，以20根木楹撑托梁架，辟成回廊。改革后的慕陵创造了一种小巧玲珑的新模式，并对后世陵寝产生了巨大的影响。

慕陵虽然外观上保持了“节俭”之意，但其材质结构却异常精美。主体建筑的大殿全部采用昂贵的金丝楠木制作，不施彩绘，保持了本色。外面烫蜡。虽然看起来不是那么富丽堂皇，但却赋予人们古朴、典雅的感觉。最令人惊叹的是在三座殿的门窗隔扇、梁柱、雀替、天花、藻井上布满了形态各异的木雕龙，尤其是天花板上都以高浮雕的手法雕成向下俯视的龙头。走进殿内，举目上望，但见群龙聚首，栩栩如生。整个雕刻构思严谨，线条流畅，刀法娴熟，制作精巧，形象生动，充满着祥和气氛，使人仿佛来到了一座雕龙博物馆，难怪有人惊叹:“慕陵是座雕刻艺术的殿堂。”

慕陵建筑面积虽没有泰陵大，建筑也不如泰陵那样宏伟，布局更不如泰陵那样完善，但别出心裁的设计以及独特的建筑手法，使其成为清代帝王陵寝中绝无仅有的艺术珍品。

Muling Tomb is built for the sixth generation of Emperor Daoguang since the Manchurian came to Central China.

Muling Tomb is located at Longquan Valley, the outmost west of Western Tombs of the Qing Dynasty. It was built by the minister, Mu Zhang'a, from the twelfth to the sixteenth year of the reign of Emperor Daoguang, using about 2.5 million taels of silver and 876000 workers. Taking the lessons from the snoozing of water in Baohua Valley, the directors chose the higher and flatter spot, Longquan Valley, as the site. With the restriction of the terrain, Emperor Daoguang innovated the construction with 27 buildings occupying 45.6 *mu*. Also, the main structure of the building was reformed. There were two gates and a Longxu Gully in the underground palace. Longen Palace was also changed to singular eave without stone rails outside. Using twenty wooden columns supporting the beam, the winding corridor was constructed. After the reform, Muling Tomb created a new pattern, small but exquisite, which affected the model of later tombs.

Although Muling Tomb maintains its "frugality" in appearance, its material and structure are very delicate. The main building uses the expensive gold phoebe but without colorful paintings. The covering of the woods is polished with melted wax, which endows the building simplicity and elegance. The most astonishing thing is that the gates, the window, the girder, the sparrow and the ceiling in the three halls are all covered with wooden dragons of different postures. Among these, the most particular one is the head of the dragon watching toward the ground carved with the technique of alto-relievo. Once entering the palace, the lifelike dragons can be seen. The rigorous carving, smooth lines, blade skill, ingenious manufacture and vivid image form a peaceful atmosphere and give people the feeling of entering a museum of carved dragons. No wonder someone exclaimed: "Muling Tomb is the place of the arts of woodcarvings."

The construction area of Muling Tomb is not as broad as that of Tailing Tomb, nor as perfect as the configuration of Tailing Tomb, but the particular design and unique means of the building cannot be outweighed, making it become the unique treasure of the imperial mausoleums in the Qing Dynasty.

(4) 崇陵

崇陵是清朝入关后第九位皇帝——光绪的陵墓，也是中国最后一座帝王陵墓。

崇陵陵址名金龙峪。崇陵在建筑规模上比其他帝陵均小，没有大碑楼、石像生、二柱门等建筑，但基本上沿袭了明、清两朝的陵寝制度，并集清朝各陵的建筑经验于一体，采用先进的建筑技术，用料考究。主要建筑的三大殿全部采用质地坚硬的铜藻、铁藻木料构成，而且地宫石门上端的管扇全部用青铜制作，素有"铜梁铁柱"之称。隆恩殿内的四根明柱采用沥粉贴金盘龙装饰，为体现帝陵的独到之处。檐下增设了通风孔，可保殿内空气流通，以防木料腐朽。就其建筑群体而论，设有较完备的排水系统，宫殿四角的散水既宽又陡，便于雨水的排放。明楼与三座门前分别挖砌了御带河，地宫内凿有十个漏水眼与之相通，为地宫排水之用。

崇陵

崇陵虽建于清末民初，但建筑规制仍宏伟壮观。在众多建筑物中，地宫工程最为浩大，崇陵地宫如同其他帝陵的地宫那样，为拱券式石结构建筑，共有四门九券。墓道全长63.19米，面积349.95米，空间2170.65立方米，四道石门是地宫的重要组成部分，每扇石门上浮雕菩萨立像一尊，佛像大小与真人差不多，各个头戴佛冠，身披袈裟，足蹬莲花座，手持法器，分别代表力量、智慧、愿望、富贵等。过了四道门便是地宫九券中最大的一个券——金券，这里是地宫的主体建筑，高大宽敞，内有宝床，上面安放着皇帝、皇后的梓宫。

1938年，一伙不明身份的武装人员盗掘了崇陵地宫。1980年，文物部门对崇陵地宫进行了清理并对外开放。虽然崇陵地宫没有乾隆的裕陵地宫那样规模宏大、雕刻精美，但它却成为研究清朝皇帝陵寝地宫规制的实物见证。

崇陵铜梁铁柱

Chongling Tomb is the tomb of the ninth emperor since the Manchurian came to Central China, Guangxu, which is also the last tomb of emperor.

The site of the tomb is named Golden Dragon Valley. Compared with the tombs of former emperors, this one is much smaller without buildings, such as the Tablet Mansion, the stone animals and the Two-column Door. But it also inherits the mausoleum system of the Ming Dynasty and the Qing Dynasty, integrating the architectural experience of the tombs in the Qing Dynasty, adopting the advanced technology and materials. The three main palaces are all made of solidified copper and iron algae woods, with the bronze fans in the upper part of the stone door in the underground palace, which is universally called "Bronze beam, iron prop". The four overt pillars in Longen Palace are decorated with gold dragon, demonstrating the uniqueness of the tomb. There are ventilating poles underneath the eaves, which keep the air circulated and resist the decay of the wood. In terms of the whole building complex, there is relatively sound drainage system. The four horns of the palace are wide enough to discharge the wastewater. A draining area is drilled respectively in front of Ming Building and the three gates, which is linked with the ten leaking holes for draining away the water in the underground palace.

Built in the late Qing Dynasty and the early years of the Republic of China, the architectural regulation of Chongling Tomb is magnificent and spectacular. Among the various buildings, the underground palace is of unparalleled size. There is no difference with others in terms of the arch-style stone construction. There are four gates and nine halls inside. The total length of the tomb is 63.19 meters, with the area of 349.95 meters and the space of 2170.65 cubic meters. The four gates constitute the significant part of the underground palace, with a relief sculpture of Boddha on each stone gate. The size of the Buddha is about the same as a real person. The decorations of the Buddha hat, the cassock, the lotus blossom, and the instrument used by the Buddha, represent power, wisdom, hope and wealth individually. Passing the four gates, one can step into the biggest hall, which is the main construction of the underground palace, tall and spacious. There is a bed inside, above which are the coffins of Emperor Guangxu and his wife.

In1938, Chongling Tomb was excavated and robbed by a group of unidentified armed people. Later, it was restored by the Department of Cultural Relics and was opened to the public in 1980. Although the underground palace of Chongling Tomb is much smaller compared with that of Yuling Tomb of Emperor Qianlong, it has become the testimony of the regulation of the tombs in the Qing Dynasty.

6. 满城汉墓

满城汉墓位于保定市满城区，是西汉中山靖王刘胜(公元前165—前113年)及其妻窦绾之陵墓。满城汉墓占地144公顷，墓室构造仿汉化宫殿形式，规模宏大，建造考究，陈设华丽，举世罕见，是目前我国规模最大、结构最复杂、保存最完整的崖墓。两墓出土金、银、铜、铁、玉石、陶、漆等器物和纺织品、银鸟篆壶、医用金针等文物10633件，举世闻名的金缕玉衣、长信宫灯、错金博山炉都出土于此。1988年，满城汉墓被国务院公布为“全国重点文物保护单位”，现为4A级旅游景区，河北省风景名胜区。

中山靖王墓室

1968年5月，解放军某部在满城县(现为满城区)陵山上施工时，偶然发现了西汉中山靖王刘胜和他夫人窦绾墓。之后，满城县就多了一个名称——金缕玉衣的故乡。

刘胜，是西汉景帝刘启之子，汉武帝刘彻的异母兄长。他在景帝三年(公元前154年)被封为中山王，死于武帝元鼎四年（公元前113年），统治中山国达42年之久。中山国位于太行山东麓，首府设在卢奴(今河北省定州市)。西汉中山国有十代王，刘胜是第一代王。

满城汉墓墓室，位于陵山主峰东坡。一为中山靖王墓，一为其妻窦绾墓。两侧南北并列，墓道口向东，相距约120米。以山为陵，依崖建墓，两墓均为人工开凿的山崖墓，这在迄今为止发现的汉代陵墓中是独一无二的。墓室构造和布局完全模仿地面上的建筑，宛若豪华的地下宫殿，规模恢宏，无与伦比。

刘胜墓全长51.7米，最宽处37.5米，最高处6.8米，体积2700立方米，由墓道、车马房、库房和后室组成。前堂长约15米，宽约12米，是一个修在岩洞里的瓦顶木结构建筑，恢宏富丽，厅堂里摆满了铜器、铁器、陶器、瓷器和金银器，还有象征侍从的陶甬和石甬，以及出行时使用的仪仗等。前厅是象征墓主人生前宴饮作乐的大厅。后室建造十分讲究，用大小不同的石板筑成，分石门、石道、主室和侧室。主室是一间石屋，内置汉白玉铺成的棺床，室内放置了许多贵重器物。

窦绾墓与刘胜墓基本相同，体积3000立方米，车马房和库房比刘胜墓大，墓内随葬有许多珍贵器物。特别是窦绾的镶玉漆棺，在我国还是第一次发现，但建造规模和坚固完整程度超过了刘胜墓，墓洞全长49.7米，最宽处65米，最高处7.9米，容积3000立方米。

两墓共出土文物10633件，其中玉石器、金银器、铜器等文物精品4000多件。满城汉墓就是以出土文物之多、品级之高、做工之精美著称于世的。下面介绍一下举世瞩目的金缕玉衣、长信宫灯、错金博山炉。

甬道

玉衣为西汉贵族死后的葬服，按当时等级制度的规定，玉衣共分为金缕玉衣、银缕玉衣、铜缕玉衣三种。据《后汉书》记载，皇帝死后才能穿金缕玉衣，而诸侯只能穿银缕玉衣。公元前154年，汉景帝刘启平定吴楚七国之乱后，封刘胜为中山国的第一代王，按规定只能穿银缕玉衣，而他穿的却是金缕玉衣，这到底是怎么回事呢？据推测有两种原因：一个是当时已有皇帝对有功侯王赐葬服的特例；另一个或许是当时玉衣使用制度不太严格。推测只能是推测，这个问题至今仍是个未解之谜。

刘胜的玉衣全长1.88米，共用玉片2498片，金丝大约1100克。全体由头饰、上衣、裤、手套和鞋五部分组成，玉片大多为长方形或方形，也有少数为三角形或梯形。玉衣制作水平十分精湛，按当时西汉时期生产力水平来推测，制作一件金缕玉衣，需一名玉工花费十多年的时间才能完成。

如果说金缕玉衣把古代工匠的血汗结晶和西汉王侯的腐朽愚俗的生活都表现出来的话，那么长信宫灯则是古代劳动人民智慧的结晶。宫灯的造型十分优美，铜质鎏金，高48厘米，为一宫女跪坐执灯状，宫女头上梳髻，戴有头巾，身穿长衣，衣袖宽大，面含幽怨，一双呆滞的双眼无神地注视着灯口，它反映了汉代宫女凄惨悲凉的生活。这些姿色端庄的女子被帝王视为私有财产，可肆意地掠夺、抛弃，地位十分低下，其中尤以像长信宫灯造型中那种持灯宫女的地位最为卑贱。

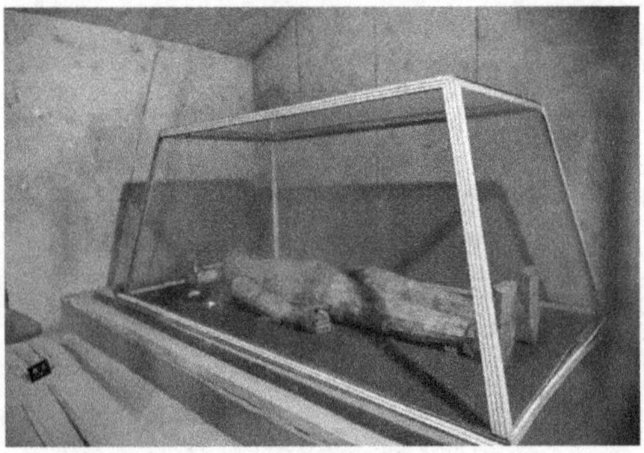
金缕玉衣

长信宫灯之所以闻名，更重要的是结构科学、合理。宫女左手托起灯盘，右手则高高吊起，宽大的袖口下垂，自然而然地形成灯罩，灯盘可以转动，灯罩可以开合，这样可以随意调节灯的照明和照射角度。更有趣的是整个宫女为一空心体，当在灯座上点燃油灯之后，油烟就会从袖口即灯罩右臂吸入体内，油烟一旦进入宫女腹腔，就会扩散，所以油泥和油灰就会自然黏附于宫女的体腔内，起到净化空气、过滤油烟的作用。那么长信女的腹腔内油泥又是如何清洗掉的呢？宫女其实是一个有机的组合体，它的头、臂、灯罩等部位是活动的，可

长信宫灯

以拆开，故此清洗油泥的难题就迎刃而解了。这一切都反映了宫灯设计的科学、巧妙、合理。宫灯的照明和通风设计，则反映了大约两千年前我国物理光学和热力学的科学水平。

经考古学家鉴定发现，在灯身上有“阳信家”“长信尚浴”等字样，表示此灯的第一位主人是阳信家。阳信家是阳信侯刘揭的简称。刘揭在位 14 年后，因其子获罪，全家被抄，这件稀世珍宝可能就是这样进入长信宫的，故此它的新主人就在灯身上铭刻“长信”等字样，因此我们才给它命名为长信宫灯。那么，它又怎么由长信宫到了靖王妃窦绾墓里呢？据资料记载，长信宫的主人是窦太后，也就是汉文帝皇后，靖王刘胜的祖母。当时，窦氏为一大望族，相传窦绾和窦太后是本家，窦太后在一次出游时识得窦绾，因窦绾生得乖巧伶俐，很招窦太后喜爱，征得同意，进入长信宫，成为窦太后的贴身侍女。后刘胜和窦绾相识，在结婚时，窦太后便把这个珍贵无比的宫灯赠予窦绾做嫁妆，窦绾视为珍宝，因此“她”才会长期陪伴在窦绾身旁，一陪就是两千多年。

错金博山炉在汉代被称作熏炉，也叫香炉，是豪门贵族的专用品。说起博山炉，首先还要联系仙境博山。相传，博山在东海中央，因它上面有仙人修炼仙丹的传说，所以在秦汉时期，一度成为人们向往的地方。据说，秦始皇就曾派徐福到那里去寻找长生不老之药，但最终还是心愿未了，所以在当时以博山形状作用品的器物极多。它表明了当时的人们向往仙境的思想。再将金丝银线嵌入器物，错入流畅、精细的纹饰，便称之为错金博山炉了，错金博山炉高 26 厘米，由炉座、炉盘和炉盖三部分组成。炉座圈足错金，作卷云纹，三条腾出波涛汹涌海面的蛟龙托着这座仙山；炉盘上的错金花纹潇洒飘逸，宛若随风起舞；自炉盘上部到炉盖，则烧筑“博山”。整个山体陡峭，峰峦交错，在整个山体上清晰可见神兽出没，虎豹奔走，猎人搭工放箭。仙风洒洒，海涛阵阵。打开炉盖，把香料放进炉内点燃，香烟便随着峰峦间的小孔袅袅上升，弥漫房中。博山炉之所以闻名中外，就是因为它设计独特，做工精湛。错金博山炉不仅是一幅富有生活气息的自然风景画，而且还反映了古代劳动人民的卓越成就。

满城陵山汉墓的出土文物品级高、数量多、科技工艺价值含量高，充分体现了古代劳动人民的勤劳与智慧，为研究西汉政治、经济、军事、科技提供了丰富的实物资料。

Being located in Mancheng District of Baoding, the Tombs of the Han Dynasty is the tomb of Liu Sheng(154 BC—113 BC), the king of Zhongshan Kingdom in the Western Han Dynasty, and his wife Dou Wan. The Tombs of the Han Dynasty, covering an area of 144 hectares. The tomb structure imitates the form of the palace in the Han Dynasty, with the grand scale, exquisite construction, and magnificent furnishings. It is the largest, most complex, and most intact protected cliff tomb in China, with 10633 pieces of unearthed cultural relics, such as gold, silver, bronze, iron, jade, pottery, lacquer wares, textiles, silver bird pot and medical gold needle, as well as the world famous Jade Clothes Sewn with Gold Wire, Changxin Palace Lamp and Boshan Censer Inlaid with Gold Decorations.

In May, 1968, in Mancheng County (Mancheng District), when Mt. Ling was under construction, the Chinese People's Liberation Army accidentally discovered the tombs of Liu Sheng, the king of Zhongshan in the Western Han Dynasty, and his wife Dou Wan. Since then, Mancheng County became the birthplace of Jade Clothes Sewn with Gold Wire.

In 1988, it was promulgated by the State Council as the "National Key Cultural Relic Protection Unit". Now it is a 4A-level scenic spot and a famous scenery area in Hebei Province.

Liu sheng is the son of Liu Qi, Emperor Jing in the Western Han Dynasty, and the half-brother of Liu Che, Emperor Wu of the Han Dynasty. He was honored king of Zhongshan Kingdom in the third year of the reign of Emperor Jing (154 BC) and died in the fourth year of the reign of Emperor Wu (113 BC), who ruled Zhongshan Kingdom for 42 years. Zhongshan Kingdom is located at the eastern foot of Mt. Taihang, and its capital is located in Lunu (Dingzhou City in Hebei Province). Liu Sheng was the first generation among the ten generations of kings in the Western Han Dynasty.

The Tombs of the Han Dynasty are located in the eastern slope of the main peak of Mt. Lingshan consisting of the tombs of the king of Zhongshan, and his wife Dou Wan. About 120 meters apart, the tombs sit side by side in the north-south direction, with the entrance facing to east. Built along the mountainside, the two tombs are both artificial excavations, which are unique in the so far found mausoleums of the Han Dynasty. The structure and layout of the burial chamber completely imitate the buildings on the ground, which are just like the luxurious underground palace with unparalleled grand scale.

The tomb of Emperor Liu Sheng is 51.7 meters long, with a maximum width of 37.5 meters and a maximum height of 6.8 meters. It consists of the tomb passage, the stable, the storehouse and the back room. The antechamber, which is 15 meters long and 12 meters wide, is a tile-roofed building which is located in a cave. Its hall is filled with copper, iron, pottery, porcelain, gold and silver wares, as well as terracotta warriors symbolizing attendants, and a guard of honor. The antechamber is a hall symbolizing the life of merrymaking and feasting. The rear room is built with slates of different size, which consists of the stone gate, the stone path, the main room and the side room. The main room is a stone house with a white marble coffin bed and many valuable objects placed inside.

The Tomb of Dou Wan is identical with that of Liu Sheng, but its scale and the degree of solidness and integrity exceed the Tomb of king Liu Sheng. The stable and warehouse are larger than that of Liu Sheng, and there are many precious burial objects. Particularly, the lacquer coffin of Dou Wan was first found in our country. The tomb is 49.7 meters long, with a maximum width of 65 meters and a maximum height of 7.9 meters.

Jade clothes are made for the dead nobles in the Western Han Dynasty. According to the provisions of the current hierarchy, jade clothes could be divided into Jade Clothes Sewn with Gold Wire, Jade Clothes Sewn with Silver Wire, and Jade Clothes Sewn with Bronze Wire. *History of the Later Han Dynasty* records that only the emperor can wear Jade Clothes Sewn with Gold Wire after death, while the feudal princes can only wear Jade Clothes Sewn with Silver Wire. After the chaos of the seven countries of Wu and Chu settled down, Liu Sheng was titled the first king of Zhongshan kingdom in 154 BC by Emperor Jing. According to the provisions, he could only wear Jade Clothes Sewn with Silver Wire; however, what he wore was Jade Clothes Sewn with Gold Wire. What happened to him on earth? There are two possible reasons, one is the special case of the burial clothing for the feudal princes bestowed by the emperor at that time, and the other is the less strict system of the use of jade clothes. But the actual reason is not clear until now.

With a total length of 1.88 meters, 2498 jade pieces, and about 1100 grams of gold wire, Liu Sheng's jade clothes can be divided into five parts of headgear, jacket, pants, gloves and shoes. Most of the jade pieces are in the shape of rectangular or square, and a few of them are in the shape of triangle or trapezoid. The production level of jade clothes was superb. Making a suit of jade clothes took over 10 years by a lapidary based on the productivity in Western Han Dynasty.

If Jade Clothes Sewn with Gold Wire manifests the blood and sweat of the ancient craftsmen and the rotten life of the feudal princes in the Western Han Dynasty, then the Changxin Palace Lamp reflects exactly the wisdom of ancient laboring people. The beautiful palace lamp is made of gold-plated bronze with the height of 48 centimeters. With a scarf around her halo of hair, long garment and loose sleeves, the court maid sits on heels and holds the lamp. With resentment on her face and dull eyes gazing at the lamp, it reflects the miserable and desolate life of the court maids in the Han Dynasty. These demure women are regarded as private property of the emperors who might willingly plunder and abandon them, thus their status are very low. The court maids who hold the lamp were down to the lowest status.

Changxin Palace Lamp is famous for its scientific and logical structure. With her left hand propping up the lamp plate, her right hand lifting, the loose sleeves of the court maid fall down and naturally form a lampshade. The lamp panel can be rotated, and the lampshade can be opened and closed, therefore one can freely adjust the illuminating angle. What's more interesting is that the body of the court maid is hollow. When the oil lamp is lit, the fumes will be sucked into the body from the sleeve, that is, the right arm of the lampshade. Once the fumes enter into the enterocoelia of the court maid, they will diffuse, so the greasy filth and putty will naturally attach to the body cavity, playing a role in purifying the air and filtering oil fumes. How to clean the greasy filth? The body of the court maid is actually an organic combination with mobile parts. The head, arm, and lampshade are detachable, so the cleaning problems can be solved. All of these reflect that the design of the palace lamp is scientific and reasonable. The function of illumination and ventilation reflects the scientific level in the field of physical optics and thermodynamics in China about 2000 years ago.

Through identification and discovery by archaeologists, there are "Yangxin Family" "Chang Xin Shang Yu" and other words on the lamp, indicating that the first owner of this lamp is Yangxin Family, the name of Liu Jie for short. 14 years after the reign of Liu Jie, his property was confiscated for his son's conviction. Perhaps this is why the rare treasure was found in Changxin Palace and was named "Chang Xin Palace Lamp" after its new owner. Then why was it found in the Tomb of Dou Wan? According to historical records, the owner of the Changxin Palace Lamp is Empress Dowager Dou, that is, the wife of Emperor Wen of the Han Dynasty, and Liu Sheng's grandmother. At that time, the Dou family is illustrious. According to the legend, Dou Wan and Empress Dowager Dou are members of the same clan. They got to know each other when traveling. Because of Dou Wan's cleverness, she got affection from Empress Dowager Dou and entered into Changxin Palace, becoming the personal maid of Empress Dowager Dou. Then Liu Sheng and Dou Wan were acquainted with each other. At their wedding, Empress Dowager Dou gave this precious palace lamp to Dou Wan as the dowry, and it had accompanied by the side of Dou Wan for over two thousand years.

In the Han Dynasty, Boshan Censer Inlaid with Gold Decorations was exclusive goods for powerful family and honorable nobility. Speaking of Mt. Bo, it is located in the center of East China Sea. Because of the immortal legend, it has once become a place that people yearned for in the Qin Dynasty and the Han Dynasty. It is said that the first emperor of the Qin Dynasty (259 BC—210 BC) sent Xu Fu there to look for the medicine of immortality, but he failed ultimately. So at that time, there were many artifacts in the shape of Mt. Bo which reflected the hope that people yearned for. With the gold and silver wire embeded inside the smooth and fine ornamentation, thus it is called the "Boshan Censer Inlaid with Gold Decorations". It is 26 centimeters high and consists of three parts, including the base, the hob and the cover. The base is mixed with gold cloud scroll patterns and three dragons jumping out of the sea to protect this huge fairy hill. The golden mixed patterns on the hob are as flexible as the wind dance. From the upper hob to the cover, Mt. Bo was created with staggered peaks. Mythical animals, running tigers and leopards, and hunters releasing the arrow can be seen clearly from the whole body of the mountain. Open the lid, put spices into the furnace, the smoke will rise from the hole and diffuse in the whole room. Boshan Censer is famous both at home and abroad for its unique design and exquisite workmanship. Boshan Censer Inlaid with Gold Decorations is not only a painting of natural landscape, but also reflects the remarkable achievements of the ancient laborers.

The unearthed cultural relics of the Tombs of the Han Dynasty with high grade, large quantities, and high value fully reflect the diligence and wisdom of the ancient people, and provide a wealth of materials of the Western Han Dynasty for political, economic, military, scientific and technological studies.

7. 北岳庙

千年古刹北岳庙始建于北魏宣武帝景明、正始年间（公元500—512年），至今有1500余年的历史，是封建帝王祭祀北岳恒山的场所。由于北岳庙内碑碣林立，古建成群，于1982年2月23日被国务院列为国家重点文物保护单位。北岳庙目前共有三大价值：古建筑、碑碣雕刻、壁画。

北岳庙规模宏大，主要建筑布局呈“田”字形，排列在一条垂直的中轴线上，由南向北依次是登岳桥、神门、牌坊、朝岳门、御香亭、凌霄门、三山门、飞石殿、德宁之殿、后宅门。北岳庙南北长542米，东西宽321米，面积173982平方米，现今保留南北长300米，东西宽139米。

北岳庙

朝岳门是在原址的基础上修复起来的，为歇山式建筑，进深二间，面宽三间。跨越朝岳门就预示着祭祀活动将要正式开始了。

御香亭始建于明嘉靖十五年（公元1536年），至今也有400余年了。此亭是皇帝在祭祀之前更衣之地，所以也称更衣亭。这里原来有一个石头做的鼎式香炉，每到祭祀当日，便早早洒满了松枝、檀香，香烟缭绕，皇帝沐浴更衣后，在这儿亲自点燃三炷清香，然后带领文武官员，前来跪拜，以谢神恩。香炉是北岳庙内施工时挖掘出来的唐代遗物，刻工精美，精雕细琢，比原物更是有过之而无不及了。此亭建筑是全木结构，坚固精巧，设计美观，亭顶为重檐三滴水攒尖顶，平面八角形，四角设有券门，到了夏季，凉风习习，也不失为一处避暑纳凉的好地方。

按照古帝王留下的传统，五岳是天子祭祀必到的地方。曲阳有北岳庙，所以历代祀事为多，其中《曲阳县志》记载的就有隋大业四年（公元608年），隋炀帝杨广曾亲临曲阳祭祀北岳。当时西域十国皆来助祭，河北道郡守也齐集于曲阳，并大赦天下。历代帝王祭祀北岳的仪式是十分隆重的。

凌霄门是北岳庙的第三道门。第一道门为神门，就是最前面的那道欧式铁栅栏门，以后要恢复原状。第二道门名朝岳门，两边都是关于北岳恒山的碑刻，它为硬山式建筑。距今700多年历史的北岳恒图记叙了北岳恒山的区域范围，河流山脉分布情况及曲阳城的部分情形。现在北岳和北岳庙已改在山西浑源。从此，曲阳只留有原北岳庙一座，不再列为国家祀典了。但当地的香火依然十分旺盛，祭祀大典仍在当地百姓中进行着，至今还能看到很多的庙宇废墟。

北岳庙内保存了200多通碑刻，从时代上说，自南北朝、北魏、北齐、唐、宋、五代、金、元、明、清和民国各代碑刻具备，跨越1500余年。碑刻内容多为历代重修北岳庙的记载和祭祀北岳庙的祭文，也有的是用诗词歌赋记录的观后感，现移入碑廊内的碑刻70余通，使这些祖国的文化遗产得到了保护。

三山门建于明嘉靖以前，为明清时期的悬山式建筑。两侧为曲阳鬼的雕刻，右边这一块是明朝曲阳知县根据唐吴道子的壁画所刻的，至今有600余年。那“曲阳鬼”是怎么回事呢？据传，从前曲阳县有个商人，他虽然是个买卖人，但武艺高强，乐于助人。一次，他去南方做买卖，在谈笑之间，船客得知他是保定府曲阳人。客船正在航行中，突然海妖作怪，一时狂风大作，波浪滔天，眼看一只小舟颠簸飘摇，随时有沉没的危险。正在这紧急关头，只见此人精神抖擞，纵身入江，没入水中，不一会儿，风平浪静，转危为安，船客得救，欢呼雀跃，但定睛看时那人却不见了，原来那个曲阳客商经过与海妖奋力搏斗，已把海妖打死，得胜远走了。后来得救的船客跋山涉水，不远万里来到曲阳，寻找救命恩人。他们一连住了数日，也未找到。一天，他们无意中来到北岳庙，忽然看到德宁殿西壁画上的飞天神与那曲阳客商长得一模一样，才恍然大悟。原来救命恩人是“曲阳鬼”。于是他们把壁画“曲阳鬼”勾摹下来，带回家去，供奉起来，从此“曲阳鬼”就远近皆知，扬名四海了。

凌霄门

庙内建筑都有严格的对称格局，重修后的洪武碑楼保留了明太祖朱元璋亲笔御题的一篇“大明诏旨”。全碑字体为楷书，笔画工整，结构匀称，刚柔适度，虽未署名，但定是出自名家之手。

北岳庙的主体建筑德宁之殿占地2009.8平方米，高25米，殿面宽九间，进深六间，始建于南北朝北魏时期，至今1500多年。各代进行过大大小小16次维修与扩建。因为它现在多存有元代建筑风格，所以被确定为我国目前“元代”木结构中最大的古建筑。1981年至1987年，国家投入资金116万元进行过大的维修，我们看到的德宁之殿依然如故。通过重修，揭开了过去一些传说之谜。传说大殿内每根砌在墙内的通天柱下压着一只乌龟，所以墙根内每一个小孔都会自动呼气吸气。原来为了每根通天柱能通风，在通天柱周围留一些空隙，便于空气上下流通，防止柱子腐朽，延长使用寿命，哪里有什么乌龟呢？实际上是一种比较科学的通风防腐措施。

北岳庙最为珍贵的是德宁之殿内的壁画。殿内北、东、西墙壁内侧皆有高大的壁画。北墙巨幅壁画高 8 米，长 27 米；东西两侧壁画各高 8 米，长 18 米，壁画总面积为 504 平方米。北墙壁画是《北岳恒山神出巡图》，东墙壁画为《云行雨施》，绘有众多天神兴云布雨，普降甘霖，为民造福的形象，最大的人物高达 3.3 米。西壁画为《万国咸宁》，画的是众天神胜利完成兴云布雨的任务后得胜回宫的情景。西壁的飞天神是全幅壁画之精华所在，肌肉矫健，相貌狰狞。

庙内建筑

北岳庙内建有雕刻艺术馆，保存古雕刻 100 多件，其作品有人物、动物、佛像等， 作品造型优美，刀工细腻，线条清晰流畅，充分展示了我国北方石雕艺术在不同历史时期的风格和特点。

庙内还建有曲阳博物馆。博物馆始建于 1998 年，2001 年正式对外开放，属于仿明、清建筑的四合院，占地 1800 平方米，建筑面积 730 平方米。为打造北岳文化品牌，更好地发挥博物馆功能，2011 年，曲阳博物馆改为北岳文化陈列馆。此馆共设三个陈列室，以精美图片和生动活泼的形式，集中展示了古北岳大茂山的自然、人文景观和北岳庙建筑、壁画、碑刻等内容，让人们更直观地认识北岳文化的起源、发展及深厚内涵。

北岳庙不仅是祭祀北岳恒山之神的风水宝地，更是一座内涵丰厚的文化艺术殿堂。它集古建、绘画、书法、石雕、定瓷等艺术之花于一身，璀璨夺目、光彩照人，向世人展现出我们伟大祖先的勤劳和智慧。

The Beiyue Temple was first established in the era of Jingming and Zhengshi during the reign of Emperor Xuanwu of the Northern Wei Dynasty (500 AD—512 AD), with a history of over 1500 years. The temple was used to make sacrifices to Mount Heng by the emperors. Due to its many ancient stelae and building complex, it was classified as "A Major Historical and Cultural Site Protected at the National Level" in February 23, 1982. Currently, the temple features its three artistic and cultural treasures: ancient buildings, ancient stelae and murals.

The Beiyue Temple is imposing and magnificent, and its main architectural layout is the shape of "田". The Beiyue temple is laid out on a north-south axis featuring ten extant buildings. From south to north, the buildings are: the Mounting Bridge, the Immortal Gate, Paifang (Chinese architectural arch or gateway), the Mount-Pilgrim Gate, the Imperial Incense Pavilion, the Cloud-Reaching Gate, the Three-mount Gate, the Flying Stone Hall, the Dening Hall, and the Inner Residence Gate. It was originally 542 meters long from south to north, and 321 meters wide from east to west, covering 173982 square meters. Now the extant complex is 300 meters in length from south to north and 139 meters in width from east to west.

The Mount-Pilgrim Gate is restored from where it once was. It has a saddle roof and is 2 rooms deep, 3 rooms wide. Passing through the gate signals that the sacrifice ceremony is about to commence officially.

The Imperial Pavilion was first established in the 15th year of the reign of Emperor Jiajing in the Ming Dynasty (1536 AD), with a history of over 400 years. The pavilion serves as the place for emperors to change clothes, so it is also known as the Pavilion of Changing Clothes. Originally, there stood a stone censer in the shape of Ding (a sacrificial tripod cauldron in ancient China). On the day of sacrifice, the pavilion was haunted with the fragrance of burning rosin and sandalwood-scented joss. After having a bath and changing clothes, the emperor would light three incense sticks in person and then led the imperial officials and military officers to kowtow to pay homage to the grace of gods. The censer was unearthed by accident during the renovation of this temple. It derives from the Tang Dynasty and has meticulous inscriptions and exquisite carvings for decoration. The pavilion is entirely made of wood, firm and solid. It is of subtle and elegant design, with a pyramid roof and triple dripping eaves. It is octagonal in shape and has archways on four corners. When the summer heat hits, the pavilion is blessed with cool draught, thus making it an ideal summer resort.

According to the convention of ancient China, the Five Great Mountains were the subjects of imperial pilgrimage by emperors. The Beiyue Temple, which is located in Quyang County, witnessed numerous sacrifices throughout ages. According to the accounts in *Quyang County Annals*, in the fourth year of Daye era of the Sui Dynasty (608 AD), Yang Guang, Emperor Yang of the Sui Dynasty, ever came to Quyang County to pay homage to the North Great Mountain, Mount Heng. At that time, ten tributary states in the regions west of Yumen Pass all came to consummate the sacrifice ceremony. Meanwhile, the emperor granted amnesty to criminals to pay respect to the grace of gods. All the rituals of the emperors' sacrifice to Beiyue are extraordinarily solemn.

The Cloud-Reaching Gate is the third gate to the Beiyue Temple. The first gate is named Immortal Gate. It has been replaced now by a European-style iron fence gate, and is yet to be restored to what it looked like. The second gate is the Mount-Pilgrim Gate. It is an archway with a gabbled roofline, and is flanked by stelae to commemorate Mount Heng. The inscription of Bei Yue Heng Tu, dating back to more than 700 years ago, records the range of the North Great Mountain, Mount Heng and the distribution of its rivers and mountain branches as well as some information about the Quyang County. Currently, an alternative Beiyue Temple has been built in the Hunyuan County, Shanxi Province, and Quyang County still retains the original Beiyue Temple. Though the Beiyue Temple in the Quyang County ceases to be included in the list of areas for national sacrifice ceremony, it continues to enjoy exuberant worship from local people.

The Beiyue Temple has hosted nearly 200 stelae. Chronically, they are composed of stone tablets covering ages from the Southern and Northern Dynasty, the North Wei Dynasty, the North Qi Dynasty, the Tang Dynasty, the Song Dynasty, the Five Dynasties and Ten Kingdoms period , the Jin Dynasty, the Yuan Dynasty, the Ming Dynasty, the Qing Dynasty and the Republic of China. They witness over 1500 years' history of China and most of them record the reconstruction of the Beiyue Temple and sacrificial rituals, others record some poetic and lyrical reviews of the visitors. Now, more than 70 stelae have been moved into a stele pavilion, allowing the valuable cultural heritage to be under better conservation.

The Three-mount Gate had been built before Emperor Jiajing of the Ming Dynasty commenced his reign. The current building was rebuilt during the Qing and Ming Dynasty, with a suspension roof. There are carvings about "Quyang Ghost" on both sides of the gate. The one in the right was carved by the magistrate of Quyang County in the Ming Dynasty based on the mural created by Wu Daozi, the famous artist in the Tang Dynasty, and it has a long history of more than 600 years. Then, who is "Quyang Ghost" on earth? Legendarily, once upon a time, there was a businessman in Quyang County. A trader though he was, he was proficient in martial arts and always ready to help others. One day, he went to the south to do business by ship. During casual talking, the passengers learned that he came from Quyang of Baoding. During the voyage, all of a sudden, a water monster made trouble, causing strong wind and billowing waves. The ship was bumpy and swaying, with an imminent risk of sinking. At this critical point, the businessman plunged himself into the water valiantly. Soon after, the violent wind and waves were quelled and the ship was saved. The passengers were exhilarated, but the Quyang businessman had vanished. Actually, the businessman, after defeating and killing the water monster, had left triumphantly. Later, some of the rescued passengers travelled thousands of miles to Quyang to look for their benefactor, but they made efforts in vain for several days. One day, when they accidentally visited the Beiyue Temple, they found out by chance that their rescuer looked exactly like the figure of celestial god in the mural, named "Quyang Ghost", painted on the west screen wall of the Dening Hall. Thereupon, they learned suddenly that they were saved by the "Quyang Ghost". Then, they copied down the mural "Quyang Ghost", and took home to worship. Henceforth, "Quyang Ghost" is universally well-known, far and near.

Buildings of the temple have a strict architectural symmetry. The restored Stele Pavilion of Emperor Hongwu houses one stele which is inscribed with one sacred edict of the Ming Dynasty, which is written by Zhu Yuanzhang, the first emperor of the Ming Dynasty. As a regular script, the inscribed characters are written tidily with moderate force and each is composed symmetrically. Though anonymous, the excellence of the handwriting tells that it must be the masterpiece of a notable calligrapher.

The main building of the temple is the Dening Hall, covering an area of 2009.8 square meters and 25 meters high. The hall measures nine bays by six bays. It was first built during the reign of the North Wei Dynasty in the medieval Northern and Southern Dynasties period, with a history of more than 1500 years. It has gone through 16 renovations of various scales through ages. Due to the fact that the extant building bears a strong architectural feature of the Yuan Dynasty, it is identified as the largest remnant wooden ancient building that dates from the Yuan period. From 1981 to 1987, the state invested 1.16 million *yuan* in the maintenance and renovation of the hall, by which some myths about the construction were resolved. The myth has it that underneath each of the pillars enclosed in the wall is placed a tortoise, which breathe through those little holes embedded in foot of the wall. In fact, those holes are designed to ventilate those pillars inside the wall so as to prevent the pillars from rot, thus prolonging their service life. Actually, there is no tortoise at all, but a scientific technique for ventilation to keep them from decay.

What value most of the Beiyue Temple are the murals painted in the Dening Hall. There are magnificent and big murals on the north, south and west inside walls. The north wall's mural measures 8 by 27 meters; and those on the south and west walls are 8 meters tall and 18 meters long respectively. They take up 504 square meters in total. The mural on the north wall is named *Patrol of the God of Mount Heng*. The east wall's mural is *Gathering Cloud and Dispensing Rain*, featuring many deities mass up clouds and dispense timely rains to benefit people, and the biggest figure on it is 3.3 meters tall. The mural on the west wall is *Universal Tranquility*, which portrays the deities, after completing their task of dispensing rains, returned to their immortal palace triumphantly. The painting of celestial god on the west wall is the gem of the whole set of the three murals, vividly presenting the god's vigorous muscle and hideous appearance.

Inside the Beiyue Temple, there is a sculpture gallery, which collects more than 100 ancient sculptures, featuring human figures, Buddhist figures and animals. These works are characterized by elegant modeling, exquisite carving and smooth outlines, fully demonstrating styles and characteristics of the stone carving art of ages in the north of China.

Quyang Museum is also built in the Beiyue Temple. The museum was constructed in 1998, and officially opened in 2001, belonging to the Chinese courtyard house with the imitation of the architectural style of the Ming Dynasty and the Qing Dynasty. It covers an area of 1800 square meters, with the floor space of 730 square meters. In order to strengthen the cultural brand of the North Great Mountain and put the role of the museum into full play, the Quyang Museum was upgraded to North Great Mountain Cultural Gallery in 2011. It has three showrooms. With exquisite pictures and other lively means, it intensively displays the natural and humanistic landscapes of the ancient Damao Mountain as well as the architecture, murals and stelae of the Beiyue Temple, thus allowing visitors to intuitively experience the origin, development and cultural connotations of the North Great Mountain.

The Beiyue Temple is not only the geomantic place for people to pay homage to the god of Mount Hengshan — the North Great Mountain, but also the art palace hosting numerous cultural treasures. It incorporates ancient architecture, paintings, calligraphic works, stone carvings and Dingzhou porcelain wares and other artistic fruits. Splendid and imposing, the temple demonstrates the diligence and intelligence of our great ancestors to the world.

8. 腰山王氏庄园

腰山王氏庄园是全国重点文物保护单位，位于保定市正西25千米处的顺平县腰山镇，庄园始建于清顺治初年，是华北现存规模最大、最完整的清代大地主兼巨商的豪门巨宅。其建筑既不同于皇宫官府，又不同于一般民居，是我国北方民居建筑的极品。《天下粮仓》等影视剧中的很多场景都在此拍摄。

腰山王氏庄园大门

顺平腰山王氏庄园是中国建筑史上一处罕见的超规制清代城堡式民居建筑群。庄园东西宽368.5米，南北长504.1米，占地面积18.6万平方米。四周城墙五尺厚，有垛口，墙上是更道，墙外有护庄沟，墙内是马道。庄园由三道中西内街隔成四大部分，由北往南依次为“北园”“中园”“南园”“场院”。北部三大部分为住宅区，建有成套庄园50余套，各类房屋500余间；核心建筑群的“仁和堂”，是由10个四合院组成的大套院，保存下来了4座正院，2座跨院，成为异常珍贵的古建文物。腰山王氏庄园文化蕴含丰富，是一座中国千雕博物馆，是一部永远读不完的书，为全国重点文物保护单位，3A级景区。

王氏家族祖居辽宁省铁岭市南关，其世祖王国福、王国卿兄弟追随清太祖努尔哈赤起兵征战，属汉军正黄旗。1638年，王氏八世祖王锡衮跟随多尔衮入关。顺治元年，清朝入主北京后，为解决八旗官兵生计，顺治帝遂下圈地之令。在这场大规模的圈地运动中，王家受封于顺平县南腰山村，用跑马圈占的方法，占据了方圆百余里的土地。

王氏解甲归田后，利用圈占的大量土地成为当地有名的豪绅。到六世王命召时，他成为冀商肇始的代表人物。他农商兼营，积累了巨大财富，遂大兴土木，建起规模宏大的庄园。王命召亲自带设计师赴北京绘制了某一王爷府建筑图。经过王家几代人的经营，从南到北，建成了南园、尚礼堂、尊义堂三部分建筑群体。现保存完整的名为“南园”，庄园内部以道为界，分南北两部分，北部为建筑区，南部为场院，场院外围辅以护庄沟和院墙。庄园现存建筑东路二进院落，中路为四进院落，西路仅存一进院落，称铺子院。各路门的左右置更房两间。庄园每进均置垂花门，门首精工雕刻覆莲垂花，青石雕成的抱鼓相对而设。正门外置影壁一座，长12米，高6米，壁座以石灰石精工雕琢成须弥座式样。据载，仅这座影壁就

雕刻

耗费白银一千两。

庄园内有东西排列四合院 4 排，每排均为三进，四合院各院前后贯通，左右相连，房屋建筑 120 间，由南而北，依次为商号、庭房、腰房、底房，另外还有书房、小伙房、伙计房、更房、畜房等。道路两旁古槐参天，遮云蔽日，俗称槐荫道。建筑每排均设二道大门，一为行人出入之门，二为车马出入门。该庄园占地面积之广，建筑规模之大，格局之考究，建筑艺术之精美，在河北省不多见。

整座庄园布局由北往南三道内街隔成四大部分，依次为北园、中园、南园、场院。庄园建成之时，总建筑面积达 3 万多平方米，成套庄园 3 处 50 多套宅院，房屋 500 余间。目前修复开放的南园部分，占地面积 2.2 万平方米，是整座庄园的九分之一。其建筑格局呈四方形，坐北朝南排列在一条直线上，是四世同堂的大院子。内有东西排列的四合院两排，九个套院，一百余间房屋建筑。

在庄园高墙内分布有多套宅院，命名为“堂”。西路“仁和堂”四进院是老主人王锡衮的住宅区，东路“梦和堂”三进院是王锡衮三儿子王佩的住宅区。四合院各院落前后贯通，左右相连。四进院正院九个门全在一条纵轴线上，一进院落的所有门廊全在一条横轴线上。道北排列正门、侧门各两座。“仁和堂”正门外建有影壁一座，壁座以石灰石精工雕琢成须弥座式样，还有虎皮纹上马石一对。庄园主要建筑立在近一米高的直壁式青石台基上，台基高三至五阶不等。房屋建筑形制为单檐硬山灰布瓦顶，抬梁式木构架。建筑色调以灰色为主，古朴大方。砖、石、木雕精妙古典，给人以庄重典雅之感。

庄园一角

腰山王氏庄园是一组古代民居精品，是研究清代民风民俗的珍贵资料和影视拍摄的重要外景地。游客除观赏豪门人家的宅院建筑外，还可看一看内设的各种展览，如大宅院的生活习俗展、顺平文物展、直隶婚俗展等；庄园还设有品茶、看戏、换装照相、坐花轿、拜花堂、唱堂会等民俗活动。

Yaoshan Manor of Family Wang, one of the national key cultural relic protecting units, is located in Yaoshan Town, Shunping County, 25 kilometers right west of Baoding City. The manor was originally built in the early years of Emperor Shunzhi by the ancestor of family Wang — Wang Xigun. Up to now, it has already had a history of more than 300 years. It is the largest and most intact gigantic residence of squire and tycoon in the Qing Dynasty. The construction of the manor is a masterwork of north civilian residential architecture, which is different from either royal palace and feudal official residence or common civilian residence. In recent years, Yaoshan Manor of Family Wang has become an important spot, where films and teleplays are shot. Many scenes in such plays as *Barns under the Sun* were shot there.

Yaoshan Manor of Fmily Wang is one of the superordinate castle style residential building complexes of the Qing Dynasty in China's architectural history. It is 368.5 meters wide and 504.1 meters long, covering an area of 186000 square meters. The walls are five feet thick with crenels. On the wall is Geng Road, and outside the walls is the ditch, and within the wall is the horse road. The manor is divided into four parts by three middle-west inner streets. And from north to south, there are "north garden" "middle garden" "south garden" and "yard". The three major northern parts are residential areas, with more than 50 sets of houses and more than 500 kinds of houses. As the core of the complex, the "Ren He Tang", a large courtyard, consists of 10 courtyards, with 4 courtyards and 2 cross-courtyards well-preserved. And it has become an extremely valuable ancient relic. It is a Chinese museum of thousands of sculptures. It is a book that will never be finished. It is a national key cultural relic protection unit and a 3A-level scenic spot.

Wang's family used to live in Nanguan, Tieling City, Liaoning Province. The ancestors Wang Guofu and Wang Guoqing followed Nurhachi, the first emperor of the Qing Dynasty, to go on an expedition. In 1638, Wang Xigun, the eighth generation of Wang family followed Duorgun to come to Central China. In the first year of the reign of Emperor Shunzhi of the Qing Dynasty, in order to solve the livelihood of the Eight Banners soldiers, Emperor Shunzhi ordered to launch the enclosure movement. In this large-scale enclosure movement, using the method of staking their claims, Wang family occupied the land with more than 50 square kilometers in South Yaoshan Villiage of Shunping County.

After returning home, the Wang family made use of large numbers of fields to become the local famous gentry. By the time of the sixth emperor's summons, Wang Mingzhao had become the representative of the Hebei businessmen. Since he had accumulated a great deal of wealth by running business together with agriculture, hence he began to construct a large-scale manor. Wang Mingzhao took the designer to Beijing to imitate the architectural drawings of a royal mansion in person. After several generations of Wang family's operation, from south to north, it is made up of three construction groups named South Park, Shangli Hall, and Zunyi Hall. Among them, the South Park is well-preserved. The manor is divided into the north and south part by the boundary of a wide road. The north part is the construction area, while the south part is the courtyard. The courtyard is surrounded by ditches and retaining walls. The existing buildings of the manor are houses with two yards to the east, four courtyards in the center, and only one courtyard in the west, which is called the shop yard. There are two side rooms on the left and right of each gate. The floral-pendant gates are carved with hanging lotus and decorated with the two drum-shaped bearing stones. Outside the door is a screen wall, 12 meters long, 6 meters high, which is carved with the Chinese traditional architectural pedestal style, made of limestone. According to the records, it cost a thousand taels of silver.

In the manor, there are four rows of quadrangle courtyard that have east-west arrangement, each row is 3 rooms deep, and each courtyard is closely linked. There are over 120 rooms in the courtyard. From south to north, it has the business house, the court room, the side room, and bottom room. In addition to that, it also has the study, the small kitchen, the dude room, the watchman room, and the livestock house, etc. On both sides of the road, there are luxuriant ancient locust trees; this is why it is called the Locust Road. Each row of the building has two gates; one is for pedestrians, and the other is for carriages and horses. With extensive area, grand scale, exquisite pattern, and elegant architectural art, the manor is such a rare place in Hebei Province.

The whole manor is divided into four parts from north to south, including the north garden, the central garden, the south garden and the backyard. When the manor was built, the total construction area was over 30000 square meters, and there were more than 50 yards with over 500 houses. At present, the south garden, which has been renovated and reopened, covers an area of 22000 square meters, which is one ninth of the entire manor. Its architectural layout is in the shape of square, sitting in a straight line and facing to south, and it is a big yard with four generations. There are two rows of quadruped courtyards, nine courtyards and more than one hundred houses.

There are many houses in the manor, which are named "Tang". "Ren He Tang", a 4-room-deep yard in the west is the residential area of the old master, Wang Xigun, and "Meng He Tang", a 3-room-deep yard in the east is the residential area of Wang Xigun's son, Wang Pei. Each yard is closely connected. The nine gates of the courtyard are all on one vertical axis, and all the porches of the courtyard are on a horizontal axis. In the north, there are two main gates and two side gates. Outside the "Ren He Tang" front gate lies a screen wall, which is carved with the Chinese traditional architectural pedestal style, made of limestone. And pair of stone is used to mount a horse with tiger skin stripe. The main building of the manor stands on a vertical pedestal nearly a meter high, namely, three to five steps. The architectural form is a saddle roofline with single eave, grey tiles and lintel timber frame. The architectural tone is mainly gray, simple and generous. The brick carvings, stone carvings, and wood carvings are exquisite and classic, giving people a feeling of elegance.

Yaoshan Manor of Family Wang is a collection of ancient houses, which is an important location for studying the folk customs of the Qing Dynasty, and it is also a film and television shooting spot. In addition to watching the buildings of the rich families, one can also watch the various exhibitions, such as the life and custom exhibition of the big house, the exhibition of Shunping cultural relics and the exhibition of the marriage custom of Zhili, etc.. The manor also has other folk activities like tea-tasting, drama-watching, wearing ancient clothes and taking pictures, bridal sedan chair sitting, performing formal bows by bride and groom in the old custom, staging a performance and so on.

9. 开元寺塔

开元寺塔是中国现存最高的砖塔，高 83.7 米，有“中华第一塔”的美誉，同时也是首批全国重点文物保护单位。开元寺塔始建于宋真宗咸平四年也就是公元 1001 年，而建成的时候，时间已经过去了 50 多年。在 1000 多年前，没有现代设备，完全依靠人力来搬运的情况下，它的出现和定州悠久的历史、灿烂的文化以及地理位置的重要性紧密相连。纵观定州上下五千年，定州历朝历代均为政治、军事重镇和商业繁华之地。北宋时期，定州地区佛教信仰极为流行，加上定州位于宋、辽交界的边陲，被称为“国之门户”。为了军事所需，瞭望敌情，同时存放从印度取回的舍利，顺应和利用广大佛教信徒的热情，于是诞生了这座佛教文化与中国实际国情相结合的建筑物——开元寺塔。

开元寺塔

这座塔的形制是八角形阁楼式建筑，外观挺拔秀丽。由塔基座、塔身和塔刹组成。塔身高十一级，从下向上按比例逐层收缩，每层用砖层层叠加挑出短檐，檐下悬挂风铃。每层的四个正方向都辟有门，门券上彩绘着火焰纹，象征着佛光普照、香火缭绕的佛门胜景。四个侧方向都辟为盲窗。但是到了十层和十一层，为了军事所需，塔的八面辟门。塔身顶部是绿琉璃剪边的屋顶，呈八坡八脊式，每脊边各站立一尊铸铁力士。屋顶以上为塔刹，塔刹是塔这种建筑与其他建筑有着本质区别的部分，同时也是塔最讲究的地方，主要用来表现佛祖崇高、佛像庄严。这座塔的塔刹高 8.56 米，由砖雕莲花瓣底座、束腰仰覆莲纹铁钵、两个铜制宝珠和一个铜制宝顶组成。

这座塔之所以叫开元寺塔，是因为建在唐朝的寺院开元寺中。大殿前边是开元寺的大门，殿后是塔，塔的后边是开元寺的后殿，开元寺塔正好建在寺院的南北中轴线上。

塔的东北门是上塔之门。第一层有 13 米多高，相当于四层楼的高度。一层的中心龛的大石座是当时放置佛像的底座。佛像在“文化大革命”时期被砸碎了。据《定州志》记载，这尊佛像“高可盈丈”，很高大，是一尊立佛。

这座塔不单单是一座雄伟高大的建筑物，它本身还蕴含了极高的美学艺术欣赏价值和历史资料参考价值，是一座内涵及其丰富的宝塔。塔的美学艺术欣赏价值主要体现在塔内的壁画和斗拱平棋的彩绘上。这几幅壁画从风格上来讲，时代很相近，都是明代绘制的；从手法上，这座塔都采用了工笔重彩的手法，有的还采用了沥粉贴金的技法。塔内最精彩的壁画在一层，那是宋代的原绘，线条清晰流畅，彩绘鲜艳如初，人物形象栩栩如生，代表了北宋时期高超的绘画水平。

这块建塔时立的“佛说金刚寿命塔陀罗尼经碑”清楚地记载了建塔的原因和时间。北宋时开元寺的大僧人，奉命前往印度求取真经和佛祖舍利，后满载而归。真宗咸平四年七月十八日，开始奉诏修建开元寺塔，用来供奉佛祖舍利。在建塔的前后几年，正是宋朝和契丹建立的辽朝决一死战的时候，碑文中提到的王显和王超是宋军方面和辽军交战的军事统帅，大权在握。这两位人物在《宋史》中都有传记，他们是在咸平年间，在修塔前二年在定州任职的，可以说是受命于危难之间。皇帝派他们在这个时候上任，目的只有一个，就是为了让他们在战场上得胜，因为当时的定州是作战的前沿。在这关键时刻，能够借助塔的高大来料敌制胜，是上至皇帝下至这些军官们一致盼望的事情。而且当时佛教信仰在民间极为流行，对于修塔老百姓肯定是非常赞同的。所以说这座塔是借佛教之名供奉舍利，行军事之实起料敌作用的一座塔。这也就是这座塔又名料敌塔的原因。

塔中现存碑刻 37 块，大部分是建塔时立的功德碑，这些碑刻是塔具有历史资料参考价值的体现物。除了这些碑刻，塔内众多的题记也是它具有历史资料、书法艺术价值的体现物。从题记里我们可以知道，北宋著名的大文豪苏东坡和当时的书画家张舜民曾登此塔并且在塔顶留下了他们的题字。但是可惜的是他们的墨迹今天已经看不到了。苏东坡曾于宋哲宗元祐八年，也就是公元 1093 年，以端明殿学士兼翰林侍读学士身份出使定州。这些墨宝应是他在做定州知州时登塔所题。由于这些名人的登临，塔的人文价值又增添了许多，所以才引得这些文人墨客不可不到绝顶。

这座塔之所以为“中华第一塔”，历千年而仍然耸立，很大的一个原因在于它建筑的科学性。这主要体现在两个方面。首先，塔的结构牢固。人们在这次维修时发现，内、外塔的八个角之间都有粗大木筋相连，而内、外塔体之间又如母子环抱，以顶部和回廊相连，逐层收缩，到塔刹部分融为一体。其次，每层的上下楼道都是从内塔体穿心而上，而且每层基本上都是在上、下楼道相对的方位，设置着佛龛，这样就不但保证了塔体的稳定，而且非常有效地减轻了塔体的重量。这次维修后新塔体和旧塔体之间主要采用了锚杆连接，这和原塔的木筋连接道理相同，所不同的是锚杆是用钢筋做成的。整个塔体又采用了圈梁加固的方法，就是在每层的檐子上都做了钢筋圈梁，这样就把新、旧塔体牢牢地连在了一起。

Kaiyuan Temple Pagoda is the highest extant brick pagoda in China, 83.7 meters high-lauded as the Greatest and Tallest Tower in China. It was declared by the State Council as among the first batch of state priority protected sites. Its construction commenced in the fourth year of Xianping during the reign of Emperor Zhenzong of the Song Dynasty, and lasted over 50 years when it was completed. Considering the absence of modern equipment and complete reliance on manpower more than 1000 years ago, the construction of this pagoda is closely associated with the long history, splendid culture and the importance of the location of Dingzhou where the pagoda is situated. Throughout the 5000 years of history of China, Dingzhou have been the strategic point of political, military and commercial significance. During the Song Dynasty, the Buddhism was exceptionally prevalent in Dingzhou. Besides, DingZhou was located on the bordering area of the Song Dynasty and the Liao Dynasty, and was known as the Gate to the Empire at that time. In order to spot enemy movements coming from the northern Liao Dynasty, and to store Sarira from ancient India to temporize and utilize the enthusiasm of the Buddhist believers, the authority of the Song Dynasty built this pagoda, which represents Buddhist culture and the actual condition of China during the Song Dynasty.

The multi-storied pagoda is octagonal, with a lofty and elegant appearance. It is composed of three parts: the pagoda base, the main body and the steeple. The body of the pagoda has eleven stories, each of which is of gradually lesser size proportionally from the bottom all the way up. All stories have the encircling short eaves, which are built by stacking tier upon tier of bricks around the body of the pagoda. Under the eaves hang wind chimes. Doors are installed on four sides of each storey, and they are decorated with flame patterns painted in bright colors, symbolizing the shining Buddha's grace and vibrating burning incense. Besides doors, there are false windows on four sides. Nevertheless, when it comes to the eleventh and twelfth storey, there are eight doors on eight directions for the military purpose. The upper-level roof has a dome ceiling made of green glazed tiles and supported by a skeleton of eight ridges and slopes, and small iron statues of celestial guards are positioned on of the corner each ridge. Above the roof is the steeple, which signifying the main difference between the pagoda and other buildings. It is the most exquisite part of the pagoda, and is usually employed to demonstrate the loftiness and solemnity of the Buddha. The steeple of the Pagoda at Kaiyuan Temple is 8.56 meters tall, composed of a subbase made of bricks carved with large lotus pedals, an inverted-bowl-shaped iron top decorated with lotus patterns, a pair of bronze beads and a bronze crown.

The reason why the pagoda is called the Kaiyuan Temple Pagoda is that it was built in the Kaiyuan Temple of the Tang Dynasty. In front of the main hall of the temple was the gate, while the pagoda stood behind the main hall. Behind the pagoda lay the rear hall. The pagoda was built on the south-to-north axis of the temple.

The northeast door of the pagoda has a winding staircase, which leads to the upper levels. The first storey of the pagoda is over 13 meters, equivalent to the height of four stories of a common building. On the center of the first storey lies a large stone base, which was originally the pedestal on which the statue of the Buddha is placed. The statue was destroyed during the "Cultural Revolution" in China. Nevertheless, according to the accounts in *Dingzhou County Annals*, it was a statue of the standing Buddha, and was enormously huge, with the height of over 11 feet.

Besides being magnificent and imposing, the pagoda itself is of high value both in artistic aesthetics and historical reference, which makes up its rich and profound cultural implication. The artistic value of the pagoda is reflected in the murals of the interior and those colored paintings on the brackets and ceilings. Judging from style, most murals belong to the Ming Dynasty. Technically, these murals are made meticulously with heavy color, and some of them employ the technique of gelled patterning and gilding. The most exquisite mural exists in the first storey. It is the original painting of the Song Dynasty, whose lines are clear and smooth, the color is as good as new and the figures are lifelike, representing the superb level of painting of the Northern Song Dynasty.

The pagoda was constructed in the fourth year of Xianping during the reign of Emperor Zhenzong of the Song Dynasty (1001 AD). The time and reason for its construction was clearly recorded on the Dharani Pillar. During the Song Dynasty, the great monk of the Kaiyuan Temple was ordered to go on a pilgrimage to India for Buddhist scriptures and the Sarira of the Buddha and returned successfully. On July 18,1001 AD, the Kaiyuan Temple Pagoda was commenced to be built under the imperial order to hold and worship the Sarira of the Buddha. A few years before and after the construction of the tower, it was crucial time for the decisive battle between the Song Dynasty and the Liao Dynasty established by the Khitan people. At that time, Wang Xian and Wang Chao were the military commanders of the Song Dynasty and held enormous power. According to the accounts of *Records of the Grand Historian*, they assumed their office in Dingzhou two years earlier than the construction of the pagoda during the year of Xianping. It can be said that they came to power in the midst of crisis. The sole aim to assign them to Dingzhou by the emperor was to win the battle, since Dingzhou was the warring frontline at that time. At the critical point, both the emperor and the military leaders unanimously hoped to take advantage of the pagoda to provide a high position for the garrison troops to watch the enemy's activities. Besides, the Buddhism was exceedingly prevalent among the people; thereupon, the common folk were extremely supportive of building a pagoda. Therefore, it is understandable that this pagoda is dedicated to the worship of the Sarira of the Buddha nominally, but actually, it acts as a watchtower. And that's why this tower is also known as the Liaodi Pagoda (Pagoda for watching for the enemy).

In the pagoda, there are 37 extant stone tablets, most of which are used to extol the merits and virtues of those contributors to the building of the pagoda. These stelae are the representation of the pagoda's worth in historical reference. Besides, the numerous inscriptions inside the pagoda are also of great importance both in history and calligraphic art. According to the inscription, it is known that Su Dongpo, the eminent literary giant of the Song Dynasty, and Zhang Shunmin, the famous calligrapher of Su's same age, had ever scaled this pagoda and left inscriptions. Regrettably, their handwritings have completely vanished now with the passage of time. In the eighth year of Yuanyou during the reign of Emperor Zhezong of the Song Dynasty (1093 AD), Su Dongpo, honored as an imperial scholar at Duanming Hall and a member of Hanli Academy, served as a magistrate in Dingzhou Prefecture. It is estimated that those inscriptions were written by Su Dongpo during his tenure in Dingzhou when he scaled the pagoda. Due to the frequent visit of these literary celebrities, the humane and cultural implication of this pagoda strengthened considerably, thus attracting more men of letters to mount the top.

Reputed as the Greatest and Tallest Tower of China, the Kaiyuan Temple Pagoda stands for hundreds of years, largely due to the fact that its architectural structure is extraordinarily scientific. The main structure of the pagoda is decidedly solid. During the maintenance, it is found that in the middle of the pagoda there is a central pillar, which is in the shape of an octagonal pagoda, called "inner pagoda". The eight angles of the inner pagoda are linked to their counterparts of the outside pagoda all the levels from the top to the base by bulky and thick wooden brackets, resembling a mother clutching her baby. The inner pagoda and the outside pagoda are also connected with corridors, shrink in size tier to tier while going up and integrate each other into the shared ceiling on the steeple. In addition, on each storey inside the pagoda a winding staircase in the middle leads to the upper levels. Each level has a niche for a statue of the Buddha around the staircase, which not only guarantee the stability of the building but also efficiently lessen the weight of the whole pagoda. After the renovation, the new parts and the old brick structure of the pagoda are connected by bolting, which models on the original structure of supportive wooden brackets, but steel bars. Moreover, the whole pagoda is reinforced by periphery beams. Steel beams are installed to support each tier of eaves, thus creating a firm connection between the newly renovated parts and the body of the original pagoda.

10. 光园

光园是一座中西合璧、造型与设计匠心独特、保卫设施严密的特殊建筑，又是一处花木掩映、富有情趣的园林式建筑。1993 年，光园被公布为河北省文物保护单位，2013 年，被列为全国文物保护单位。作为国家级文物保护单位，位于保定市区的“破烂”光园一度为市民和媒体诟病。2014 年 9 月，市政府决定将方志馆建在光园，一改其多年闲置的窘迫局面。2015 年，光园修复如新，正式开放。2015 年 3 月底，方志馆正式投用。自此光园成为一个挖掘、研究保定地情、历史、文化的平台，宣传展示保定的窗口。

光园原为明代大宁都司右卫署和断事司。康熙八年(公元 1669 年)直隶巡抚由正定迁到保定后，巡道司狱署驻此，雍正二年(公元 1724 年)改为按察使司狱署。1917 年，直系军阀首领曹锟改建为公馆。因曹锟敬慕明朝抗倭名将戚继光的英名，故冠其名为“光园”。

光园原占地总面积为 20 000 多平方米，是一座以单层建筑为主的建筑群。由曹锟的天津幕僚刘氏仿照天津流行的小洋楼风格，融入传统四合院建筑格局设计并主持建造，使光园成为当时乃至现代仍颇具时代特色的建筑组群。从建筑功能上看，南部多为办公、会议用房，北部则是花厅、花圃、居室、客房等建筑。光园正门高约 6 米，毛石结构，拱形券门，门外有一对高大雄伟的石狮相对而立，正门与迎门主建筑之间，用小型园林式庭院绿化作为过渡空间。大门及庭院已被拆除，盖起办公用楼。主体建筑是表为单层实为双层的四阿式顶“工”字形建筑，高 7~8 米。建筑的前立面东西两侧为两座突出前墙基线，有着多角形屋顶的正圆形房屋所围护。室内天花板上及墙面装饰物均留有防卫用的枪眼，天花板顶上和地面地板下也留有保卫人员活动的空间和地道。主楼门前设有一个直径 1 米左右的德国造的铜球，球中空，可与墙体天花板顶及地道相通，是为主楼设置的特殊警卫设置。铜球西南侧地面上用 7 块异常名贵的花箭石砌成北斗星形，正对着铜球，隐含北斗星开口面对天帝居住的无极星的寓意。主楼有内廊通向装饰华丽的小剧场(现已拆毁)，剧场也有地道口可出入。主楼室内外墙壁、立柱、门、窗及檐角采用木雕、石雕、砖雕作为装饰，技艺高超，造型生动。而中国的花鸟图案配以西式水泥雕或石雕，中国式木结构外廊配以西式木花边，中式女儿墙配以西洋瓶装饰等中西合璧的建筑风格则极富时代特点，也充分显示了主人的身份与地位。主楼的西北部有几套坐北向南的建筑，据说是曹锟家属、亲友的住所。现仅存部分房舍，成为民居。

光园是直系军阀穷兵黩武、争权夺利、发动战争的大本营，直皖战争、第一次直奉战争都是在这里策划的。光园自建成后，随即成为直系军阀策划重大事件的大本营。1920 年 6

月，曹锟在光园促成了直、苏、鄂、赣、奉、吉、黑、豫八省同盟；1922年4月，曹锟、吴佩孚在光园策划了第一次直奉战争；1923年，臭名昭著的曹锟贿选大总统的丑闻也策划于此，同年10月10日，曹锟正式出任北京政府大总统(民国第八任总统)，至此直系军阀的大本营从保定迁往北京。

自曹锟离开光园后，光园成为更迭的军阀、民国政要临时办公和居住之地。1926年9月，奉军将直系赶出河北，张学良入驻光园；1928年6月，阎锡山在光园就职京津卫戍总司令；此外，吴佩孚、冯玉祥、蒋介石等政坛要人均曾在光园策划过重要历史事件；1933年，蒋介石在保定建立行宫，钱大钧为行营主任，也以光园为公馆，蒋介石在保期间，也住此园。

保定光园原建筑规模较大，现仅剩融东西方建筑风格于一体的正厅。保留光园历史建筑风貌，既是对民国史的回顾，更是进行爱国主义教育，让人们对光园历史内涵有一个真切的了解，并借此弘扬传统文化，呼吁要留住古城的一些老旧建筑，保留一座独具历史内涵的古城，也保留了古城独特的城市记忆。

The Guang Garden is a unique building complex with a combination of both Chinese and Western styles, with ingenious pattern and design and with secure safeguarding facilities. Meanwhile, it also resembles a landscape painting luxuriant with flowers and trees and registers elaborate taste. The Guang Garden was listed as the "Major Historical and Cultural Site Protected at the Provincial Level" by Hebei government in 1993, and in 2013, it was listed as the historical and cultural site under state protection. Despite the honors as cultural relics, the garden have been criticized and despised by media and individuals due to its shabby appearance. In September, 2014, the government of Baoding decided to build a Museum of Local Chronicles in Guang Garden to improve its idle distress. In 2015, on the completion of renovation of Guang Garden, it was opened officially to the public; then by the end of March of the same year, the Museum of Local Chronicles was put into use. Thereafter, the Guang Garden has become a platform to excavate and study the condition, history and culture and a channel to promote Baoding.

Guang Garden was initially the resident office of the Right Regional Military Defense and Judicial Commission of Daning. In the eighth year of the reign of Emperor Kangxi of the Qing Dynasty (1699 AD), the governor of Zhili Province moved his office from Zhengding to Baoding, and then the governor positioned his governmental office, Grand Coordinator Commission, in Guang Garden. Later, in the second year of the reign of Emperor Yongzheng of the Qing Dynasty (1724 AD), the office was renamed Provincial Surveillance Commission. In 1917, Cao Kun, the warlord of the Zhili clique in the Beiyang Army converted it into a private mansion. Because Cao Kun admired Qi Jiguang, the prominent hero in the anti-Japanese war in the Ming Dynasty, he renamed it Guang Garden.

Guang Garden is basically a single-storey architectural complex, originally covering an area of about 20000 square meters in total. The current Guang Garden was designed and built by Liu Shi, one of Cao Kun's aides, who came from Tianjin. It incorporated the constructional style of Chinese Courtyard (a courtyard surrounded by buildings on all four sides) into the style of the western mansions that were popular at that time in Tianjin. This has made the garden a building complex with age characteristics at that time even today. The garden has multiple functions. Most of the buildings in the southern part are offices and conference rooms, while those in the north are reception rooms, flower garden, bedrooms and guest rooms. The main entrance of Guang Guard is a stone archway about 6 meters high, and outside it stands a pair of magnificent stone lions facing each other. Between the archway and the main buildings, a miniature garden-like courtyard serves as the transition. Now, the archway and the small courtyard have been demolished and official buildings have been built there. Seeming to be one-storey, the main building is actually a two-storey H-shaped construction, which has a gabled roof with one positive ridge and four inclined ridges. It is 7 or 8 meters high. The front elevation of the main building is flanked by outstanding footing of front walls, surrounded by circular houses with a polygonal roof. Inside these houses, shooting holes for defense are made in ceilings and wall decorations, and there are space and tunnels for security personnel above the ceiling and under the floor. In front of the main building is a bronze ball made in Germany about 1 meter in diameter. The ball is hollow and is connected to the interior ceiling and the underneath tunnel. It is a special set to guard the main building. On the ground southwest of the bronze ball, 7 pieces of extremely precious and rare Huajian stones are piled together to make a pattern of Big Dipper, which faces the ball to symbolize that the Big Dipper faces itself to the Infinite Star where the supreme god lives. The main building has an inner corridor leading to the ornate small theater (now demolished), which also has a tunnel for retreat. The main building's interior and exterior walls, pillars, doors, windows and cornices are all decorated with vivid carvings made of wood, stones or bricks, all displaying lofty craft. The combination of Chinese pattern of birds and flowers with Western cement carvings or stone carvings, the combination of the Chinese-style wooden gallery with western-style wooden lace, the Chinese-style parapet wall with Western-style bottle decorations and other Chinese and Western architectural features have displayed fully the characteristics of that era and fully reveal the owner's social and political status. In the northwest part of the main building, there are several sets of buildings that face south, which are said to be the residence of Cao Kun's families and relatives. Now, the extant houses have become homes of common people.

Served as the military headquarters of Zhili clique, it is in Guang Garden that Cao Kun, who is indulged in armed force, launched many wars in order to seize power. For instance, the Zhili-Anhui War and the Zhili-Fengtian War were plotted here. Since the completion of this garden, it immediately became the headquarters of warlords of Zhili clique to plan major operations. It is in this garden that Cao Kun, in June, 1920, initiated the military alliance of eight provinces, involving Zhili, Jiangsu, Hubei, Guizhou, Fengtian, Jilin, Heilongjiang, and Henan. In April 1922, it was also in this garden that Cao Kun and Wu Peifu planned the first Zhili — Fengtian War. In 1923, the political scandal of Cao Kun's running for the presidency via bribery was also schemed here in Guang Garden. On October 10 of the same year, Cao Kun officially assumed the office of the President of Beijing Administration (the sixth president of the Republic of China), and thereupon the military headquarters of Zhili clique moved to Beijing from Baoding.

Since Cao Kun's leaving, Guang Garden has become home and temporary office of many warlords and senior officials of the government of Republic of the China. After driving Zhili clique out of Hebei in November, 1926, Zhang Xueliang, the head of Fengtian clique, began to live in Guang Garden. In June, 1928, Yan Xishan assumed his office as Commander-in-chief of Beijing and Tianjin Garrison Command in Guang Garden. In 1933, Chiang Kai-shek established a palatial palace in Baoding and converted Guang Garden into his private mansion, and General Qian Dajun was appointed the director to be in charge of the security and live of Chiang Kai-shek during his stay in Baoding. Besides, some important political figures in the history of China, such as Wu Peifu, Feng Yuxiang and Chiang Kai-shek, all once planned important events in this garden.

The original complex of Guang Garden is huge, while what is left now is the main hall alone, which incorporates the technique and features of both China and West. Conservation of this garden can allow people not only to pay their respect to the history of the Republic of China, but also to enhance their patriotism. Gaining historical insights by appreciating the authentic building of Guang Garden, people can carry forward the traditional culture of China. In this respect, it is advocated that some ancient buildings in Baoding should be protected and preserved, thus consummating the cultural and historical implication of this old city and never making its distinctiveness of pale.

11. 淮军公所

淮军公所全称为“淮军昭忠祠暨公所”，从这个名字上可以看出，这座建筑分为两大部分，一是为追念在镇压太平天国和剿灭捻军时阵亡的将士而建的淮军昭忠祠，再就是淮军的办公驻地。淮军公所这座建筑始建于公元1888年，由李鸿章创建。这是历史上最后一次为淮军修建的祠堂。这座建筑是目前北方保存唯一完好的一座徽式建筑群。1993年，这座建筑被国家建设部、文化部评为河北省唯一的一处国家优秀近现代建筑。

该处原为清苑县(现为清苑区)城隍庙、土地祠的故址。咸丰初年（公元1851年），庙宇废弃。李鸿章从江南请来能工巧匠，仿照徽式祠堂风格修建。自光绪十四年五月至光绪十七年十月(公元1888年—1891年)，历时三年有余，工程才得以告捷。祠堂建成后，随即举行了盛大的典礼活动。从京城请来戏曲名角在刚建成祭场内的戏楼上演戏数天，以表庆贺。

淮军公所

这座公所规模宏大，风格独特，整个区域呈不规则梯形，南北长200米，东西宽约140米，总占地面积40亩，有南、北、西门各一座。房屋200多间，大致分为祭场区、办公区、神厨库区、生活区、操场区、小广场区、花园区七大区。祠堂的大门是一面牌坊似的高大门墙，左、中、右三座大门就开在这面门墙的下面。门墙中心顶部高十多米。而用白色条石做成门框的三道大门高不过两米，宽也只有一米左右。中门白色石坊上端的中心位置有一个长方形大型匾额，当年是蓝底金色大字“敕建李文忠公祠”，如今依稀可见。

两侧高低错落的山墙就是徽州的马头墙，马头墙是徽州居民最显著而鲜明的一个标志。马头墙的别称是五岳朝天，这一别称表达的应该是徽州人对天的敬畏和虔诚，也是徽州人对生活的自信和神圣。这组迎门建筑给我们的第一印象是宏伟、壮观、气势磅礴。进入南门后为迎宾院，南北房各7间，东西房各3间，成为一个四合院。此院北房为轿厅，东、西、南房为休息厅称下房或客厅。

游客从该院再往北走，穿过一条小巷就到了主祭场（也称戏楼），戏楼正门为清水墙门。高宽尺寸较小，贴墙起脊，鱼龙吻，筒瓦屋面，檐下带花篮，重柱。罩面防砖刻松鼠，葡萄垂头上刻有花篮，一块玉上刻福、禄、寿三星，兜肚到狮子，间柱上刻吉祥图案。沿门枋镶贴的一组剔透而立体感很强，长约20余米的砖雕山、水、人物画卷。整组石雕构思浪漫而潇洒，工艺娴熟而自然。花鸟、人物、走兽，一丝不苟的刀法，切割有痕，斩削无迹，细若传神，使人看后会赞叹不已。其工艺价值很高，进入此门便到了戏楼内。

整个戏楼的规模较大，东西南北长约各30多米成方形，面积大约1000多平方米，四周是二层庑廊。中间为空场，是搞大型活动的地方，如集会、演戏、祭祀。这个祭场大约能容纳500人，戏台上屏风、隔扇、护栏等物品用料讲究，雕木非常精细。祭场内四周是二层看台，原来是用隔扇隔成包厢，供不同身份的人看戏时应用。

祭场北侧中间有一屏风斗门，通往后院则是中路的北院，该院明亮宽大，两侧走廊直通北房，这也是享殿。是摆放灵牌和平时祭祀之地。在建成初期，这里摆放的是战死的淮军将领的牌位。1901年，李鸿章去世以后奉诏改为了“李文忠公祠”，这里就成了专门祭祀李鸿章的场所。

翻开保定淮军公所的历史会发现，捻军被镇压是在公元1868年，李鸿章为什么在事隔20年之后才奏请筹建淮军昭忠祠暨公所呢？鸦片战争以后，清政府国势日趋衰落，阶级矛盾和民族矛盾日益激化，相继爆发了太平天国起义和捻军起义。清政府在两次农民起义的打击下极其腐朽，虽然尽全力将这两次农民起义镇压下去，但是两百年以前曾经以弓马夺取天下的劲旅“八旗子弟”和“绿营兵”表现得极其庸腐，在镇压农民起义的两次用兵中，基本上是依靠湘、淮两支地方武装。太平天国起义被镇压以后，湘军很快败落，而淮军却在平稳战争中进一步壮大，从而成为清政府尤为依中的武装力量，作为淮军统帅的李鸿章于公元1870年9月被清政府实授北洋大臣，总督直隶等处的河道、粮饷、长芦盐政，并驻节在保定。因此从各方面讲，淮军这支从封建地主阶级中崛起的武装力量，被清政府用以保卫京畿和镇守海防都将是最好的力量，保定北控三关，南达九省咽喉，是保卫京师的南大门，因此在保定建立淮军的大本营和安抚将士的昭忠祠，乃是政治和军事的需要。

这座宏伟的建筑作为祠堂只运行了十年。1912年，民国建立，该祠废弃。1924年，私立志存中学在此建立，祠堂的东部被县立第一小学占用，后开办织布厂。1937年，日本侵占保定后，此处为日军兵营。1948年11月，保定解放，冀中军区司令部驻此。1949年8月，改为河北省军区司令部。1958年5月，省军区司令部随省委迁驻天津，后为河北省财经干部学校。20世纪70年代，市房屋管理局在此院空闲地方建造了不少红砖排房，迁入了很多新住户，变成了一个地道的大杂院。1993年7月，淮军公所被河北省人民政府公布为省重点文物保护单位，给淮军公所的有效保护提供了重要保证。

The full name of the Huai-Army Office is the “Loyalty Memorial Shrine and Office of the Huai-Army ”. From this name, it can be seen that the building is divided into two parts. One is those memorial temples to commemorate the officers and soldiers of Huai-Army killed in the suppression of the Taiping Heavenly Kingdom and the suppression of Nian Army in the Late-Qing Dynasty, the other is the Huai Army office. Huai Army Office was built by Li Hongzhang in 1888 AD, and was the last shrine built for the Anhwei Army in history. This building is a currently well-preserved ancient building with Anhwei style in the north of China. In 1993, the building was rated as the Outstanding Contemporary Building at national level by the Ministry of Construction and the Ministry of Culture, and this honor is inimitable in all the counterparts in Hebei Province.

The Huai Army Office was built on the ruins of the Temple of the City God and the Altar of Tudigong(God of the soil and the ground) in Qingyuan County (Qingyuan District). During the early years of the reign of Emperor Xianfeng (1851 AD), those temples were abandoned, thereafter; Li Hongzhang built this shrine modeling on the building of Anhwei. Constructed by the proficient artisans from the south of China, the building was completed after three years, from May, 1888 to October, 1891, in the reign of Emperor Guangxu. On the completion of the construction work, grand celebration ensued. Many opera celebrities were invited from Beijing to present wonderful performances for several consecutive days in the newly established Chinese Opera Theatre which is located on the sacrifice square within.

This Huai-Army Office is of grand scale and a unique architectural style. The whole building area is trapezoidal. The overall length of it is 200 meters from south to north, while approximately 140 meters from east to west in width, and covering an area of around 2700 square meters in total. There are three gates to it, on the north, south and west side respectively. It is composed of about 200 rooms and is roughly divided into seven areas, that is, sacrificial field, office area, the god kitchen, living area, playground, the small square, and the garden. The gateway to the shrine is a tall wall like a paifang (memorial archway), under which three gates, namely, the left gate, the right gate and the central gate, are built. The peak of the doorway reaches over 10 meters, sharply in contrast to the three white-stone-framed gates which are no more than 2 meters in height and 1meters in width. A large oblong plaque is embedded in the central part above the stone frame at the top of the central gate. Having faded, golden Chinese characters meaning the Shrine of Liwengong Built by the Order of the Emperor were inscribed on a blue background and can still be identified on the plaque now.

The courtyard is flanked by uneven corbie gables or horse-head walls, which is a noticeable characteristic of the vernacular architecture of Huizhou. The corbie gable is also known as "five overturned sacred mountains saluting heaven", which registers

Huizhou people's awe and piety for heaven as well as their self-confidence and holy spirits. What these gates impress visitors first is their grandeur and magnificence. Entering the south gate, one will see the guest-meeting courtyard. There are 7 houses facing south and north respectively as well as 3 side houses facing east and west respectively, thus forming a typical Chinese quadrangle. The north house serves as the place to accommodate sedan chairs and the others are for rest, known as sitting room or living room.

Going through this courtyard and heading northward via a narrow lane, one will reach the main sacrificial field (also called the Chinese Opera Theater). The front door to the theater is built in a range of brick wall. The door is of moderate size both in width and height, and topped with a ridge of tiles joining the side wall. The ridge is decorated with the pattern of fish kissing dragon. The roof is covered with round tiles and supported by heavy pillars. Under the cornice, the pattern of corbel is carved. The doorpost is embedded with carved bricks featuring mountains, rivers and figures, which represents exquisite skills as well as natural and unrestrained composition. No matter it is the image of a flower and a bird, a figure, or an ordinary animal, all display the meticulous carving craft, with the trace of dividing but smooth joint. Nobody fail to get impressed by the vivid representations and its high artistic quality. Passing the gate, one will come to the inside of the Chinese Opera Theater.

The whole theater is grand and square-shaped with each side over 30 meters in length, covering an area of approximately 1000 square meters. The theater is enclosed with two-storey porch and the central part of the theater is an open space, where some mega-events such as gathering, opera performance and sacrifice are held. It can hold about 500 people. As for the opera stage, it is equipped with such facilities as screens and handrails, all of which are made of fine materials with elaborate carvings. The second storey of the surrounding porch serves as the auditorium, which was originally divided into private boxes by partition boards in order to provide tailored service to those of different status.

After going through the screen door set up in the central part of the north wall of the sacrificial field, visitors will come to the backyard, which is positioned to the north of the constructional axis. The yard is spacious with flanked corridors leading to the north house. The north house functions as the shrine, where spirit tablets are placed and worshipped during the peace. Initially, the spirit tablets of the officers killed in battles in Huai-Army enjoyed the honor to be worshipped here. Whereas in 1901 when Li Hongzhang, the minister of the Qing Dynasty and the head of Huai-army, passed away, this shrine, by the order of the Emperor, was converted into the Ancestral Hall of Li Wenzhong, specially dedicated to the sacrifice-offering to Li Hongzhang.

The history of the Huai-Army Office tells that the Nianarmy was suppressed in 1868 AD, and then a question arises. Why did Li Hongzhang seek to build this memorial shrine 20 years later? After the Opium War, the power of the Qing Dynasty declined gradually, and the conflicts of different social classes and nations got worse off, thus triggering the Taiping Rebellion and Nian Rebellion. Under the heavy blow of these two revolts of farmers, the authority of the Qing Dynasty was undermined considerably. Though these rebellions were quelled, Eight Banners Soldiers and Green Standard troops, who had been famous for their vitality and powerful warhorses and arrows 200 years ago, proved to be unable to put down the unrest. The two military operations mainly depended on the local armed forces: Xiang Army and Huai Army. After the suppression of the Taiping Rebellion, the Xiang Army quickly collapses, while the strength of Huai Army was reinforced during battles, and become the elite force of the Qing Dynasty. As the commander of Huai Army, Li Hongzhang was appointed "Beiyang Trade Minister", overseeing military and civil affairs of Zhili such as waterway maintenance, military provision and salt trade administration of Changlu. And Li Hongzhang's administrative center lay in Baoding. Therefore, in light of the aforementioned, Huai Army, which derived from the local forces of landlords, was the best choice to be assigned to safeguard the area surrounding the imperial capital. Baoding, joining three important military passes in the north and nine important provinces in the south, is referred to the Last Shield of Beijing in the South, so it is understandable that Huai Army, to meet the requirement politically and militarily, set up its headquarters and loyalty memorial shrine in Baoding.

As a shrine, this building operates only ten years. In 1912, the Republic of China was founded, and this shrine was abandoned. In 1924, Zhicun Private School was set up on the site, and its east part of the shrine was taken up by the First Primary School of the County, later being converted into a textile mill. In 1937, when Baoding was captured by Japanese aggressors, this building was expropriated by force and used a military barrack as the station of Japan soldiers. In November, 1948, Baoding was liberated, and the headquarters of Jizhong Military Region was stationed here, and then renamed Hebei Provincial Military Region Command in August, 1949. After the Command was moved to Tianjin in May, 1958, the place was occupied by Hebei Financial and Economic Cadres School. In the 1970s, many rows of red brick houses were constructed in the open space of the courtyard of Huai-Army Office by the Municipal

Housing Administrative Office, and thereafter, many common residents moved to live here, thus making it a thorough residential compound. In July, 1993, Huai-Army Office was conferred the title "A Major Historical and Cultural Site Protected at the Provincial Level", which guarantees the effective protection of it.

12. 药王庙

安国药王庙始建于东汉建武年间，到北宋太平兴国年间拓址建立新庙，是中国目前规模最大的纪念历史医圣的庙宇古建筑群体。建中靖国元年（公元1101年），追封庙神为“灵贶候”，后改封公，南宋咸淳六年（公元1270年），加封庙神为“明灵昭惠显佑王”。乾隆年间东阁大学士刘墉为庙题写门额谓“药王庙”。庙中所祀之神药王，姓邳名彤，字伟君，信都(今河北省冀州市)人，原为下曲阳(今河北省晋州市西)卒正，后为汉光武帝刘秀部下二十八将之一，因战功显赫，官至太常少府。《祁州志》载邳彤死后葬于安国南关，生时常行医于民间，死后在宋朝“显灵”，为宋秦王治愈顽疾，被立庙祀之，并加封为王。

药王庙全貌

药王庙是我国少有的纪念历史医圣的庙宇。自北宋建庙后，经历代扩建修葺，汇集了宋、明、清时代的建筑特色，形成了一座民族风格鲜明的建筑区，全部建筑结构严谨，浑然一体。

药王庙分前院、中院、后院三进院落，另有两个跨院，占地14亩，有马殿、药王墓亭、正殿、后殿、名医殿、碑房、钟鼓楼等单体建筑17座。庙前的铁铸旗杆建于清朝道光九年，每根高24米，重15吨，上铸有两条盘龙，昂首远望，栩栩如生。每根旗杆上有三个吊斗，各悬十二枚风铃，微风吹动，“叮铃”作响。每根旗杆顶端都有一只遥望西天展翅欲飞、引颈似鸣的金凤凰，造型奇妙，瑰丽无比。

正中的木质牌楼建于嘉庆二十三年(公元1818年)，为三栋四楹庑殿顶结构，高8.4米，琉璃瓦面，斗拱飞檐，逼真的浮雕，优美的木质绣花图案，技术精湛的苏式彩画，风格典雅凝重。牌楼正面额书“显灵河北”，背面额书“封加南宋”各四个贴金大字。

穿过牌楼，为药王庙正门，门楣上悬有“药王庙”匾额，笔迹遒劲，别有韵味，乃乾隆年间东阁大学士刘墉题写。跨入正门，进入马殿(大门过庭)，为硬山顶叠梁式结构，后出廊。殿内南北各立泥塑战马一匹，南白北赤，马前各有两个马童，造型生动，温馨可亲。

前院内，古柏参天，掩映着钟鼓二楼，南为钟楼，北为鼓楼，均为两层，二层上置放钟、鼓。晨钟暮鼓，声震四方，两楼南北相望，大小一致，规矩相等，长宽各4米，高8.1米，基座呈四方形，均为青砖砌成，其顶为银锭玲珑脊，布瓦歇山顶，正脊上饰有吻兽。

穿过垂花门为中院，垂花门为悬山顶，两侧建单面廊，由 8 根大红明柱等距离支撑，设计奇特精巧。院落正中，矗立着高 6.3 米的墓亭，即药王之墓，为琉璃歇山顶，斗拱飞檐，金碧辉煌，檐下饰有珍禽异兽及戏曲人物，雕画工艺精熟，内容朴实有趣，古意盎然。墓亭内有一幢套色穿龙透花枣木碑，上刻“敕封明灵昭惠显佑王之墓”十一个贴金大字，熠熠生辉。

墓亭南北两侧为名医殿，塑有我国古代十大名医像，北殿内塑有华佗、孙林、张子和、张介宾、刘河间的塑像；南殿塑有扁鹊、张仲景、孙思邈、徐文伯、皇甫谧的塑像，装束不一，姿势各异，神态自然，和蔼可亲。

药王正殿是药王庙的主要建筑，其外貌宏伟壮观，为叠梁式硬山顶结构。大殿面阔三间，进深三间，八角明柱，殿内泥塑彩绘像 11 尊，正位药王像，黄袍金面，手持圭牌，神态庄严。两厢文臣武将，昂首挺胸，英姿勃勃，后殿，为药王寝殿，面积与正殿等同，正中为药王便装像，神态慈祥，和蔼可亲。两旁为药王夫人及侍女塑像，表情生动逼真，端庄秀丽。后殿壁画很珍贵，殿顶山尖处绘有八仙过海及其先前济世救人故事，八仙过海图案，人物立于宝器之上，乘风破浪于大海之中，立体感极强，共有 14 幅，画面形象逼真，故事动人，让人看后不由浮想联翩。此壁画为明代遗存，虽经数百年沧桑，依然清晰如初，乃罕见之珍品。

药王庙香火旺盛

药王庙在战争年代和“文化大革命”中曾惨遭破坏。1985 年，安国市政府在上级文化部门和全国中药界以及安国市广大群众赞助下，对药王庙进行了修复，庙貌焕然一新。药王庙修复后善男信女上香祭祀，香火甚盛，后来逐渐发展成庙会，四方商客云集，百货交流，形成全国规模最大的药材市场。而后安国被誉为“药都”和“天下第一药市”，所以有安国药业起源于药王庙之说，药王庙已经被列为国家重点文物保护单位。

Anguo Drug King Temple was originally built during Jianwu period of the Eastern Han Dynasty. It was rebuilt during the Taiping years of the Northern Song Dynasty. It is by far the largest complex of ancient temples in China commemorating the historically medical sage. In the first year of Huizong period (1101 AD), the god of this temple was ennobled “Lingkuang Nobleman”, and later, it was titled the Duke. In the sixth year of

Xianchun of the Southern Song Dynasty (1270 AD), the god of the temple was ennobled "the king of Ming Ling Zhao Hui Xian You". During the reign of Emperor Qianlong, Liu Yong, a scholar of the East Pavilion, wrote the inscription "Drug King Temple". The drug king in the temple, whose name is Pi Tong, word of Wei Jun, was from Xindu(now Jizhou City in Hebei Province). He was originally the prefecture in Qu Yang (now west of Jizhou City in Hebei Province), and later served as one of the 28 generals under Emperor Liu Xiu's command in the Han Dynasty. Due to illustrious military exploits, Pi Tong got promoted. According to the *Qi Zhou Records*, Pi Tong was buried in Nanguan of Anguo County after his death. Since he practiced medicine among people, Pi Tong was believed to have supernaturally appeared in the Song Dynasty and cured Emperor Qin of his chronic disease. Thus he was worshipped in the temple and titled the Drug King.

The Drug King Temple is one of the few temples in China that commemorates the medical sage. Since the building of the temple in the Northern Song Dynasty, through extension and renovation of various dynasties, it integrates the architectural features of the Song, Ming and Qing Dynasties, forming a distinctive national style building complex, with rigorous and integral structure.

The Drug King Temple is divided into three courtyards, including the front yard, the middle yard and the back yard, together with two side courtyards, covering an area of 14 *mu*. There are 17 individual buildings, including the horse hall, the tomb pavilion of the Drug King, the main hall, the back hall, the famous doctors' hall, the tablet house, the Bell and Drum Tower, etc..

The iron-cast flagpoles in front of the temple were built in the ninth year of the reign of Emperor Daoguang of the Qing Dynasty, with each flagpole a height of 24 meters and a weight of 15 tons. On the flagpole are two spiral dragons whose heads are raised and alive with vitality. Each of which hung twelve bells, and there is a golden phoenix at the top of each pole, marvelous and magnificent.

The wooden building was built in the twenty-third year of the reign of Jiaqing of the Qing Dynasty (1818 AD), which is the hip roof structure with four principal columns. It is 8.4 meters high, with glazed tile, stone eaves, lifelike reliefs, beautiful wooden embroidery patterns, and fine skills. The Su-style painting is elegant and dignified. The decorated archway writes "Apparition Hebei"and has four gold characters "Feng Jia South Song Dynasty" at the back.

Passing through the archway, it is the main gate of the Drug King Temple, and there is a plaque on the lintel, the bold and elegant handwriting of which is inscribed by Liu Yong, the scholar of the Eastern Pavilion. Going through the main gate, the horse hall is of a saddle roofline and folded beam timber frame structure. There are two clay horses in the north and south which are in white and red respectively, and there are also two vivid stable boys in front of the horses.

In the front yard, the tall ancient cypress trees reach towards the sky. The Bell Tower is in the south, while the Drum Tower is in the north. On the second floor of each tower are bells and drums. Morning bell and evening drum can spread around the town. The Bell Tower lies in the south of the Drum Tower. With the same size, they are 4 meters wide, 4 meters long and 8.1 meters high. The pedestal is square, decorated with blue bricks, and its top is covered with pieces of silver and exquisite ridges decorated with beasts, and the hip roof is covered with cloth tiles.

The floral-pendant gate is covered with suspended roof. On both sides are single-sided porches supported by eight big red columns, with strange and ingenious design. Going through the floral-pendant gate to the central courtyard, in the middle stands a tomb pavilion with the height of 6.3 meters, the Tomb of Drug King. The glazed hip roof is magnificent. The eaves are decorated with rare birds, exotic animals and opera characters, with exquisite arts of carvings, and the content is simple and interesting. In the tomb pavilion, there is a jujube tablet decorated with a dragon and the inscription "The Tomb of Chi Feng the King of Ming Ling zhao Hui Xian You" is engraved with gold letters, shining brightly.

The tomb pavilion has famous doctors hall on its north and south sides, sculpting ten famous doctors in ancient China, including Hua Tuo, Sun Lin, Zhang Zihe, Zhang Jiebin in the north hall. The south hall consist of Bian Que, Zhang Zhongjing, Sun Simiao, Xu Wenbo, and Huang Fumi. The clothes and the posture are various, and the manner is natural and affable.

The main hall of the temple is the main part of the Drug King Temple. Its appearance is magnificent with the structure of folded beam saddle roofline. The hall is 3 rooms wide, and 3 rooms deep, with eight pillars, and it also has 11 clay figure statues. The Drug King, with the golden face and the yellow robe, holds an elongated pointed tablet of jade in hands with solemn manner. The two officials standing in the wing-rooms raise their heads proudly. The back hall is the bedroom of the Drug King, which has the same size with the main hall. The Drug King Statue is in the middle, whose appearance is kind and affable. On both sides of the statue stands his wife and maid, and their expression is vivid, dignified and beautiful. The 14 frescoes there are precious, depicting the ancient stories, such as the eight immortals crossing the sea and relieving the common people. With the eight figures standing on their instruments and sailing beautifully in winds, the painting is in complex three-dimensional form. The lifelike images and touching stories let people have random thoughts. The frescoes are relics of the Ming Dynasty. Though having weathered hundreds of years, they are still as clear as the time when they were painted, which is so rare in the world.

The Drug King Temple was once destroyed in wartime and the period of "Cultural Revolution". In 1985, sponsored by the Cultural Department and National Traditional Chinese Medicine Group, as well as boundless common people in Anguo city, the Drug King Temple was renovated. After the establishment of the Drug King Temple, numerous religion believers went to the temple to pray. Gradually, the temple fair was developed, where merchants gathered together to form the largest market of medicine materials in China. Thus Anguo City was reputed as the "Drug Town" and "the first drug market of the world". Since the Drug King Temple is the origin place of the pharmacy industry of Anguo city, the historical site has been listed as a national key cultural relic protection unit.

（二）古城的前世今生

1. 太行水镇

太行水镇位于易县，是具有中国本土特色的乡村旅游小镇，包括太行水镇核心区、休闲农场、长寿村、芳香养生区、田园康养区、养心谷、文化创意区、滨水休闲区、综合服务区、生态涵养区。十大功能区汇于一体，既是农村三产融合的产业园区，又是乡村文化传承基地。

太行水镇

太行水镇核心区一期工程于 2016 年 8 月底投入运营，总投资达 2.6 亿元，以太行山民俗文化为内涵。搭建风情小吃街、传统工艺十二坊、大师工坊街、民俗文化广场、房车露营地等游览项目。

传统十二坊带大家穿越时光，回到前店后坊的古老商业形式——油坊、酸奶坊、豆腐坊、面坊、粉条坊、挂面坊、醋坊、香油坊。游客可以亲自操作太行特色的手工艺，见证食材在碾压蒸煮下的蜕变，感受小时候的街肆文化。

公司创新经营模式，建立农村资源变资金、资金变股权、农民变股东机制，推动农村三产融合、文化传承、旅游扶贫、双创平台，打造可推广、可复制的美丽乡村综合体。

太行水镇项目建成后，其培育孵化个体户 500 余个，提供劳动就业岗位 5000 个，为本地解决剩余劳动力 3000 余人，年接待游客量达 500 万人次，年旅游收入达 20 亿元，年举办民俗活动 100 次，实现本地农副产品深加工后进城市 1 万吨。

风情小吃街

Being located in Yixian County, it is a rural tourism town of Chinese local characteristic. There are Mountain Water Town, Leisure Farms, Long-living Village, Aromatic Health-care Area, Rural Health-care Area, Yangxin Health-care Valley, Cultural Creativity Area, Waterfront Recreational Area, Comprehensive Service Area, and Ecological Conservation Area. The ten major functional areas are integrated in one, which is not only the industrial park of the rural industry integration, but also the heritage base of the rural culture.

The first stage project in Taihang Water Town core area was put into operation at the end of August, 2016, with a total investment of 260 million *yuan*. With the connotation of Taihang Mountain folk culture, many sightseeing project were built such as Local-snacks Street, Traditional Twelve Crafts Workshops, Master Workshop Street, Folk Culture Square, Car Campsites, etc..

The traditional twelve crafts workshops may remind you of the time when it was operated in ancient commercial form, producing and selling were done in the same workshop. There are Oil Workshop, Yogurt Workshop, Flour Workshop, Vermicelli Workshop, Vinegar Workshop and Sesame oil Workshop. Visitors can make Taihang characteristic crafts personally, witnessing the change of ingredients when being grinded and experiencing the street culture.

The innovation management model of the company is to establish the mechanism of turning the rural resources into capital, turning the capital into stock rights and turning the villagers into shareholders, so as to promote the integration of three industries, cultural inheritance, tourism supporting, management platform, and create scalable and replicable beautiful village complex.

After the completion of Taihang Water Town, there are more than 500 incubators and 5000 employment posts, which solve the surplus labor force of more than 3000 people. The annual number of visitors is 5 million, the annual tourism income is 2 billion *yuan*, and the folklore activities are held 100 times in the year, and 10 thousand tons of local agricultural and sideline products are provided for the city.

2. 百里峡艺术小镇

百里峡艺术小镇位于涞水县，按照“低碳、高端、乡村资源旅游化”理念，打造乐享生活、文化沙龙、艺术创客的乡村旅游特色小镇，是全国旅游扶贫示范项目。香雪故事村以怀旧和人文情怀为主题，七彩小镇把原来100多户的农家旅馆整体包装，突出色彩情调，“赤橙黄绿青蓝紫，犹如彩练山间舞。”

百里峡艺术小镇

作为河北省旅游发展大会主会场，涞水县紧抓河北省首届旅游发展大会契机，打造全域旅游，积极推进景区全面升级，创建特色旅游小镇，位于三坡镇苟各庄村的百里峡艺术小镇项目就是其一。苟各庄村正依托百里峡的门户地位，努力打造集接待服务、食疗餐饮、康体度假、休闲娱乐于一体，低碳、高端，具有太行部落风格的色彩艺术小镇。

全村主要分为注重古法新入、修旧如旧的香雪故事村和融入时代元素的百里峡七彩小镇两大部分，同时打造台湾美食一条街、舌尖上的中国一条街、创客一条街、工艺美术一条街和酒吧一条街5大特色街区。

七彩小镇是百里峡艺术小镇建设的重点项目之一，该项目由中国建设集团规划设计院、中央美院等多家单位设计施工。设计师对每家每户进行编号，以七种颜色为基础色调，为每一户设计特有的颜色，通过对村内庭院进行建筑外立面精装和色彩设计与喷漆，使全村形成一户一色、色彩纷呈的欧式小镇。同时，百里峡艺术小镇也将成为中国唯一一家以色彩为主题的七彩小镇。

Being located in Laishui County, in accordance with the “low carbon, top level, rural tourism resources” concept, Baili Canyon Art Town is a rural tourism characteristic town full of pleasant lifestyle, culture salon, and artistic creation, aiming at the national tourism poverty-relieving demonstration project. Xiangxue Story Village sets nostalgia and humanity as the theme. Colorful Town integrates more than 100 rural inns as a whole series, highlighting the theme “colorful shining rainbow in the sky, colorful dancing ribbon around the mountain."

As the main venue of the provincial tourism development conference, Laishui County firmly seized the opportunity of the first session of the Hebei Tourism Development Conference to build the region-based tourism, which actively promoted the overall upgrading of the scenic area, and created characteristic tourist towns. Baili Canyon Art Town in Gougezhuang Village of Sanpo Town is one of them. With the status of gateway of Baili Canyon, Gougezhuang Village is striving to create an low-carbon, top level art town of Taihang tribal style, functioning as a place for reception services, diet therapy and catering, tourist spot, and entertainment.

The whole village is divided into two parts, including the nostalgic Xiangxue Story Village and the fashionable Baili Canyon Colorful Town. Meanwhile, 5 characteristic streets were built, including Taiwan delicacy street, Chinese food street, maker street, arts street and bar street.

The construction of Colorful Town is one of the key projects in the construction of Baili Canyon Art Town. The project was designed and construt by many units, such as Planning and Design Institute in China Construction Group, Central Academy of Fine Arts. The designers numbered each household based on seven colors, and designed a unique color for every household. Through the decorating, color designing and paint spraying of the facade building, the whole village was formed into a colorful European-style town. At the same time, Baili Canyon Art Town will also be the only colorful town with the theme of color in China.

3. 京南体育小镇

京南体育小镇位于高碑店市，包括攀岩馆、户外极限运动广场、户外攀岩运动展示步行街、国家登山博物馆、展览展示中心、夜光健身步道、七彩花海等。以“珠峰”为原型的世界上最高赛道最多、体积最大的人工单体攀岩馆，将助力项目在京南形成“世界攀岩在中国，中国攀岩看保定”的格局，提升城市影响力和旅游竞争力。

京南体育小镇是在京津冀协同发展的战略背景下，国家体育总局与河北省对接的第一个项目，将建设“体育+旅游”双产业导向的特色小镇。

小镇建设融合了新加坡新镇开发、产城一体、绿色建筑的设计理念，由国家体育总局、新加坡建设局、高碑店市人民政府以及新加坡投资商，联合北京嘉华宏远集团共同打造，总占地面积 657.67 公顷，投资总额 180 亿元，主要建设内容有国家登山训练基地、绿色食品产业基地、现代生态农业休闲观光园三大项目。

国家登山训练基地落户高碑店，使高碑店成为全国登山户外产业示范城市，并成功举办了 2016 年竞技攀岩入奥后的第一届全国攀岩锦标赛。经国家体育总局批准，自首届旅游发展大会起连续 3 年在登山训练基地举办全国青年攀岩锦标赛。

“京南体育小镇”全部建成后将形成体育休闲旅游、户外运动赛事及培训、展览展示、户外运动装备研发制造、健康疗养等板块，直接带动就业人口 1.2 万，为当地带来良好的社会和经济效益。无论是国际国内赛事的举办、攀岩及户外运动训练、参观游览，还是紫泉河康体公园、国家登山博物馆及展览展示中心等景观的呈现，都极大地提升高碑店市的城市旅游竞争力，引领高碑店成为中国攀岩及户外极限运动之都，打造国内全域旅游新样板。

Being located in the city of Gaobeidian, South Beijing Sports Town consists of Rock-climbing Gym, Outdoor Extreme Sports Square, Ourdoor Rock-climbing Show, National Mountaineering Museum, Exhibition Center, Luminous Fitness Trails, and Colorful Flowers Garden. The highest and largest artificial rock-climbing gym, as the Mount Everest for the prototype, will promote the best rock-climbing project of China in Baoding, south of Beijing, enhancing the city tourism competitiveness and influence.

South Beijing Sports Town is the first project making National Sports Bureau and Hebei Province butt joint against a background of the coordinated development of the Beijing-Tianjin-Hebei region. It will build the “sports + tourism” double industry oriented town.

The construction of the town integrates the design idea of Singapore new town development, the combination of industrial function and urban function, and green building, jointly created by the State Sports General Administration, Singapore Construction Bureau, Gaobeidian Municipal People's government and Singapore investors, and Beijing Jiahua Hongyuan Group, with a total area of 657.67 hectares, a total investment of 18 billion *yuan*. The main content of the construction consists of national mountaineering climbing training base, green food industry base, and modern ecological agriculture sightseeing garden.

The national mountaineering training base was settled in Gaobeidian, making Gaobeidian a national demonstration city for mountaineering outdoor industry, and successfully held the first national rock climbing Championships after it was subsumed by the Olympic Games in 2016. With the approval of the State General Administration of physical education, the National Youth Rock Climbing Championships were held for 3 years at the mountaineering training base since the first conference of Tourism Industrial Development.

"South Beijing Sports Town" will form sports leisure tourism, outdoor sports competitions and training, exhibition, outdoor sports equipment R & D and manufacturing, health recuperation and other sectors after its construction, with a direct employment population of 12 thousand, bringing good social and economic benefits to the locals. Whether it be international and domestic competitions, climbing and outdoor sports training, sightseeing, or Ziquan River sports park, national mountaineering Museum and Exhibition Center, it will greatly enhance the competitiveness of Gaobeidian city tourism, leading Gaobeidian into Chinese climbing and outdoor extreme sports center, so as to build a new model for domestic region-based tourism.

4. 昌利农业旅游示范园

保定昌利农业旅游示范园是河北昌利农业科技开发集团有限公司的子公司，位于定兴县李郁庄乡杨各庄村，距定兴县城 7 千米，园区占地 1080 亩。园区始建于 1998 年 10 月，2000 年 5 月开始接待游客。

园区以河北农业大学为技术依托，发展农业种植，生产、经销名优特果蔬、花卉、苗木。其中水果有爱宕梨、苹果、太阳杏、葡萄等；蔬菜有结球生菜、番茄、黄瓜、茄子、五色椒、西葫等；花卉有鲜切菊花、火鹤、一品红、仙客来等；苗木有七叶树、银杏树、黄杨等。集团公司注册了昌利果蔬商标并获得了河北省著名商标称号。这些种植起到了很好的示范带动作用，为定兴县成为省政府指定的蔬菜生产基地县打下了坚实的基础。为此，园区被誉为“全国农业技术推广先进单位”“国家级蔬菜生产标准化示范区核心示范基地”“河北省科技园区”“省市县三级农业产业化经营重点龙头企业”。

随着经营范围的拓展，园区不失时机地引入了农业旅游功能，将生产经营的过程作为旅客观赏、采摘、体验的农业旅游活动内容，并筹建了十几处人文景观和购物、餐饮场所，最大限度地使园区具有旅游的功能，以满足游客的需求。2004 年 4 月，园区被国家旅游局命名为“全国农业旅游示范点”。2012 年 12 月，园区获得“全国休闲农业与乡村旅游示范点”称号。

通过十几年努力，园区已具备了农业旅游功能。园区采取封闭式管理，外部环境优美，园内游路纵横，各景观四通八达。园区辟为 4 个常设功能区，即观赏采摘体验区、休闲游乐区、旅游购物区、餐饮休闲区；并设有两个专项旅游活动项目功能区，农机博物馆和王实甫书院。

这里也是一个有机、绿色、生态环保、安全、和谐的旅游乐园，主要的特色项目有生态乐园、观景平台、特色养殖中心、问道精舍、修身茶社、迷宫、水上游乐、五谷苑、百花坛、养心阁、浪漫屋、手工坊、民俗馆等。

昌利农业示范园

王实甫书院是园区的文化底蕴的核心所在。西厢文化是定兴非遗的主要组成部分。园区修葺书院并在院内以雕塑的艺术形式还原主要戏剧场景，旨在让游客受到西厢文化的熏陶，愿天下有情人终成眷属。

农机博物馆是园区独特的亮点，集农机

具大全。馆内以实物、声、光、电等媒介，图文并茂地展示了各历史时期不同种类的农机具，旨在使游客了解我国农机的发展历程，从农机这一侧面了解农业发展史，寓爱国主义教育于游乐之中。此举在全省乃至全国独树一帜。

Being located in Yanggezhuang Village, Liyuzhuang Town, 7 kilometers away from Dingxing County, Baoding Changli Agricultural Tourism Demonstration Park is the subsidiary of Hebei Changli Agricultural Science and Technology Development Group Co., Ltd, covering an area of 1080 *mu*. The park was built in October, 1998, and visitors were received in May, 2000.

The Park develops agriculture planting, production and distribution of high-quality fruits and vegetables, flowers, nursery stocks with the backing of technical support of Hebei Agricultural University. The fruits include Aidang pear, apple, apricot, grape, etc.. The vegetables include lettuce, tomato, cucumber, eggplant, pepper, squash, etc.. The flowers include fresh-cut anthurium, chrysanthemum, poinsettia and sowbread. The nursery stocks include horse chestnut, ginkgo tree, boxwood, etc..The company registered the trademark of Changli and won the famous brand name of Hebei Province. These plants play a good demonstration role, and lay the solid foundation of vegetable production base in Dingxing County designated by the provincial government. For this reason, the park is known as the "National Advanced Agricultural Technology Extension Unit" "the Core Demonstration Base of the National Vegetable Production Standardization Demonstration Area" "Hebei Provincial Science and Technology Park" "Agricultural Industrialization Operation Key Leading Enterprises in Cities and Counties".

With the expansion of business scope, agricultural tourism was introduced to the park. The process of production and operation was served as agricultural tourism activities, such as watching, picking and experiencing. Moreover, a dozen cultural landscapes and places for shopping and dining were built to maximize the tourism function and meet the needs of tourists. In April, 2004, the park was named "National Demonstration Point of Agricultural Tourism" by the National Tourism Bureau. In December, 2012, the park got the title of "National Leisure Agriculture and Rural Tourism Demonstration Point".

Through more than ten years' effort, the park has already had the function of agricultural tourism. The park is managed with a closed form, with beautiful external environment, criss-crossed pathways in the garden and landscapes in all directions. The park is divided into 4 permanent functional areas, namely, the ornamental picking experience area, the recreational area, the shopping area, the dining and entertainment area, and there are two special tourism activities functional areas, namely, Agricultural Machinery Museum and Wang Shifu Academy.

Here is an organic, green, environmental protection, safe and harmonious tourist park. The main characteristic items include ecological park, viewing platform, characteristic breeding center, Vihara, teahouse, maze, aquatic amusement, grain garden, flowers altar, Yangxin pavilion, romantic room, workshop, folk museum, etc..

Wang Shifu academy is the core of the cultural background of the park. The Culture of the Romance of West Chamber is the main part of the intangible cultural heritage in Dingxing County. The academy was repaired and the main drama scene was restored in the form of sculpture arts, so that visitors can enjoy the the Culture of the Romance of West Chamber.

The Agricultural Machinery Museum is a unique highlight of the park, which is a collection of agricultural machinery tools. The museum displays different kinds of agricultural machinery tools in different historical periods with physical, acoustic, optical and media graphics, aiming at making tourists understand the developmental process of Chinese agricultural machinery, and the history of agricultural development from the perspective of agricultural machinery, and incorporating patriotic education with amusement. This move is unique in the whole province, even in the whole country.

5. 世界门窗小镇

世界门窗小镇位于高碑店市，总占地面积1500亩，包括中国门窗博物馆、门窗物理性能体验中心、中国被动式建筑发展历程馆、未来生活园被动式科技馆、被动式建筑材料产业基地等，是以门窗文化、被动式建筑技术展示、体验为主题的特色工业景点。

世界门窗小镇是我国唯一以展示建筑节能新产业、新技术、新工艺为核心的公益性工业旅游景区。

小镇包括节能门窗产业科技文化展示区和超低能耗建筑产业科技文化展示区两大板块。

作为中德合作的典范，小镇已经吸引入驻国内外企业400多家，成功举办了三届中国国际门窗博览会，累计接待游客30万人次。小镇通过打造汇集全球1000多家行业知名企业合作交流的国际平台，形成了“欧洲门窗看纽伦堡，亚洲门窗看高碑店”的世界行业新格局。

2011年，小镇被河北省旅游发展委员会评为首批工业旅游示范点；2012年，被河北省科技厅认定为“科普基地”；2016年，通过河北省旅游发展委员会4A级工业旅游景观质量评审；同年，被京津冀三地联合认定为“科普之旅精品路线”。

中国门窗博物馆于2011年6月在中国国际门窗城内落成。博物馆展区面积7000平方米，已征集到上至汉唐、下至当代的古今门窗展品619件，其中以明清门窗展品居多，诠释了古今门窗的发展历史。馆内分为古代门窗、近代门窗、当代门窗、高科技门窗四个展区，并设立节能门窗演示区、未来之家智能化门窗区、遮阳体验区等。在这里，游客可以领略到中国几千年的门窗发展史，感受到中国门窗精湛的制作工艺。中国门窗博物馆的建成，填补了中国门窗类综合博物馆的空白，是中国建筑文化领域的新成就。

中国门窗博物馆

Being located in the city of Gaobeidian, covering the total area of 1500 *mu*, International Door and Window Town is the industrial scenery exhibiting the culture of door-and- window and passive building, composed of the Chinese Door-and-window

Museum, Physical Properties Experience Center, Chinese Passive Building Museum, Prospective Passive Technology Museum, and Passive Building Materials Industry Park.

International Door and Window Town is the only public welfare tourism scenic spot which exhibits the new industry and technology of architecture and energy saving in our country.

The town includes the exhibition areas of science and technology culture, energy-saving doors and windows industry and ultra low-energy building industry.

As a model of Sino-German cooperation, the town has attracted more than 400 domestic and foreign businesses, and has successfully hosted three International Window and Door Fairs in China, which has received 300 thousand tourists. It has created an international platform for gathering and communicating among more than 1000 well-known companies worldwide, and has formed a new pattern of the world industry, which is "Nuremberg is the city which is famous for windows and doors in Europe, whereas Gaobeidian is the town which is famous for windows and doors in Asia".

In 2011, the town was named by the Hebei Tourism Committee as the first industrial tourism demonstration sites. In 2012, it was identified as "Science Base" by Hebei Science and Technology Department. In 2016, it passed through the review of 4A-level industrial tourism landscape quality assessment by the Hebei Tourism Commission. In the same year, it was identified as "Boutique Route in Science Tour" by Beijing-Tianjin-Baoding jointly.

The Chinese Door-and-window Museum was completed in the international door and window city of China in June, 2011. The exhibition area of the museum is 7000 square meters. It has collected 619 pieces of ancient and modern door and window exhibits up to the Han and Tang Dynasties. Doors and windows in the Ming and Qing Dynasties are in the majority, which explains the developmental history of ancient and modern doors and windows. The museum is divided into four exhibition areas: ancient doors and windows, modern doors and windows, contemporary doors and windows, high-tech doors and windows, and energy-saving doors and windows demonstration area, future home intelligent door and window area, shading experience area and so on. Here, visitors can appreciate the history of the development of doors and windows for thousands of years in China, and feel the exquisite craftsmanship of China's doors and windows. The construction of Chinese Door and Window Museum has filled the blank of the comprehensive museum of doors and windows in China. It is a new achievement in the field of Chinese architectural culture.

6. 刘伶醉工业文化旅游景区

占据全国索具行业 70%份额的中国巨力集团主要有六个产业：索具、新能源、影视文化、刘伶醉景区、多晶硅料、地产商贸，并已开辟了多个展区。

(1) 刘伶醉展区

竹林七贤里刘伶被称为“酒仙”，在徐水一醉三年。现今刘伶醉有千年古烧锅遗址，是国家重点文物保护单位，有中国第一古烧锅之称。刘伶醉获“中华老字号”“中国驰名商标”称号。

(2) 刘伶醉新工业园区

刘伶醉新工业园区是集工业旅游观光和白酒酿造生产于一体的现代化工业园区，2011 年 4 月底开始筹建，2012 年 9 月全部竣工。园内占地面积 400 亩，成品酒设计生产能力 5 万吨，共分五大功能区：原辅材料储存加工区、白酒酿造区、基酒陈贮区、白酒灌装区、成品库存区。

刘伶醉

新工业园区建设突出以人为本的思想和传承、创新、发展的理念，建成了一座安全、卫生、绿色、环保、高效、节能的花园式工业园区。园区在各工艺过程中尽量采用先进的、机械化程度高的技术装备以减轻工人的劳动强度，改善工人的工作环境，提高工作效率；同时注重在继承传统工艺的基础上，不断引进现代先进技术，使刘伶醉酿造技艺得到进一步的发展。

园区内生产工艺过程有完善的质量保障体系，先进的检验方法和检测手段以及分析仪器，以确保产品质量和安全。

(3) 万坛酒林

万坛酒林目前为中国第一酒林，已被列入上海大世界吉尼斯之最，是刘伶醉新工业园区中一道亮丽的风景线。它占地 180 多亩，埋有 500 升、1000 升陶坛近 2 万个。林区内布满青松翠柏、绿柳银杏、玉兰桂花，碧草如茵、绿荫蔽日、喷泉涌流、溪水淙淙，形成了一个天然氧吧，为原浆酒创造了一个富氧的成熟条件，并形成了一个相对恒温恒湿的贮酒环境。再采用透气性较好的陶坛封存陈贮，更有利于原浆酒的老熟。在贮存过程中刘伶醉原浆酒经历酷暑严寒的陶冶和雨雪风霜的洗礼，在各种自然条件下完成各种物理变化和化学反应，酒体更加香味突出、舒适醇和、丰满浓郁、自然协调，真正体现了“林中一秋，洞藏五载”的效果。

⑷ 灌装车间

灌装车间共有三座，均为无菌无尘车间。14 条白酒灌装线，均为目前中国白酒行业比较先进的灌装流水线。原辅料储存加工区有辅料库、曲料库各一座，原料储存筒仓 15 个，每座容原粮 500 吨。从入仓、温度检测、通风控温，至出仓加工、搅拌混合、输送至车间采用全自动控制。

⑸ 酿造车间

酿造车间占地面积将近 70 亩，共有 3000 余个发酵池，为目前我国长江以北最大的浓香型白酒酿造车间，于 2011 年 12 月开始陆续投产。车间酿造生产在传承刘伶醉传统酿造技艺的同时，最大限度地采用机械化的工艺设备，大幅降低了劳动强度，提高了生产效率。

酿造车间

⑹ 刘伶醉古烧锅遗址

刘伶醉古烧锅有近千年的白酒酿造历史。该古烧锅历史上名为“润泉涌烧锅”，因其位于县城南城门内第一家，因此又名“南门里烧锅”，在明清乃至民国时期的《徐水县志》上都有明确的记载。该古烧锅起源于金元时期，距今已有近千年的历史。2006 年，刘伶醉古烧锅遗址被国务院公布为国家重点文物保护单位，为中国目前已知历史最早的白酒酿造遗址，为研究我国白酒的起源和发展提供了有力的实证，有非常重要的考古价值。

最珍贵的是，自金元时期以来的千百年虽经朝代更替，战乱频繁，刘伶醉古烧锅却一直连续生产使用至今。古发酵池自然驯化和繁衍了非常丰富的微生物菌群，形成了独特的酿酒微生物环境。其中两种微生物是目前世界其他各地从未发现过且对酿造优质浓香型白酒非常有益的菌种，为酿造高品质的刘伶醉酒提供了先决条件，有相当重要的科学研究价值。

Juli Group, which occupies 70% share of the national cable industry in China, has six main industries: sling, new energy, film culture, Liulingzui scenic spot, polysilicon, and real estate. It has opened up a number of exhibition areas.

2.2.6.1 Liulingzui Exhibition Area

Liu Ling is called "Winebibber" among the seven sages of the bamboo grove, who had drunk in Xushui District for three years. Now the Site of Ancient Distilling Still is listed as the national key cultural relics protection units and the first ancient distilling still in China. Liulingzui had won the title of "China's Time-honored Brand" and "Chinese Well-known Trademark".

2.2.6.2 Liulingzui New Industrial Park

It is a modern industrial park, functioning as industrial tourism and white wine brewing and producing. It was built at the end of April, 2011, and completed in September, 2012. The park covers an area of 400 *mu*, and the design and production capacity of finished wine is 50 thousand tons. The park is divided into five major functional areas: raw and auxiliary materials storage and processing area, white wine brewing area, base liquor storage area, liquor-filling area and finished product inventory area.

The construction of the new industrial park highlights the idea of "people-oriented" and the idea of inheritance, innovation and development, and has been built into a safe, hygienic, green, environmentally friendly, efficient and energy-saving garden type industrial park. With the adoption of advanced and mechanized technology and equipment, the park is aimed to reduce the intensity of labor, improve the working environment and work efficiency; at the same time, on the basis of inheriting the traditional process, the park is constantly introduced advanced technology, making Liulingzui brewing technology gain further development.

The production process in the park has perfect quality assurance system, advanced inspection methods, testing means and analytical instruments to ensure the quality and safety of the product.

2.2.6.3 Wantan Wine Woods

At present, the Wantan Wine Woods is the first in China. It has been listed as the Guinness of the great world of Shanghai. It is a beautiful scenery line in Liulingzui New Industrial Park. It covers an area of more than 180 *mu*. More than 20000 crockery jars with a total capacity of 500 litres and 1000 litres were buried there. The woods area is covered with pines, cypresses, green willows, Ginkgoes, Magnolia and osmanthus, springs and streams, forming a natural oxygen bar, which creates a mature condition of rich oxygen for the raw wine and forms a relatively constant temperature and humidity of the wine storage environment. It is more beneficial to the maturing of the raw wine by sealing permeable crockery jars. In the process of storage, Liulingzui wine is exposed to the extremely hot or severely cold environment and years of harsh weather. After completing a variety of physical change and chemical reaction in various natural conditions, the wine is more fragrant and purer, which truly reflects the fitness of the environment in the woods.

2.2.6.4 Filling Workshop

There are three filling workshops, all of which are aseptic and dustless workshops. The 14 liquor filling lines are all the more advanced filling lines in China liquor industry. There are 2 material storehouse and 15 raw material storage silo in the raw material storage and processing zone with a capacity of 500 tons each. Automatic control is used for warehousing, temperature detection, temperature control, ventilation, processing and delivering.

2.2.6.5 Brewing Workshop

The workshop covers an area of nearly 70 *mu*, with more than 3000 fermentation pools. It is the largest highly flavored liquor brewing workshop in the north of the Yangtze River in China, and has been put into operation since December, 2011. When inheriting Liulingzui's traditional brewing technology, the workshop's brewing production adopts mechanized equipment to the maximum extent, greatly reducing labor intensity and improving production efficiency.

2.2.6.6 The Site of Liulingzui Ancient Pot

It has nearly a thousand years of liquor brewing history. The ancient pot was called "Run Quan Yong Pot" in history. Being located at the South Gate, it is also known as the "South Gate Pot", which has a clear record in the *Xushui Records* of the Ming and Qing Dynasties. The ancient pot was originated from the era of the Jin and Yuan Dynasties, dating back nearly a thousand years. In 2006, it was published by the State Council as a national key cultural relics protection unit, being the earliest known site of white wine in China and providing a strong physical evidence for the origin and development of white wine in China. It has very important archaeological value.

Most preciously, since the Jin and Yuan Dynasties, with the replacement of different rulers and frequent wars, Liulingzui Ancient Pot is still in use up till now. The ancient fermentation pools naturally domesticate and multiply a very rich microbial flora, forming a unique microorganism environment for brewing. Among them, two kinds of microflora that have never been found in other parts of the world are very useful for brewing high-quality liquor and provide a prerequisite for brewing high-quality Liulingzui wine, which are of important scientific value.

7. 四季圣诞小镇

四季圣诞小镇位于涞水县，是华北地区第一个以“雪花”为主题，以“趣味”为灵魂，以“祝福”为文化的新业态项目。户外运动乐园主要是冬季的冰雪运动和夏季的自行车运动；圣诞小镇以梦幻雪花为核心元素，突出奇幻，营造“乐趣享受”；冰雪奇缘乐园致力打造滨水乐园、热气球乐园、萌萌乐宠物乐园、麋鹿乐园、跑马乐园以及生态农庄、生态观光园等，可以让游客在与山水、动物、花草、田园的亲密接触中体会到自然的乐趣。

Being located in Laishui County, Four Seasons Christmas Town is the first new format project in northern China, setting “Snowflake” as the theme, “Fun” as the soul, and “Bless” as the culture. The Outdoor Sports Park mainly aims at winter snow sports and summer cycling. The Christmas Town is the core element of dream snowflake, highlight fantasy, and fun enjoyment. The Snow Garden consists of Waterfront Park, Hot air Ballons Park, Cute Pets Paradise, Deer Park, Horse-racing Park and Ecological Village and Garden, providing the natural intimate contact with landscapes, waters, animals, flowers and gardens.

8. 易水湖康养小镇

易水湖康养小镇位于易水湖中心，引入易文化中医养生理念，强调中国传统养生文化的体验，立足打造成心灵的栖息地、身心的能量场。自然养生区主要以养生游步栈道、养生民宿客栈等元素组成；调理养生区主要由经络理疗村落、中医饮食养生、动形健身区等组成；五行养生区主要由中医堂、户外静养、疗养住宿等元素组成。

易水湖风光

Being located in the center of Yishui Lake with the concept of Chinese medicine culture in Yi culture, the experience of traditional Chinese culture, it is aimed at the soul habitat and the energy field of mind and body. The Natural Health-care area consists of the Leisure Walkway and Health-care Hotel. The Adjustment and Health Area consists of Meridian Physiotherapy Village, Traditional Chinese Medicine Diet, Dynamic Fitness Area and so on. And the Taoism Health-care Area consists of Traditional Chinese Medicine Hall, Outdoor Retreat, Recuperation and Accommodation.

9. 中华非遗小镇

定兴县计划以拒马河谷为依托，向西扩张，以优质的环境、水系文化、戏曲公园为特色亮点，综合打造全国知名、美誉度高、市场辐射力强、特色主题性强、富有创造性的非物质文化遗产小镇。

该项目规划占地面积 3 平方千米，建筑面积 1.4 平方千米，以非遗文化创意产业和非遗文化旅游产业为基础，打造 4A 级非遗文化特色旅游景区。重点建设黄金台历史文化博物馆、非物质文化遗产产业园、非遗风情街巷、非遗培训中心、西厢戏曲文化园等五大功能板块。

黄金台历史文化博物馆总高 29 米，由地下一层和地上三层组成，第三层为元代风格建筑。整体建筑含黄金台大殿、四个角亭和连廊。占地 15 亩，建筑面积 14602 平方米，总投资 4000 万元人民币。博物馆名源于定兴县著名古迹“黄金台”(亦称招贤台)。据载，公元前 333 年，燕昭王继位时，燕国人才匮乏、国力较弱。燕昭王听从定兴籍谋士郭隗的策略，筑黄金台招贤纳士，名士邹衍、名将乐毅、贤士剧辛等先后投奔燕国，使燕国迅速壮大，并一度占领齐国 70 余座城池。昔日燕昭王所筑黄金台，在今定兴县城西南 15 千米的高里乡北章村台上，目前遗址尚存。

中华非遗小镇的建设，不仅对讲好本地故事、发展本地旅游文化事业起到重要推动作用，成为广大游客了解定兴、体验传统文化的新窗口，还将为当地甚至周边入驻这里的非物质文化遗产传承人提供文化交流、产业创新和发展生息的广阔平台。

Dingxing County plans to rely on the Juma river valley to expand westward. With the shining point of quality environment, water culture, and opera park, it aims to create a well-known, high-reputed, strong market radiation, thematic, and creative town of intangible cultural heritage.

The project covers an area of 3 square kilometers and a building area of 1.4 square kilometers. Based on the intangible cultural heritage industry and intangible cultural tourism industry, the 4A-level intangible cultural heritage scenic spot is to be built with the focus on the construction of Golden Platform Museum of History and Culture, Intangible Cultural Heritage Industrial Park, Intangible Cultural Heritage Style Streets, Intangible Cultural Heritage Training Center, West Room Opera Culture Park and other five functional blocks.

The Golden Platform Museum of History and Culture is 29 meters high, consisting of one floor underground and three floors on the ground, and the third layer is the style of the Yuan Dynasty. The whole building consists of a golden hall, four corner pavilions and a corridor. It covers an area of 15 *mu*, with a building area of 14602 square meters and a total investment of 40 million *yuan*. The museum originates from the historical site "Golden Platform" (also known as Zhaoxian Platform) in Dingxing County. According to the records, in 333 BC, when the king of Yanzhao was succeeded to the throne, the talent of Yan State was scarce and the national strength was weak. Listening to the strategy of his advisor Guo Kui, whose hometown is Dingxing, the king of Yanzhao built Golden Platform to recruit talents. The celebrity Zou Yan, famous general Yue Yi, and wise man Ju Xin defected to the state of Yan, making the Yan state develop rapidly, and once occupied more than 70 cities of the state of Qi. The former Golden Platform built by the king of Yanzhao is in Beizhang Village of Gaoli Town 15 kilometers southwest of Dingxing County, with the remaining sites preserved.

The construction of the intangible cultural heritage of the town plays an important role in promoting not only local stories, but also the development of local tourist culture. It will become a new window of understanding and experiencing Dingxing traditional culture for the majority of visitors, and it will also provide a broad platform for cultural exchanges, industrial innovation and development for people who inherit intangible cultural heritage.

10. 涿州影视城

涿州影视城位于京石高速公路涿州市东侧，总占地2200亩，包括唐城、汉城、铜雀台以及清代皇宫和四合院景区；梅园、桃园、竹园、梨园四处民居区及两座各为1200平方米的摄影棚。涿州影视城既是一处为影视拍摄提供场景和制作服务的场所，又是旅游观光、观赏影视剧拍摄场景的好去处。

影视城1991年建成以来，已先后拍摄了《唐明皇》《武则天》《三国演义》《文成公主》《开国领袖毛泽东》等2000多部(集)电影、电视剧。有上百万海内外游客来此观光。占地13616平方米的大型摄影棚具有世界一流水平。同时棚内建有现场拍摄观赏走廊，采用单向反射玻璃设备，做到拍摄、旅游互不影响，从而使其成为集拍摄旅游于一体的、独具特色的旅游景观。

影视城建有外景区、内景区和传统民居区。外景区建有中国唐汉两个朝代的建筑群，风格各异。民居区建有体现明清历史风格的梅、竹、梨、桃园招待所和一处祠庙风格的梨园餐厅以及艺苑多功能厅，随时为剧组和游人提供食、宿、娱乐之方便。

影视城内的建筑，在建筑手法上具有虚实结合、真假并用的特点。影视城最吸引剧组和游人的景点是铜雀台，独特的建筑风格为当今世界罕见。登主台要上84个台阶，到配台可通过两架桥梁，台上有院，院中有楼，楼间有亭，台前是碧波荡漾的湖泊，湖泊中有绿草茵茵的小道，山、湖、岛、台、阁、楼、廊、桥、青松翠柏相互呼应，浑然一体，颇为壮观。

铜雀台

不远的将来，这座影视城展示给人们的不仅是一个拍摄基地，而是一个集影视文化、历史文化、民族文化、异域风情于一体的具有多功能的影视城、历史城、文化城和旅游城。

Zhuozhou World Studios lies in the east of Zhuozhou by the side of Beijing-Shijiazhuang speedway. It occupies an area of 2200 *mu* and includes such scenery spots as Tang City, Han City, Copper Sparrow Platform and royal palace of the Qing Dynasty and Siheyuan as well. Zhuozhou World Studios also includes four residential areas:

Plum Garden, Peach Garden, Bamboo Garden and Pear Garden and two studios, the respective area of which is 1200 square meters. It is not only a place to provide scene and service for film and television shooting, but also a good place for sightseeing and viewing the scene of film and TV play.

Since the establishment of Zhuozhou World Studios in 1991, over 2000 films, teleplays and numerous advertisements were shot here, such as *Emperor Li Longji*, *Wu Zetian Regina*, *the History of Sanguo Period*, *Wen Cheng Princess*, *Father Figure of New China — Mao Zedong*", and so on. Millions of tourists from home and abroad visited here. The large studio that covers an area of 13616 square meters has a first-class advanced level. With the sightseeing corridor built inside, it combines shooting and tourism together, by using the specular reflection glass equipment to make it a unique landscape.

It consists of outdoor scene area, indoor scene area and folk dwellings area. The building complex of the Tang and Han Dynasties is built in the outside area. In the folk dwellings area, there are 4 gardens named as plum, pear, bamboo and peach with the style of the Ming and Qing Dynasties, a restaurant in the Pear Garden with the style of temple, and a multifunctional hall, which can provide the basic necessities for the crew and visitors at any time.

The buildings inside feature the architectural techniques of virtual-real and true-false combination. What impresses the crew and tourists most is the Bronze Sparrow Terrace, whose unique architectural style is rare in the world. One has to climb 84 steps to get to the main stage, and pass through two bridges to get to the side stage. There is a yard on the stage, with buildings and pavilions inside. In front of the stage is a rippling lake, in which lies a trail. The scenes of mountain, lake, island, stage, pavilion, loft, corridor, bridge and green pines and blue cypress form a unified spectacular.

In the near future, Zhuozhou World Studios will show us a multifunctional place that combines the culture of film and TV play, history, nationality and exotic customs.

(三)红色之城巡礼

1. 冉庄地道战遗址

冉庄地道战遗址位于保定市清苑区冉庄镇，是中国人民抗击日本侵略者的一处重要战争遗址。抗日战争时期，冉庄人民在无险可守的冀中大平原地下建起了长达 16 千米的地道网，形成了能打能藏、可攻可守、进退自如的地下长城，成为世界战争史上的奇迹。遗址保护面积 20 万平方米，重点保护区 2.26 万平方米，当年对敌斗争的大部分工事、地下设施、兵工厂等保存完好。遗址内现保留着 20 世纪三四十年代冀中平原的村落原貌和当年构筑的地道及各种作战工事，建有冉庄地道战纪念馆。电影《地道战》《烈火金刚》《平原游击队》等多部电影都是在此拍摄的。

村头大钟

⑴ 双向地道

冉庄地道网中有一条双向地道，这条地道内有两扇可以活动的门，可以将地道关闭，通道两端有翻板陷阱，敌人到了这里就如同进了囚笼，这就叫“堵住笼子抓鸡，关起门来打狗”。为防敌人用水灌地道，冉庄的地道与水井相连，正如电影《地道战》中说的“水是宝贵的。从哪里来还回到那里去”。无论敌人从哪口水井里灌地道，水都会流回原处。

⑵ 地下兵工厂

抗日战争时期，冉庄民兵为了解决弹药不足的问题，自己动手建立起地下兵工厂。地道口通到炕上，可以从屋内炕上的地道口进入地下兵工厂。民兵们用简单的工具制造了大量的土武器。地下兵工厂分工比较细，主要有锻轧组、铸造组、机加工组。锻轧以烘炉为主，在这里锻造打制大刀、长矛、土枪及各种武器配件。炭窑是制造火药原料的。铸造组通过各种关系将焦炭从解放区搞来，利用废铁等铸造地雷、手榴弹。机加工组用土旋床加工地雷、手榴弹把柄等木制配件，还用来加工制造镗床、土枪、火枪筒等武器零部件。各种零件制造好后，就在地下土兵工厂里装组成土枪、掷弹筒、地雷、手榴弹、子弹等武器。当时制造武

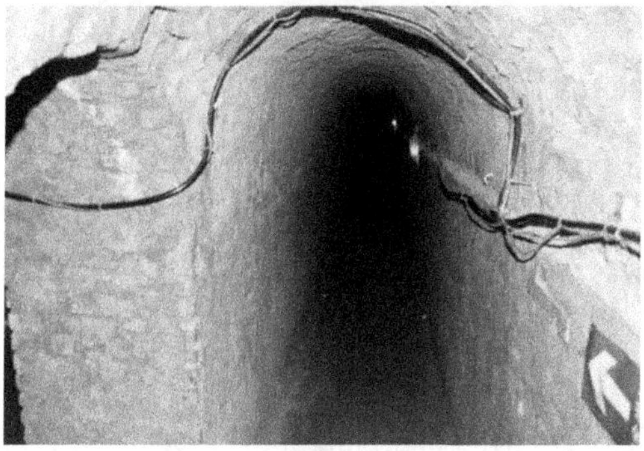
地道口

器的工具和方法比较简单和落后，所以，民兵还在工厂里挖了一口防爆井，弹药万一在组装中出事，可以立即投入井中，以防伤人。工厂里，每道工序完全是由人力来完成的。武器制成后，存放在地下库房里。战斗过程中，地道内的交通员通知兵工厂某工事需要什么武器，土兵工厂就可以在敌人的脚底下运送过去。土坦克是数层用水浸湿的棉被盖住木桌做成的，抱炸药包的人在木桌下顶着桌子冲锋，用以防子弹。1945 年，冉庄民兵拿下黑风口据点时就用了这种土坦克。冉庄民兵利用自己的聪明才智办地下兵工厂，制造武器打击敌人，为抗战做出了很大的贡献。

⑶ 翻眼

翻眼是地道内的一种防御设施。翻眼有两种，一种是向上翻的，另一种是向下翻的。向下翻眼可以用来防毒气，因为毒气比较轻，只向上走。虽然只是这样一个小小的东西，就可以将毒气隔开，使两面地道不会相互影响。而且它还是地道内的一处很好的防御设施，当敌人进入地道，民兵可以在口上等着他，居高临下，来一个打一个。

⑷ 卡口

卡口是地道内的一种防御设施，因为它比较矮小，如果敌人放毒气或放水，民兵就可以在很短的时间内把口堵上，将地道隔离。此外，敌人进入地道，一个人在此把守，敌人过来就得爬，那样把守的就很容易消灭他们。可谓“一夫当关，万夫莫开”。但是卡口在地道内不能太多，那样会限制民兵的行动。

⑸ 三官庙

三官庙原是供奉尧、舜、禹的庙宇。旧时有泥塑神像，神像前香火不断，但却救不了我们。民兵们拿起武器开展地道战，来保卫家园，抵抗侵略。为方便作战，他们把泥塑神像拉倒，庙内筑地道口通地道，在庙墙上筑暗枪眼，垒墙堵住庙门，就这样把庙宇改装成作战工事。地道战期间，三官庙工事成为把守清水河南大桥的重要射击堡垒，并与青神庙工事及两侧民居暗枪眼相配合，形成一道阻击敌人的屏障。

⑹ 冉庄抗日村公所

冉庄抗日村公所原是冉庄村公所，始建于民国年间。1938 年，冉庄建立党组织和抗日政权，改称为冉庄抗日村公所。这里是冉庄抗日活动的中枢，下设“五大会”：冉庄抗日武装委员会、冉庄农民抗日救国会、冉庄工人抗日救国会、冉庄妇女抗日救国会、冉庄青年抗日救国会。

1938 年秋，冀中军区司令员吕正操来到冉庄，在这里谈判收编清苑县西片联庄会，把

“不抗日、不降日、打土匪、保家乡”的地方武装改编成共产党领导下的抗日力量。这批武装力量(清苑县5000余人)，在抗日战争和解放战争中转战南北，为抗御外侮，为祖国解放，立下汗马功劳。

⑺ 冉庄十字街

冉庄十字街是地道战的中心地带之一，地下设有指挥室、休息室等，十字街四壁墙根设暗枪眼若干。

冉庄始建于隋唐，至宋代时，传说杨继业之子杨延昭部将在村北河畔荒原筑营戍守，冉庄因此而一度繁荣，初具小镇规模，故冉庄素有唐村宋镇之说。街上两棵老槐树，距今已有1000多年的历史。历史变迁，沧海桑田，当年栽下槐树的冉、曹两姓在冉庄村已无后人。

抗日战争时期，村民在街头古槐上悬挂北大寺的铁钟，用以报警。在1965年拍摄电影《地道战》时，这两棵老槐树枝繁叶茂，过往行人都愿在树下歇脚。有间屋子原为一个店铺，柜台下面有地平面地道口与地道相连，作战时就成了地面指挥中心。西南隅房顶为高房指挥中心，并有高房工事通夹壁墙至地道，这里的地道口为墙根壁地道口。1950年，冉庄民兵曾以实战的形式迎接来自36个国家的青年代表团，外国青年代表团找了好长时间，仍没找到地道口。

⑻ 冉庄抗日武装委员会

抗日战争期间，冉庄抗日武装委员会设在关帝庙。冉庄抗日武装委员会曾在此办公，这里是冉庄决策和指挥武装斗争、地道斗争的主要指挥所，又是为我主力部队组织和输送兵员的地方，从抗日战争到解放战争，冉庄共有200多名优秀青年加入了正规军。这里同时又是组织支前的办公地。在关公神台一侧有一处极为隐藏的地道口——地平面地道战口。电影《地道战》中的假武工队来冉庄刺探地道斗争情报的故事情节就发生在这里，这个地道口下面的地道通往战斗地道的四面八方。

抗日战争时期日军在冉庄常吃败仗，老乡们传说是关公保佑。其实地道战的胜利，是先辈们运筹帷幄，指挥有方，冉庄民兵英勇奋战的结果。

⑼ 清苑县抗日武装委员会

这里是一处普普通通的民居，是抗日战争年代的一家堡垒户，现在院内仍保持着战争年代环境风貌。南屋子是马槽地道口，现在仍然养着马，气息仍似当年。抗日战争中，清苑县抗日武装委员会在此办公，是发动全县抗日武装和民众破坏敌交通、坚壁清野、割电线、炸桥梁、开展游击战、地道战等武装斗争的指挥中心。伪装奇巧的马槽地道口与地道相通，当遇到紧急情况时，干部们便从这里转入地道。

1961年，冉庄地道战遗址，被国务院列为全国重点文物保护单位；1994年，被河北省委、省政府命名为河北省爱国主义教育基地；1995年1月26日，被共青团中央命名为全国青少年教育基地；1997年6月，被中宣部定为全国百家爱国主义教育示范基地之一；2003

年9月，被河北省政府、省军区命名为第一批省级国防教育基地。地道战以其独特的战略战术，在抗日战争和解放战争中，建立了不朽的历史功勋，在世界反法西斯战争史上谱写了光辉的一页。

Being located in the Ranzhuang Town, Qingyuan District of Baoding, the Site of Tunnel Warfare in Ranzhuang is one of the most important sites of the Chinese People's War of Resistance against Japanese Aggression. During the war, the inhabitants dug a tunnel network, 16 kilometers long, under the great plains of Hebei, where there is no natural shelter, forming the miracle in the history of war worldwide, for its capacities of fighting, hiding, attacking and defending, just like underground Great Wall. The relic covers a total area of 200000 square meters, with the key protected area of 22600 square meters. Most of the sites, such as fortifications, underground facilities and arsenals are well-preserved. At the site still remain the original looks of the villages in the Middle Plain of Hebei Province in the 1930s and 1940s, including the tunnels constructed in those years and various fortifications. The Memorial Hall of the Site of Tunnel Warfare in Ranzhuang was right built here. Movies such as the *Tunnel Warfare*, *Never Yielding* and *the Plain Guerrilla* were all filmed here.

2.3.1.1 Bi-directional Tunnel

There is a bi-directional tunnel among the Ranzhuang tunnel network. Inside the bi-directional tunnel are two movable doors that can close the tunnel. Since there are traps that have a drop leaf on both ends of the channel, the enemies would be locked in the tunnel when arriving, just like a bird in a cage. A saying of blocking the cage to catch the chicken and closing the door to beat the dog was on the lips of the local inhabitants. In order to prevent enemies from using water to irrigate the tunnel, the tunnels are linked with the well, as what is said in the film *the Tunnel Warfare*, which is, let the precious water flow back to its original place. No matter which well is used by the enemies, the water would flow back to its original place.

2.3.1.2 Underground Arsenal

During the Anti-Japanese War, the militiamen in Ranzhuang Town set up an underground arsenal to solve the problem of the shortage of ammunition. The tunnel entrance was linked with the heatable brick bed where people can enter into the underground arsenal. The militiamen used simple tools to produce a large number of weapons. The underground arsenal had a fine division of labor, including the forging group, the casting group and the machining group. By means of baking, the forging group made broadswords, spears, guns and various weapon fittings. The charcoal kiln was used for making gunpowder. Through relation activities, the casting group managed to get cokes from the liberated areas, using scrap iron to make minted mines and grenades. The machining group used lathe to process the wooden fittings, such as landmines and hand grenade handles, and also weapons parts, such as boring mills, guns and fire barrels. After various parts were made, they assembled them into guns, grenade launchers, mines, grenades, bullets and other weapons in the underground arsenal. At that time, the tools and methods were simple and backward, so the militiamen also dug an explosion-proof well in the arsenal in case the accident happened. In the arsenal, each process was completed by manpower. After the weapons were made, they were kept in the storeroom underground. In the course of the battle, the underground messengers informed the arsenal of the needed fortifications, and then the weapons would be conveyed under the feet of the enemies. The folk "tank" was made of a wooden table covered with several layers of wetted blanket. The militiamen with an explosive package charged forward under the wooden table to resist bullets. This "tank" was used in 1945 when the Black Draught fortified points were occupied. Ranzhuang militiamen made a great contribution to the War of Resistance against Japanese Aggression by using their intelligence to build an underground arsenal, and manufacture weapons to fight against enemies.

2.3.1.3 Fan Yan

It is a defensive facility in the tunnel, which has two kinds: one is upward, the other is downward. The downward Fan Yan can be used to prevent lighter poison gas. Although it is only such a small device, it can separate the poison gas, so that the two sides of the tunnel would not be affected mutually. And it is advantageous when enemies enter the tunnel, because the militiamen are waiting for them by the entrance with a dominant position to beat one after another.

2.3.1.4 Guarding Entrance

It is a defensive facility in the tunnel. If the enemies release poison gas or water, the militia could block up the guarding entrance and isolate the tunnel in a short time since it is relatively small. In addition, if the enemies enter the tunnel, they have to crawl, thus they would be easily defeated by the militia guarding there. That is, one man can hold the pass against ten thousand enemies. But there shouldn't be too many guarding entrances for the movements of the militia would be limited.

2.3.1.5 The Temple of Three Officials

It was originally a temple of Emperors Yao, Shun and Yu. In ancient times, there were clay statues worshipped by numerous people, but their efforts were unavailing. Since then, the militiamen took up the weapons and carry out the tunnel warfare to guard their homeland against aggression. In order to facilitate the war, they pulled down the clay statues and built tunnels and concealed gun eyes on the walls of the temple, with temple gate blocked up. In this way, the temple was converted into combat fortifications. During the tunnel warfare, the fortifications of The Temple of Three Officials became an important shooting fortress guarding the south bridge of Qingshui River, and formed a barrier against the enemies with the combination of the fortifications of Qingshen Temple and the concealed handgun eyes on both sides.

2.3.1.6 Ranzhuang Anti-Japanese Village Association

It was the original Ranzhuang Villiage Association built in the year of the Republic of China. In 1938, the party organization and the anti-Japanese government were established in Ranzhuang Village. And it was renamed as Ranzhuang Anti-Japanese Village Association, which is the central area of the Ranzhuang anti-Japanese activities, consisting of five branches: Ranzhuang Anti-Japanese Armed Committee, Ranzhuang Farmers Anti-Japanese and National Salvation Association, Ranzhuang Workers Anti-Japanese and National Salvation Association, Ranzhuang Women Anti-Japanese and National Salvation Association, Ranzhuang Youth Anti-Japanese and National Salvation Association.

In the fall of 1938, the commander of the military region of central Hebei Province, Lv Zhengcao, came to Ranzhuang Village to negotiate incorporating the Lianzhuang Association in the west part of Qingyuan County, the local armed forces, into the anti-Japanese forces under the leadership of the Communist Party. This group of armed forces (more than 5000 people in Qingyuan County), fought north and south in the War of Resistance against Japanese Aggression and the War of Liberation, and made a great contribution to the liberation of China.

2.3.1.7 Ranzhuang Cross Street

It is one of the central areas of the tunnel warfare. There are a commanding room and a lounge underground. The walls of the cross street have a number of concealed bullet holes.

Ranzhuang Village was first built in the Sui and Tang Dynasties, until the Song Dynasty, the military officer Yang Yanzhao, the son of Yang Jiye (a famous general in the Northern Song Dynasty), set up camps to guard the riverside wasteland in the north of the village. Thereafter, Ranzhuang Village flourished and began to take shape. The two old locust trees in the street have a history of more than 1000 years. With historical changes, the tree planters whose family names are Ran and Cao have no descendants in Ranzhuang Village.

During the Anti-Japanese War, the villagers hung the iron bell of Beida Temple in the street as an alarm. When shooting the film *Tunnel Warfare* in 1965, the two old locust trees were luxuriant, under which passers-by were all willing to have a rest. Under the counter of the abandoned store, there is an entrance to the tunnel, which is the ground command center in battle. The high-room command center is built on the southwest roof of the store, in which the high-room fortification is connected to the tunnel. In 1950, Ranzhuang militiamen received the youth delegations from 36 countries in the form of actual combat. And it was hard for them to find the entrance to the tunnel.

2.3.1.8 Ranzhuang Anti-Japanese Armed Committee

During the Anti-Japanese War, Ranzhuang Anti-Japanese Armed Committee was set up in the Temple of Guan Yunchang, which is the main command post of decision-making, armed struggle and tunnel struggle. It is also the place of organizing and conveying soldiers for the main body of the troops. From the Anti-Japanese War to the War of Liberation, more than 200 outstanding youths joined the regular army. It was also the office dealing with supporting the front. There is a hidden tunnel entrance on one side of the altar in the Temple of Guan Yunchang, namely, the ground entrance to the tunnel. The plot of the fake military team spying out military secrets in the movie *the Tunnel Warfare* was shot here, and the underground tunnels lead to all directions.

During the Anti-Japanese War, the Japanese were often defeated in Ranzhuang Village. The fellow villagers said it was because of Guan Yunchang's blessings. In fact, the victory of the Tunnel Warfare is the result of the heroic deeds of the commanders and militiamen.

2.3.1.9 Qingyuan County Anti-Japanese Armed Committee

It is a common residence and a base for protecting and storing the forces of the War of Anti-Japanese Aggression. It still maintains the style and features in times of war. The room in the south is a manger tunnel entrance, where there are still horses in it, just like the scene in those years. During the Anti-Japanese War, the Anti-Japanese Armed Committee took office here, which was the command center for calling in all the armed forces and people in the county to destroy the transportation, strengthen the defenses, cut wire, blow up the bridge, and carry out guerrilla warfare and tunnel warfare. Since the disguised manger tunnel entrance was interlinked with the tunnel, the cadres could go down to the tunnel in an emergency.

The Site of Tunnel Warfare in Ranzhuang was listed by the State Council as a national key cultural relic protection unit in 1961. In 1994, Hebei Provincial Party Committee and Provincial Government named it as Hebei Patriotic Education Base. On January 26,1995, it was named as the National Youth Education Base by the Communist Youth League. In June, 1997, it was designated as one of the national hundred Patriotic Education Demonstration Bases. In September, 2003, it was named as the first batch of Provincial Defense Education Base by Hebei Provincial Government and Provincial Military Area. The Tunnel Warfare, with its unique strategies and tactics in the Anti-Japanese War and the War of Liberation wrote a glorious page in the history of the World Anti-fascist War.

2. 阜平城南庄纪念馆

阜平城南庄纪念馆位于阜平县城南20千米处，是中国第一个敌后抗日根据地——晋察冀边区政府的诞生地。解放战争时期，这里曾为中共中央机关驻地。纪念馆有前后两院，前院有6个展览室，后院为当年晋察冀军区司令部机关和毛泽东、周恩来等中央领导的住房和办公室，共陈列文物247件，现为全国重点文物保护单位。2017年1月，该纪念馆入选《中国红色旅游经典景区名录》。

纪念馆掠影

阜平城南庄由晋察冀军区司令部旧址、晋察冀边区革命纪念馆、聂荣臻元帅铜像、花山毛主席旧居组成，总占地面积14.2万平方米，分展览馆和旧址两部分。其中展览馆建筑面积达2000平方米，展线长240米，共展出文物338件，历史图片342幅。展览紧扣"模范抗日根据地"主题，充分利用现代化陈展手段和景观、雕塑、油画等艺术手法，突出展示了晋察冀军区首创抗日根据地、开展敌后游击战、党的建设、政权建设、经济建设、文化建设等伟大实践，集中反映了1937年至1948年期间晋察冀根据地的光荣历史和晋察冀军民的丰功伟绩。毛泽东诗词匾刻展示了毛泽东在不同时期的书法作品，共110幅。战地摄影记者作品展展出抗战照片80余幅。晋察冀军区司令部旧址建于1947年，面积为1760平方米，共三排，21间土坯房，其中包括毛泽东、周恩来、任弼时等中央领导同志使用过的宿舍、办公室、电话室、作战室和128米长的防空洞。这一旧址是晋察冀军区司令部在河北唯一完整保留的机关旧址，也是毛泽东进京之前在河北保留最完整的居住旧址，成为爱国主义教育和革命传统教育的重要课堂。

毛泽东纪念馆距阜平县城20千米，南临胭脂河，北依菩萨岭，始建于1972年，占地面积5250平方米，分前后两院。前院中矗立着聂荣臻元帅铜像。聂荣臻是农民的儿子，在青年时期曾赴法国、比利时、苏联等国勤工俭学，回国后在黄埔军校担任教官，先后参加和领导了广州起义、南昌起义，在白色恐怖下曾做过地下党的领导工作，在江西革命根据地与林彪搭档，担任红军政治干部的高级职务。丰富的阅历使他集军事和政治才能于一身。抗日战争爆发后，他以五台山及阜平为基地，以3000兵力为火种，遍燃抗日烽火，开创了华北第一块抗日根据地——晋察冀边区。根据地在极其残酷的环境下得到不断的巩固和发展，最终形成地跨冀、晋、绥、察、热、辽，辖160多个县区4000多万人口的纵横千里的广阔区域，成为夺取全国革命胜利的重要战略基地之一。这片屹立在华北敌后的红彤彤的新天地，被中共中央和毛主席誉为“模范抗日根据地”。

晋察冀边区革命纪念馆是国家4A级景区、全国爱国主义教育示范基地、全国百家红色经典景区之一、河北最美三十景之一。纪念馆以“模范抗日根据地”和“全国解放战争的战略基地与指挥中心”为主题，按照历史脉络，运用大量珍贵的照片、文物，使用先进的声、光、电等手段，采取景观复原、幻影成像、触摸屏、雕塑等多种形式，对展览内容进行详细、生动的说明，展示了晋察冀边区军民可歌可泣的英雄事迹。

About 20 kilometers to the south of Fuping County, Fuping South City Town Memorial is the site of headquarters of Shanxi-Chahar-Hebei military area, the birthplace of China's first enemy's rear area, Shanxi-Chahar-Hebei border area government, and the station of the central department of China Party during the Liberation War. There are foreyard and backyard. The foreyard includes 6 exhibition rooms, and the backyard is the house and office of central leaders such as Mao Zedong and Zhou Enlai and also the headquarters of Shanxi-Chahar-Hebei military area in those years. There are 247 cultural relics on show. Now it is one of the National key cultural relic protection units. In January, 2017, it was selected as an entry on *The List of China's Classic Red Tourist Attractions.*

It is made up of the sites of the Shanxi-Chahar-Hebei Military Region Command, the Shanxi-Chahar-Hebei Border Region Revolutionary Memorial Hall, the Bronze Statue of Marshal Nie Rongzhen, and the Former Dwelling of Chairman Mao Zedong. The total area is 142000 square meters, including two parts, the exhibition hall and the former sites. The exhibition hall covers a construction area of 2000 square meters, and the exhibition line is 240 meters long. There are 338 pieces of cultural relics and 342 historical pictures on show. With the theme of "exemplary anti- Japanese base" and the full use of modern exhibition methods and artistic techniques, such as landscape, sculpture and oil painting, the exhibition highlights the great practices of the first anti-Japanese base, post-enemy guerrilla warfare, the construction of the party and political power, the economic and cultural construction in the Shanxi-Chahar-Hebei military region. It reflects the glorious history of the Shanxi-Chahar-Hebei strongholds and the great achievements of the army and the people from 1937 to 1948. The calligraphy works of Mao Zedong are displayed with a total of 110 pieces. More than 80 anti-Japanese photos taken by war photographers are exhibited. Built in 1947, the site of the Shanxi-Chahar-Hebei Military District Command covers an area of 1760 square meters, with three rows of 21 mud houses, including the dormitories and offices used by Mao zedong, Zhou Enlai and Ren Bishi, as well as the telephone room and the 128-meter-long bomb shelter. This site is the only official site in Hebei Province, which is also the most complete site of dwellings in Hebei Province before Mao Zedong went to Beijing. It has become an important class of patriotic and revolutionary education.

Mao Zedong Memorial Hall is 20 kilometers away from Fuping County, south to the Rouge River, and north to the Bodhisattva Ridge. It was built in 1972, covering an area of 5250 square meters. There are foreyard and backyard. In the front yard, there stands the Bronze Statue of Marshal Nie Rongzhen, the son of a peasant. He went to France, Belgium, the Soviet Union and other countries to work and study in his youth. After returning to China, as a teaching officer in Whampoa Military Academy, he successively led the Guangzhou Uprising and Nanchang Uprising, and worked as the leader of the underground party during the period of the white Terror. Worked with Lin Biao, he served as a senior officer of the Red Army in the Jiangxi Revolutionary Base. The rich experience made him a combination of military and political talent. After the outbreak of the Anti-Japanese War, based on Mt. Wutaishan and Fuping County, with 3000 armed forces, he established the first Anti-Japanese Base in northern China — the Shanxi-Chahar-Hebei Border Region. In the extremely cruel environment, the base has been continuously consolidated and developed, and finally formed a vast area of more than 40 million people covering more than 160 counties, which is one of the important strategic bases for the victory of the national revolution. This new world, which stands in the enemy's rear area in north China, was reputed by the Central Committee of the Communist Party of China and Chairman Mao as an "exemplary anti-Japanese base".

The Shanxi-Chahar-Hebei Border Region Revolutionary Memorial Hall is a national 4A-level scenic spot, a national patriotism education demonstration base, one of the hundreds of red classic scenic area, and one of the most beautiful 30 scenes in Hebei Province. With the theme of "model anti-Japanese base" and "strategic base and command center of the National Liberation War", in the form of advanced sound, light, electricity and other means, such as the landscape restoration, the phantom imaging, the touch screen and sculpture, a large number of precious photos and cultural relics in accordance with the historical context are displayed with detailed and vivid description, showing the heroic deeds of the military and people in the Shanxi-Chahar-Hebei border region.

3. 白求恩、柯棣华纪念馆

白求恩、柯棣华纪念馆位于唐县县城北 2 千米的钟鸣山下，面积约 4.6 万平方米，建筑面积 2300 平方米。整座建筑采用中国传统与现代建筑风格，庄严肃穆，雄伟壮丽。馆内有白求恩、柯棣华两个展厅，有珍贵的历史图片 300 多幅、实物 100 余件，详细介绍了白求恩、柯棣华光辉战斗的一生，以大量生动感人的事例反映了两位国际主义战士的高尚情操、精湛医术、无私奉献的精神、高度的责任心和满腔的工作热忱。1988 年，该馆与加拿大白求恩纪念馆结为姊妹馆。该馆现为全国爱国主义教育基地。

纪念馆掠影

为了纪念伟大的国际主义战士白求恩，1940 年，晋察冀边区军民在唐县县城西北 35 千米处的军城南关修建了白求恩陵墓，并分别在 1941 年和 1943 年先后修建了晋察冀边区抗战烈士公墓和柯棣华墓。新中国成立后，这里定名为晋察冀边区烈士陵园。陵园原建有烈士纪念塔、六棱纪念碑、碑楼、纪念碑坊和烈士传略碑等。1985 年，由中央和河北省投资 230 万元，在唐县县城北 2 千米处的钟鸣山重建白求恩、柯棣华纪念馆。1986 年 11 月 12 日，纪念馆落成并对外开放，时任中共中央总书记胡耀邦为该馆提名。它是全国规模最大的白求恩、柯棣华纪念馆，为全国爱国主义教育示范基地。

Bethune & Kotnis Memorial is located at the foot of Zhongming Mountain, 2 kilometers north of Tangxian County, occupying an area of 46000 square meters. The construction area of it is 2300 square meters The whole architecture is in a modern style combined with Chinese traditional form, it looks majestic and sublime, vigorous and attractive. The memorial includes two exhibit halls, Bethune exhibit hall and Kotnis exhibit hall. There are more than 300 precious historical pictures and over 100 material objects. It introduces these two internationalists' brilliant fighting life with a lot of vivid touching stories about their noble sentiments, superb medical skills, selfless dedication, strong sense of responsibility and incessant enthusiasm. In 1988, this memorial allied with the Canadian Bethune Memorial. Now it has become a national patriotic educational base.

In order to commemorate the great internationalist fighter Bethune, in 1940, the soldiers and civilians in the Shanxi-Chahar-Hebei border area built a mausoleum at the South Gate of Jun Cheng, 35 kilometers northwest of Tangxian County. In 1941, the tombs of the martyrs were built and the tomb of Kotnis was built in 1943. After the founding of the People's Republic of China, it was named the martyr cemetery in the Shanxi-Chahar-Hebei border area. The cemetery originally has the martyr monument, six-wing memorial tablet, stele monuments, etc.. In 1985, with the investment of 2.3 million *yuan* by the central and provincial government, Bethune & Kotnis Memorial was rebuilt at the foot of Zhongming Mountain, 2 kilometers north of Tang County. The memorial was reopened to the public in November 12, 1986. At that time, the Central Committee General Secretary Hu Yaobang entitled the museum. As the largest memorial in China so far, it is a national patriotic educational demonstration base.

4. 布里留法工艺学校

布里留法工艺学校位于保定市高阳县西演镇布里村东南部，始建于1917年8月。其创办者为留法勤工俭学运动的发起人之一李石曾和老同盟会会员段子均。这里共培养留法学生200多人，为中国共产党和新中国培养了一大批栋梁之材，在伟大的勤工俭学运动和新文化运动中占有重要的历史地位。

学校大门

布里留法工艺学校布局合理，坐北朝南，原有3排平房，共41间，占地10亩左右，现存2排平房，前排为大门、伙房和实习工厂，后排为办公室暨宿舍。旧址现保存基本完好，蔡和森旧居和学校教室、办公室保存了历史原貌，其中西合璧的建筑风格在中国北方独树一帜。有代表性的单体文物为蔡和森办公室和学校旧址大门。

学校旧址大门是一处北方农村罕见的、富有哥特式风格和传统中国特色的建筑物，大门上部为欧美哥特式建筑风格，富于“团块式”结构，一高耸的砖塔，顶部呈尖状，寓意进取和希望，下为两个半圆形的扇面式墙体，意为团结和互助；大门下方为中国传统的建筑式样，拱门、磨砖带有园林式建筑风格。大门中部为当地著名书法家张卓甫书写的校名“留法工艺学校”。书体为隶书，古朴苍劲、精致典雅，与整座建筑风格浑然一体。

20世纪初，蓬勃于中华大地上的留法勤工俭学运动，是我国旧民主主义革命和新民主主义革命交替之际，广大有识之士和进步知识分子为输入西方科学文化技术，寻求救国真理而开展起来的一场影响深远的群众运动，是我国近代史上的一件大事，是新文化运动的重要组成部分，也是中国共产党历史上的重要一页。

在留法勤工俭学运动兴起和发展的过程中，河北省高阳县曾起了特殊作用，亦可称是“留法勤工俭学运动”的发祥地之一。在运动早期的倡导者中，李石曾是一位核心人物。从巴黎豆腐公司华工的招募，到“勤工俭学”主张的提出；从“勤于工作，俭以求学，以尽劳动者之智识”为宗旨的勤工俭学会的成立，到布里留法工艺学校的成立，李石曾功不可没。

高阳县布里留法工艺学校作为留法勤工俭学运动中的第一所预备学校，先后为留法勤工俭学运动培养了200多名学生，其中便有近代史学家公认的勤工俭学的佼佼者蔡和森。留法勤工俭学运动起源于教育，更对中国近代教育史产生了巨大的影响。留法勤工俭学运动，摒弃了官办教育和早期留学教育的陈腐观念，为脑力劳动与体力劳动的结合，知识分子与工人的结合，教育与生产劳动的结合，树立了光辉的榜样。

抗日战争时期，校舍遭日军破坏。1950 年，在段子均所办的北京日实工厂做工的布里籍人士捐款重修校舍。1980 年，省政府出资落架重修。1982 年，布里留法工艺学校被河北省人民政府公布为首批省重点文物保护单位；2006 年，被国务院确定为全国重点文物保护单位。

Being located in the southeast of Buli Village, Xiyan Town of Gaoyang County in Baoding City, the Polytechnic School for Students Studying in France was founded in August, 1917. Its founder were Li Shizeng, one of the sponsors of the Work-and-Study in France Program, and Duan Zijun, the member of the Chinese Revolutionary League. It trained more than 200 students studying in France. They later played important roles in the establishment of the Communist Party of China and occupied an important historical position in the great Work-and-Study in France Program and the New Culture Movement.

The Polytechnic School for Students Studying in France has a rational layout, facing to south, which originally had 3 rows of bungalows with 41 houses. It covers an area of about 10 *mu*, with 2 rows of extant bungalows. In the front row are the school gate, the kitchen and the internship factory. In the back row are the offices and dormitories. The old site is now well-preserved, among which the Former Dwelling of Cai Hesen, the classrooms and the offices are all kept in its original historical landscape. The combination of western and eastern architectural style is unique in the north of China. The representative monomer artifacts are the Former Dwelling of Cai Hesen and the site of school gate.

The school gate is a construction with gothic style and traditional Chinese characteristics that is rare in the northern countryside. The upper part of the gate is built with the European and American gothic architecture style and “block-style” structure, with the shape of a towering brick tower and pointed top, meaning progress and hope. The lower part is built with two semicircular fan type walls, meaning unity and mutual aid. The lower part of the gate is in the traditional Chinese architecture style, the arch and the grinding bricks are in the garden-architectural style. In the center of the gate, one can see the school name “the Polytechnic School for Students Studying in France”, which was written by the famous calligrapher, Zhang Zhuofu. The calligraphy is official script, ancient and simple, exquisite and elegant, and the style is in perfect coherence with the whole building.

The Work-and-Study in France Program, which thrived at the beginning of the 20th century, at the turn of the old-democratic revolution and the new-democratic revolution in China, was a far-reaching mass movement of scholars and progressive intellectuals and young people learning western science and technology and in search of the truth of national salvation. It was an important event in the modern history of China, and an important part in the New Culture Movement and the history of the Communist Party of China.

In the course of the rise and development of the Work-and-Study in France Program, Gaoyang County played a special role as one of the cradles of the program. Among the early advocates of this program, Li Shizeng was the core figure. He made great contributions to the program due to various activities, such as the recruitment of Chinese laborers in the Tofu Company in Paris, the proposition of "work-and-study program", the foundation of Work-and-Study Organization and the Polytechnic School in Buli Village.

The Polytechnic School in Buli Village, Gaoyang County, as the first preparatory school for the Work-and-Study in France program, successively trained more than 200 students. Among them, Cai Hesen was one of the best recognized by modern historians. The program was originated from education, and it also had a great influence on the history of modern education in China. Getting rid of the outworn ideas of official education and early overseas education, this program set a good example for the combination of mental and physical labor, intellectuals and workers, as well as education and productive labor.

During the Anti-Japanese War, the school buildings were destroyed by the Japanese army. In 1950, people from Buli Village, who worked in the Rishi factory in Beijing made by Duan Zijun, donated money to rebuild the school buildings. In 1980, the provincial government paid for the restoration. In 1982, it was registered by the Hebei Provincial People's Government as one of the first batch of provincial key cultural relics protection units. In 2006, it was registered as one of the national key cultural relics protection units by the State Council.

5. 辛庄烈士陵园

辛庄烈士陵园位于高阳县城南15千米处，南、北辛庄两村之间，1957年落成，属省重点保护烈士建筑物。该陵园占地10500平方米，建筑面积335平方米，南北长150米，东西宽70米。主要建筑物有烈士纪念塔、碑亭、烈士墓、烈士纪念碑等。这座烈士陵园园址，旧为黄文寺，民国初期改为高阳县南区高级小学，并在此处设有第三区警察所。1932年8月下旬，在北方党组织的领导下，这里爆发了闻名华北的高蠡起义。8月31日，起义遭到反对军队的围剿，宋洛署、蔡书林等十七名烈士在此壮烈牺牲。尔后国民党反动派又疯狂剿杀突围的战士，有29人惨遭杀害。1946年2月，当地群众在党和政府的领导下，拆庙宇、运转石，在北辛庄村东为烈士修墓立碑。1957年，县人民委员会在此建造殉难烈士纪念塔，1978年，重新修葺，改名为辛庄烈士陵园，1981年，将烈士墓移入陵园，始成现在之规模。

烈士陵园掠影

高蠡起义殉难烈士纪念塔为八棱三层砖。塔的外径长9.3米，高16米。塔顶装有大型红色五星，塔门上部刻有“高蠡起义殉难烈士纪念塔”。塔脚铺有132平方米的平台，设有四步台阶和八角花墙，供游人留步瞻仰。

塔内底层设有碑亭，迎门中立三块纪念碑分别镌刻着当场就义的17名烈士和主要领导人宋洛署、蔡书林两位烈士的传记。三碑并排组成一体立于亭中，中间碑上刻“浩气长存”，中刻“高蠡起义殉难十七烈士之墓”，左下边刻“中华民国三十五年二月修，由高阳蠡县全体民众敬立”。塔内墙壁装潢肃静，记有高蠡起义的简史、行动路线，29名烈士名录。二、三层画有反映高蠡起义的背景和过程的彩色连环壁画和六角木亭，二层亭内写有高阳县人武部、博野县人武部的悼赠词，高蠡殉难烈士英明永驻、永垂不朽、浩气长存。

烈士墓为圆形钢筋水泥结构，直径4.5米、高2米，葬有高蠡起义当场就义的17名烈士的遗骨。墓的周围装有水泥栏墙，中间铺有水泥平台，塔墓前树立着1946年2月敬立的纪念碑。碑上刻有革命先锋，中刻高蠡起义殉难烈士名录。碑背面有原高阳县县长常程撰的碑文，记载了高蠡起义的经过。

每年清明节和“八·二七”高蠡起义纪念日，广大干部、工人、农民和学生纷纷到此扫墓谒碑，缅怀烈士。烈士的革命精神永远激励着后人奋进。

The Cemetery of Martyrs in Xinzhuang, 15 kilometers south of Gaoyang County, between the two villages of South and North Xinzhuang, was built in 1957, and it is one of the provincial key protection martyrs buildings. The cemetery covers an area of 10500 square meters with a building area of 335 square meters, 150 meters long from north to south and 70 meters wide from east to west. The main buildings include the memorial tower of martyrs, the pavilion, the tombs of martyrs and the monument memorial. The site of the cemetery of martyrs, formerly known as Huangwen Temple, was changed into a senior primary school in the southern district of Gaoyang County in the early days of the Republic of China, and was equipped with the third district police station. In late August, 1932, under the leadership of the Northern Party Organization, the famous Uprising in Gaoyang and Lixian County in North China broke out. On August 31st, it was besieged by the opposition forces. Song Luoshu, Cai Shulin and other 17 martyrs sacrificed their lives bravely and gloriously here. Then the Nationalist Party crazily slaughtered 29 soldiers who attempted to break through. In February, 1946, the local people, under the leadership of the party and the government, tore down temples and carried stones to build monuments of martyrs in the east of the village. In 1957, the People's Committee of Gaoyang County built a monument of martyrs. In 1978, it was renovated and renamed as the Cemetery of Martyrs in Xinzhuang. In 1981, the tombs of martyrs were moved to the cemetery.

The Memorial Tower of Martyrs in Gaoli (Gaoyang and Lixian County) Uprising is 3 stories in an octagonal shape and made of brick. The outer diameter of the tower is 9.3 meters long and 16 meters high. The top of the tower is equipped with a large red star, and carved with the name of "The Memorial Tower of Martyrs in Gaoli Uprising". With a platform of 132 square meters at the foot of the tower, it has four steps and octagonal walls for visitors to watch with reverence.

At the bottom of the tower, there exists a pavilion, where three tablets are inscribed with the names of the 17 martyrs who were killed on the spot and the biographies of the two main leaders, Song Luoshu and Cai Shulin. The three tablets, established by the people of Lixian County and Gaoyang County, stand side by side. A brief introduction of history and 29 martyrs in the Gaoli Uprising is carved on the walls of the tower. The chromatic serial murals which reflect the background of Gaoli Uprising and its process are painted on the second and third floors. On the second floor, there are memorial speeches made by Army Office of Gaoyang County and Boye County, praising the immortal martyrs in Gaoli Uprising.

The tombs of martyrs are made of circular reinforced concrete with a diameter of 4.5 meters and a height of 2 meters. It is buried with the remains of 17 martyrs who were killed in Gaoli Uprising. The tombs are surrounded with a cement wall, with a cement platform in the center and a tablet erected in front. The tablet is engraved with the revolutionary vanguard and a list of martyrs in the Gaoli Uprising. The inscription on the back of the tablet was written by the magistrate of Gaoyang County, which recorded the story of Gaoli Uprising.

On the annual Tomb-sweeping Day and the anniversary of "8.27" Gaoli Uprising, the mass cadres, workers, peasants and students flocked to the tombs to recall the heroic deeds of the martyrs. Their revolutionary spirits would always inspire the later generations.

6. 留法勤工俭学纪念馆

留法勤工俭学运动纪念馆位于保定市区。该馆通过500余幅文物史料真实地再现了1917—1927年留法勤工俭学运动的始末，热情讴歌了以蔡和森、周恩来、李维汉、邓小平等同志为代表的老一辈无产阶级革命家在留法勤工俭学期间崇高的爱国主义精神与光辉业绩。该馆现为河北省爱国主义教育基地。

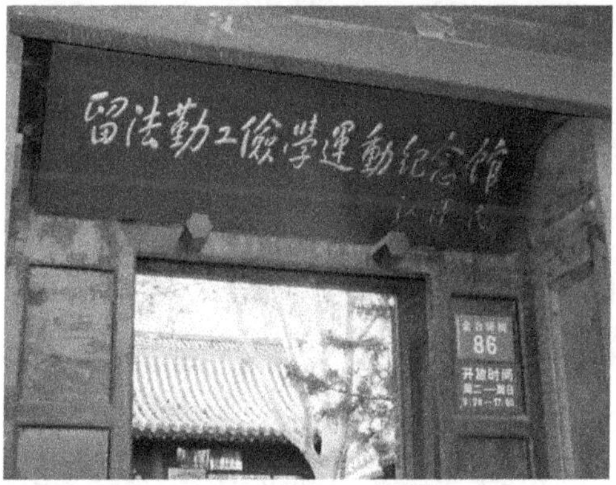

留法勤工俭学纪念馆

留法勤工俭学纪念馆占地面积2400平方米，建筑面积1100平方米，是一座典型的清末时期砖木结构的四合院形式建筑。大门坐西朝东，门楣上挂着一方棕底金色匾额，上面是江泽民的亲笔题词。踏上石阶，穿过门楼，步入青砖墁地的四合院。院子中间那座面阔三间的过厅，把一个四合院隔成前后两部分，过厅的两边与前后院相通。这所小建筑群规模虽说不大，但严整对称。南北瓦房原是育德中学的教务处所，现已辟为纪念馆的展厅。院内松柏苍翠，花木繁茂，碑石矗立，幽静清雅。保定是留法勤工俭学运动的发祥地。1995年，纪念馆被中共河北省委、河北省人民政府命名为“河北省爱国主义教育基地”，是2A级旅游景区。

五四时期兴起的留法勤工俭学运动是在辛亥革命前后，旅法中国人提倡并组织的留法俭学，巴黎中国豆腐公司工人工余求学，以及欧战期间旅法华工教育的基础上，逐步发展起来的。李石曾祖籍河北省高阳县，是清末大学士、军机大臣李鸿藻的儿子，是一位思想非常浓厚的教育家，一生致力于教育事业，是留法勤工俭学运动的主要领导者和组织者。1902年，他到法国留学，因为对大豆的研究非常成功，遂把中国的豆制品技术引入了法国，1908年，在法国巴黎西郊创办了一所“巴黎中国豆腐工厂”，豆腐工厂里的工人都是他的家乡高阳县一带没有文化的农民。为了提高工人的文化知识水平和生产劳动力，李石曾在厂内成立了一所夜校，工人们白天做工，晚上学习。经过几年的“以工兼学”实践，夜校里提出了“勤于工作，俭以求学”的宗旨，这就是我们现在所说的勤工俭学的由来。1912年初，李石曾和吴稚晖、蔡元培等在北京发起成立了“留法俭学会”，目的是鼓励青年学生以低廉的费用和节俭苦学的精神赴法留学，从而把西方的文明输入国内，以改良中国社会。后来由于遭到袁世凯政府的破坏，留法俭学会因李石曾、蔡元培等人被迫流亡法国而停止活动。在李石曾等人的组织下，“勤工俭学会”于1915年在法国巴黎成立。

在第一次世界大战期间，法国遭受严重的战火侵袭，中国向法国派遣了十几万战地华工，这些华工到法国以后，对法国社会造成了很大的影响，中法教育界人士认为有必要对这些华工进行教育。于是1916年，李石曾、蔡元培、吴玉章等人在法国巴黎成立了“华法教育会”，并创办了华工学校。

1913年5月，留法俭学会第三班学生赴法前合影

留法勤工俭学生赴法前，需要在国内进行必要的准备，学习一些法语、西方习俗和一般工艺技能，以便赴法后的交流、做工和学习。

1916年，袁世凯倒台后，被迫流亡海外的蔡元培、李石曾、吴玉章等人相继回国，开始在国内大张旗鼓地宣传和组织赴法勤工俭学。经过艰苦的努力，全国先后建起了20余所留法预备学校和预备班。

1917年，在保定高阳县布里村成立了第一所留法工艺学校。学校设有实习工厂，中国共产党早期创建人之一蔡和森就毕业于此校。

1917年秋，保定育德中学附设了留法高等工艺预备班，该班教学质量之高，赴法人数之多，是其他学校不能与之相比的。革命前辈刘少奇、李维汉、李富春等先后毕业于此班。

在李石曾等人的帮助下，育德中学留法预备班开始招生，招生对象为初中以上文化程度的青年，由学校录取31名青年为第一期留法预备班学生。同年8月，留法预备班正式开学，变革了陈腐的教育内容，“以法文及铁工为主要科目，机器原理、工艺图画、土木工程等科副之”。为巩固学习内容，帮助学生掌握实际生产技能，为将来“以工求学”做准备，育德中学在校内建起了手工教室，并聘请校外工匠传授生产技术。1918年，学校筹建了实习工厂。在筹建过程中，学校得到了法国驻华公使赫尔利、直隶督军曹锟、在保定高等师范工作的法国教员法斯德等人的赞助。实习工厂分锻工、锉工、翻砂、机械四部，每部再分四组，学生按工种分组。实习内容每周更换一次，循序轮换。每位学生以学一种工种为主，兼学别样。学生通过实习，学习掌握了生产知识和生产技能。

第一期留法预备班学生于1918年7月毕业，其中22名学生经上海赴法国勤工俭学。同年8月，育德中学留法预备班招收第二期学员。这期学员共86人，其中湖南学生就有74人，所以被人称为“湖南班”。这批湖南学生到育德中学不是偶然的。俄国十月革命后，随着马克思主义在中国的传播，留法勤工俭学运动进入了新时期。1918年6月，蔡和森受毛泽东和湖南新民学会的委托，以学习欧洲工人运动的经验，寻找科学的救国真理为目的，从长沙到北京为湖南学生联系留法勤工俭学。之后，毛泽东率领 20 余名湖南学生抵达北京，经法华教育会的同意，其中多数湖南学生分到保定育德中学留法预备班。9 月初，李维汉、李富春、张昆弟等作为第一批湖南学生，由北京到保定育德中学留法预备班学习。9 月 18 日，湖南籍学生组成了勤工俭学湘分会旅保支部，“以联络湘同学感情”。10 月 6 日，赴蠡县布里村留法工艺学校学习的 30 名湖南学生由湖南抵达保定。李维汉、李富春等人到车站迎接，毛泽东、蔡和森也专程从北京赶到保定，住在保定西大街的第一客栈。10 月 7 日下午，毛泽东、蔡和森与留法预备班、布里村留法初级班的全体湖南学生同游了古莲花池。当晚，毛泽东、蔡和森与李维汉、张昆弟等人商谈了初级班学生去布里的时间和办法。10 月 10 日，毛泽东送走布里村留法初级班学生后，于当日返回北京。蔡和森到布里村留法工艺学校教学。

育德中学第二期留法预备班的学生受俄国十月革命的影响，抱着“改造中国与世界”的目的，一面刻苦学习文化，一面认真阅读各种进步书刊。他们经常和育德中学的进步学生一起举行读书报告会，交流思想，探讨社会问题，研究适合中国国情的革命途径。五四运动中，以李富春为代表的留法预备班学生积极参加保定的反帝国主义爱国运动。他们走上街头，宣传讲演，并联合各界人士，举行大规模示威游行。

1919 年 6 月，北京政府教育部根据育德中学上报的修正留法高等工艺预备班简章及新生履历表，向直隶省省长起草咨文，获得批复后，留法预备班开始招收第三期学生，并在报刊上刊登了招生广告，全国各地青年纷纷报名。这期共招收了 63 名学生，其中有刘少奇。经过一年的学习，该期学生于 1920 年 6 月毕业，其中有 23 名学生赴法国勤工俭学。刘少奇在留法预备班学习期间，思维敏捷，学习刻苦，没有等到毕业就去俄国留学了。1920 年暑假，育德中学留法预备班招收第四期学生，共招生 33 人。当时正值第一次世界大战后，法国物价高涨，经济萧条，找工作很困难，北京政府对勤工俭学学生采取漠不关心、听之任之的态度。

留法勤工俭学在五四运动后短短一年的时间内形成了全国规模的热潮。毛泽东为了联系勤工俭学事宜走上革命道路。据不完全统计，从 1919 年 3 月 17 日至 1920 年 12 月 15 日不到两年的时间，共有 20 批学生赴法，约计 2000 人。留法勤工俭学运动于 1921 年初基本结束，育德中学留法预备班也于 1921 年 6 月停办。

在这个组织里涌现了一大批中国共产党的优秀干部，他们献身于中国人民的解放事业。例如，我国改革开放的总设计师邓小平就是从留法期间投入解放事业中去的。除此以外，留法勤工俭学活动还为中国革命建设培养了一批科技人才，他们为祖国的科技事业的发展和民族工业的兴起做出了巨大贡献。

The Work-and-study in France Program Museum is located in the downtown of Baoding. The museum, through over 500 historical materials, reveals the beginning and ending of the work-and-study movement from 1917 to 1927, eulogizes the lofty patriotic spirit and glorious achievements during the period of work-and-study in France, of the old working class revolutionaries represented by Cai Heshen, Zhou Enlai, Li Weihan, and Deng Xiaoping. Now it is the patriotism education base in Hebei Province.

The Work-and-study in France Program Museum covers an area of 2400 square meters and a building area of 1100 square meters. It is a typical quadruped courtyard with brick and wood structure in the late Qing Dynasty. The gate faces to east, with a golden brown plaque hung over the frame, which is inscribed by Jiang Zemin. Step on the stone steps, then pass through the gatehouse, one can enter into the courtyard which is made of black bricks. In the middle of the courtyard, there was a three-room hall, which separates the courtyard into two parts, and the two sides of the hall are connected with the front and back yard. The size of this small assortment of buildings is not very large, but it is symmetrical. The north and south tile-roofed houses were the academic affairs office of Yude Middle School, which is now the hall of the memorial. In the quiet and elegant courtyard, there are green pine and cypress, luxuriant flowers and trees, as well as standing monuments. Baoding is the birthplace of the Work-and-study in France Program. In 1995, the memorial hall was named as "the Patriotism Education Base in Hebei" by Hebei Provincial Party Committee and Hebei Provincial People's Government, which is a 2A-level scenic spot now.

The Work-and-study in France Program sprung up during the May Fourth Movement period. Around the Xinhai Revolution, the Work-and-study in France Program was advocated and organized by the Chinese people staying in France. Li Shizeng, whose ancestral home is Gaoyang County, is the son of Li Hongzao, the Grand Secretary and the military governor of the late Qing Dynasty. He is a great educator with deep thoughts, as well as a major leader and organizer of the Work-and-study in France Program, who devoted his lifetime to education career. In 1902, he went to study abroad in France. Since his study of tofu was very successful, the technology of Chinese soy products was introduced to France. In 1908, the China Tofu Factory was set up in the western suburbs of Paris, in which workers are those illiterate farmers from their hometown, Gaoyang County. In order to improve their knowledge and productivity, Li Shizeng established a night school in the factory. The laborers could work during the day and study in the evening. After several years of work-and-study practice, the night school put forward the tenet of "Diligent in work, thrift in study", which gradually became the guideline of the work-and-study program. At the beginning of 1912, Li Shizeng, Wu Zhihui, Cai Yuanpei and others launched the "League of Work-and-study in France Program" in Beijing, which aimed at encouraging young students to study abroad with low cost and the spirit of frugality, so as to input western civilization into China to improve Chinese society. Later, Li Shizeng and Cai Yuanpei were forced to live in exile abroad because of disruptive activities. In 1915, League of First Work-and-study Program was established in Paris.

During the First World War, flames of war spread everywhere in France. One hundred thousand Chinese workers were dispatched to France. They had a great influence on French Society. Therefore both the China and France educators believed that the education for Chinese workers was indispensable. Thus, in 1916, Li Shizeng, Cai Yuanpei, and Wu Yuzhang set up the "China-France Education Association" in Paris, and founded the school for Chinese workers.

Before going to France, students needed to make necessary preparations in China, such as learning French, western customs and general technical skills, so as to enable them to communicate, work and study after reaching France.

After the fall of the government in 1916, Cai Yuanpei, Li Shizeng, and Wu Yuzhang returned to China to publicize and organize the Work-and-study in France Program. With arduous efforts, more than 20 preparatory schools and preparatory classes were set up around the country.

In 1917, the first polytechnic school for students studying in France was established in Buli village, Gaoyang County. This school had an internship factory, and Cai Hesen, one of the early founders of the Communist Party of China, graduated from the school.

In the autumn of 1917, a higher polytechnic preparatory class for students studying in France was set up in Yude Middle School of Baoding, the teaching quality and the number of people of which cannot be exceeded by other schools. The revolutionary predecessors such as Liu Shaoqi, Li Weihan, Li Fuchun and others successively graduated from this class.

With the help of Li Shizeng and others, the preparatory classes began to recruit students whose educational level was above junior middle school, and 31 youngsters were admitted to the first phase of preparatory class. In August of the same year, the preparatory class was officially opened, and the banal education was revolutionized with the main subjects of French and blacksmithing, with the minor subjects of machine theory, crafts and drawings, and civil engineering. To consolidate the learning content, help students master the productive skills, and prepare for the future work and study, Yude Middle School set up handwork classrooms and employed craftsmen to teach production techniques. In 1918, the school set up an internship factory. In the process of preparation, the school was sponsored by Hurley, the French ambassador, Cao Kun, the warlord of the Zhili clique, and Fasid, a French teacher who worked in Baoding Higher Normal School. The internship factory consisted of four branches of forging, filing, casting and machinery, each of which is divided into four groups, and the students were grouped according to the type of work. The content of the internship changed once a week. Among all of the types of work, each student took one type as the main course from which they acquired plentiful practical knowledge and skills.

The first phase of students graduated in July, 1918, 22 students of which went from Shanghai to France. In August, the second phase of students in preparatory classes of Yude Middle School was enrolled. There were 86 students in this phase, and among them 74 students were from Hunan Province, so it was called "Hunan class". It was no coincidence that Hunanese students took up a large majority. After the October Revolution, with the widespread of Marxism in China, the Work-and-study in France Program entered a new era. In June, 1918, in order to learn the experience from the working-class movement in Europe and seek for the truth of saving the nation, Cai Yuanpei, authorized by Mao Zedong and Hunan Xinmin Institute, came from Changsha to Beijing and made contact for Hunanese students with the Work-and-study in France Program. Later, Mao Zedong led more than 20 students from Hunan to Beijing. With the approval of the France-China Education Association, most of them were assigned to the preparatory classes of Yude Middle School in Baoding. In early september, Li Weihan, Li Fuchun and Zhang Kundi, as the first group of students from Hunan, came to study at Yude Middle school in Baoding. On September 18, the Hunanese students constituted the Hunan group of the Work-and-study in France Pogram in order to make close contact with each other. On October 6,30 Hunanese students arrived at Baoding. Li Weihan, Li Fuchun and others met at the station. Mao Zedong and Cai Hesen also came from Beijing to Baoding to greet them, living in the First Inn at Baoding West Street. In the afternoon of October 7, Mao Zedong, Cai Hesen and all the other Hunanese students visited the Ancient Lotus Pond. That night, Mao Zedong, Cai Hesen , Li Weihan, Zhang Kundi and others discussed when and how those students in the primary class would go to Buli. On October 10, Mao Zedong returned to Beijing after he sent the students of the primary class to Buli Village. Cai Hesen went to teach at the Polytechnic School of Buli Village for students studying in France.

Under the influence of the October Revolution, with the purpose of "transforming China and the world", the second phase of students in preparatory classes studied hard and read various progressive books at the same time. They often held book seminars with progressive students, exchanged ideas, discussed social issues, and studied revolutionary approaches to China's national conditions. In the May 4th Movement, the students, represented by Li Fuchun, took an active part in the anti-imperialist patriotic movement in Baoding. They went to the street, gave speeches, and drew support from people from various circles to hold mass demonstrations.

In June, 1919, according to the correction of the general rules of higher polytechnic preparatory classes for students studying in France and new curriculum vitae, Ministry of Education of the Government of Beijing made drafts to the governor of Zhili Province. After approval, it began to recruit the third phase of students, and published education advertisements on newspapers and magazines. Young people from all over the country signed up. Liu Shaoqi was among the 63 students enrolled. After a year's study, this phase of students graduated in June, 1920, and 23 of them went to work and study in France. Liu Shaoqi, with quick thoughts and hard work, went to Russia to study before graduation. In the summer holiday of 1920, the preparatory class of Yude Middle School received its fourth phase of students with a total enrollment of 33. After the First World War, it was difficult to find a job due to a rise in French market and the economic depression. The Beijing Government took an indifferent attitude toward those work-and-study in France students.

The Work-and-study in France Program formed the nationwide upsurge one year after the May 4th Movement. Mao Zedong took the revolutionary road in order to contact the Work-and-study Program. According to incomplete statistics, from March 17, 1919 to December 15, 1920, in less than two years, a total of 2000 students went to France. The program was basically completed at the beginning of 1921, and the preparatory class at Yude Middle School suspended in June, 1921.

A large number of outstanding cadres of the Communist Party of China emerged in this organization. They dedicated themselves to the career of liberation of the Chinese people. And their merits and achievements would never be lost. For example, Deng Xiaoping, the chief designer of China's reform and opening up, devoted to liberation career when studying in France. In addition, the practice of Work-and-study in France Program also cultivated a number of scientific and technological talents for the construction of Chinese revolution. They have made great contributions to the development of science and technology and the rise of national industry.

参考文献

1. 保定市旅游局. 保定旅游十座城[M]. 北京：新华出版社，2016.

2. 赵静. 导游保定［M]. 北京：解放军文艺出版社，2005.

3. 金惠康，罗向阳. 汉英旅游服务实用手册［M]. 广州：广东旅游出版社，2006.